EYEWITNESSES AND OTHERS

Readings in American History
Volume 1: Beginnings to 1865

HOLT, RINEHART AND WINSTON
Harcourt Brace & Company
Austin • New York • Orlando • Atlanta •
San Francisco • Boston • Dallas • Toronto • London

Reviewers

James H. Bell
Teacher
Poway High School
Poway, California

Thomas R. Frazier
Professor of History
Baruch College
City University of New York
New York, New York

Mary Ellen Godfrey
Adjunct Instructor in History
Palomar College
San Marcos, California

James M. McPherson
Director of Graduate Studies
Department of History
Princeton University
Princeton, New Jersey

Malcolm Moore, Jr.
Teacher
Thomas Jefferson Middle School
Decatur, Illinois

Acknowledgments

For permission to reprint copyrighted material, grateful acknowledgment is made to the following sources:

Doubleday, a division of Bantam Doubleday Dell Publishing Group, Inc.: "Many Thousands Gone" from *The Folk Songs of North America*, lyrics in the English Language by Alan Lomax; melodies and guitar chords transcribed by Peggy Seeger. Copyright © 1960 by Alan Lomax.

Encino Press, Austin, Texas: From "Working on a Texas Plantation" (Retitled: "Six Texas Slave Narratives") from *The Slave Narratives of Texas*, edited by Ronnie C. Tyler and Lawrence R. Murphy. Copyright © 1974 by The Encino Press.

Harper & Row, Publishers, Inc.: Adapted from *History of the Indies* (Retitled: "Bartolomé de las Casas Condemns Spanish Treatment of the Indians") by Bartolomé de las Casas, translated and edited by Andrée Collard. Copyright © 1971 by Andrée Collard. From "The Upper World" (Retitled: "A Native American Trickster Tale") from *Nine Tales of Coyote* by

(Acknowledgments continued on page 433)

Contents

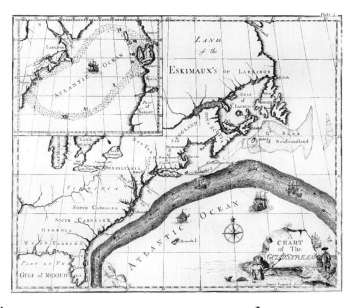

Introduction   1

1 Columbus Discovers America (1492) . .   2
Excerpts from the explorer's journal,
abridged by Las Casas

**2 Bartolomé de las Casas Condemns
Spanish Treatment of Indians
(ca. 1510)**   8
An excerpt adapted from Las Casas' book
on the history of the Indies

**3 Coronado Explores the Southwest
(1541)** 11
Excerpts from a report to King Charles I
of Spain*

4 A Speech by Powhatan (1609) 16
Excerpts from a speech to the English at
Jamestown

**5 Bradford Describes the Founding of
Plymouth Plantation (1620)** 18
Excerpts from Bradford's journal*

* Spelling has been made
consistent with current
practice.

6 An Indentured Servant Writes Home
   (1623) 26
   An excerpt from a letter describing
   conditions*

7 A Poem by Anne Bradstreet (1666) . . . 30
   Her reaction to the destruction of her home*

8 The Importance of Indian Corn (1600s) 33
   Excerpts from a nineteenth-century
   historian's account

9 Tapping the Sugar Tree (1600s) 40
   A description of the making of maple sugar
   by a nineteenth-century historian, with recipes

10 Madam Knight Travels by Horseback
   (1704) 44
   Excerpts from Knight's diary

11 The Secret Diary of William Byrd II
   (1709) 49
   Excerpts from Byrd's diary

12 Slavery in Virginia (1720s) 55
   Excerpts from the journal of a plantation
   tutor and the Virginia law codes

13 Publisher John Peter Zenger's Trial in
   Colonial New York (1738) 60
   An excerpt adapted from Zenger's record

14 A Collection of Runaways (1740s) . . . 66
   Advertisements from newspapers

15 Jonathan Edwards Describes the Peace
   of Christ (1741) 71
   An excerpt from a sermon

16 A Slave's Story (ca. 1750) 77
   Excerpts from Olaudah Equiano's
   autobiography

17 Novelist James Fenimore Cooper Writes
   of the Frontier (1750s) 83
   An excerpt from The Last of the Mohicans

18 A Cherokee Legend: How the World Was Made (ca. 1750) 92
A Native American creation myth

19 Andrew Burnaby Forecasts the American Future (1760) 96
An excerpt from Burnaby's book about his American travels

20 Women Fight for Liberty (1760s) 100
Excerpts from a modern historian's analysis

21 Patrick Henry Takes a Stand (1775) . . 103
An excerpt from Henry's speech before the Virginia Convention

22 Thomas Paine's "The Crisis" (1776) . . 108
Excerpts from Paine's pamphlet

23 Mercy Otis Warren Ridicules British and Tories (1776) 113
An excerpt from Warren's play *The Blockheads**

24 A Surgeon's Diary of Valley Forge (1777–1778) 118
Excerpts from the diary of Albigence Waldo

25 The British Surrender at Yorktown (1781) 123
An excerpt from James Thacher's journal

26 Harassment of Tories After the British Surrender (1781) 126
Excerpts from a young girl's diary

27 An Englishman Visits Washington After the War (1785) 130
Excerpts from a diary about a visit to Mount Vernon

28 Benjamin Franklin Urges the Adoption of the Constitution (1787) 136
An excerpt from James Madison's records

* Spelling has been made consistent with current practice.

29 Patrick Henry on the Constitution (1788) 141
Excerpts from debates

30 A Debate on the Constitution (1788) . . 144
Excerpts from three speeches by
Massachusetts citizens

31 Noah Webster Argues for a National Language (1789) 148
Excerpts from Webster's book *Dissertations on the English Laguage*

32 Thomas Jefferson Describes Washington's Character (1790s) 153
Excerpts from a letter

33 George Washington's Farewell Address (1796) 158
Excerpts from Washington's final speech as president

34 Mike Fink *vs* Davy Crockett (early 1800s) 162
A tall tale

35 Ranch and Mission Days in Spanish California (ca. 1800) 165
Excerpts from an early settler's reminiscences

36 Meriwether Lewis Records a Narrow Escape (1805) 172
Excerpts from Lewis' journal

37 A Slave Is Resold to South Carolina (ca. 1805) 176
Excerpts from Charles Ball's narrative

38 Tecumseh Opposes White Settlement (1810) 180
Excerpts from a speech to William Henry Harrison

39 The British Burn Washington (1814) . . 183
Excerpts from a British officer's account

40 Red Eagle Surrenders to Jackson (1814) 188
Excerpts from a speech to General Jackson

**41 Portrait of a Country Schoolteacher,
"The Legend of Sleepy Hollow" (1820)** 190
An excerpt from Irving's story

Feature: A Colonial Scrapbook 196
A visual record of home and social life

42 Fur Hunters of the Far West (ca. 1820) 198
An excerpt from an account by a fur trapper

**43 The First American Steam Railroad
(1830)** 201
Excerpts from the recollections of a
railroad official

**44 "On The Starry Heavens," a Reading
from _The Columbian Orator_ (1830s)** . . . 206
A selection from an early textbook

45 An Abolitionist Takes a Vow (1831) . . 209
A newspaper article by William Lloyd Garrison

46 The Confessions of Nat Turner (1831) 213
An excerpt from Turner's confessions to
his lawyer

**47 Frances Kemble Travels by Boat, Stage,
Railroad, and Canal (1832–1833)** 219
Excerpts from Kemble's account of an
American visit

**48 Frederick Douglass Is Sent to the Slave-
Breaker (1833)** 225
An excerpt from Douglass' autobiography

**49 Old Time Religion at the Camp Meeting
(1835)** 231
An excerpt from a book on American life
by Thomas Low Nichols

**50 A Mexican Account of San Jacinto
(1836)** 236
Excerpts from a soldier's reminiscences

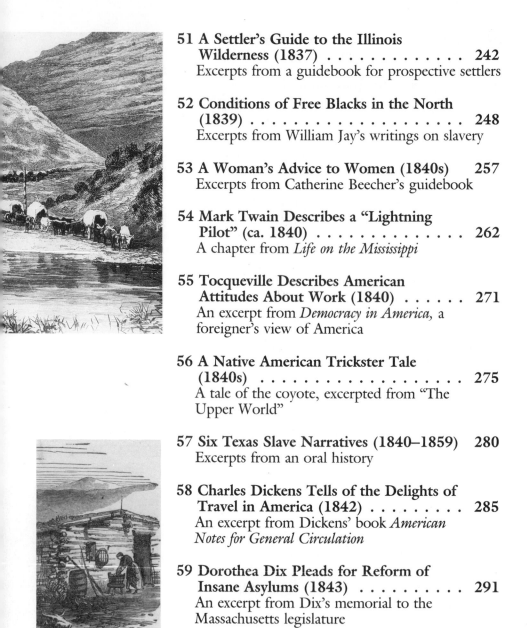

51 A Settler's Guide to the Illinois Wilderness (1837) **242**
Excerpts from a guidebook for prospective settlers

52 Conditions of Free Blacks in the North (1839) **248**
Excerpts from William Jay's writings on slavery

53 A Woman's Advice to Women (1840s) **257**
Excerpts from Catherine Beecher's guidebook

54 Mark Twain Describes a "Lightning Pilot" (ca. 1840) **262**
A chapter from *Life on the Mississippi*

55 Tocqueville Describes American Attitudes About Work (1840) **271**
An excerpt from *Democracy in America,* a foreigner's view of America

56 A Native American Trickster Tale (1840s) **275**
A tale of the coyote, excerpted from "The Upper World"

57 Six Texas Slave Narratives (1840–1859) **280**
Excerpts from an oral history

58 Charles Dickens Tells of the Delights of Travel in America (1842) **285**
An excerpt from Dickens' book *American Notes for General Circulation*

59 Dorothea Dix Pleads for Reform of Insane Asylums (1843) **291**
An excerpt from Dix's memorial to the Massachusetts legislature

60 A Teenage Bride on the Santa Fe Trail (1846) **294**
Excerpts from Susan Shelby Magoffin's diary

61 Emily Dickinson Describes Mount Holyoke Seminary (1847) **301**
An excerpt from a letter

62 Henry Thoreau Goes to Jail (1848) . . . 306
Excerpts from "Civil Disobedience"

63 Horace Mann on Education and Poverty
(1848) 313
Excerpts from a report to the
Massachusetts Board of Education

64 The Seneca Falls Declaration of
Woman's Rights (1848) 316
Excerpts from the declaration

65 Notes From a Forty-Niner's Diary
(1849) 322
Excerpts from Alonzo Delano's diary

66 Mexicans in "the Diggings" (1849) . . . 327
An excerpt from a modern historian's analysis

67 The Blackfoot Genesis (1800s) 332
A Native American creation myth

68 On the Underground Railroad
(ca. 1850) 335
Excerpts from an account by an
underground railroad organizer

69 A Contemporary Account of Harriet
Tubman (1850s) 341
Excerpts from newspaper interviews

70 A Visit to Uncle Tom's Cabin (1851) . . 347
An excerpt from Harriet Beecher Stowe's
Uncle Tom's Cabin

71 Frederick Douglass Describes the Songs
of Slavery (1855) 351
Excerpts from Douglass' autobiography,
with song lyrics

72 Lucy Stone Calls for Woman's Rights
(1855) 355
Excerpts from a speech

73 Senator Seward Foresees an
"Irrepressible Conflict" (1858) 358
Excerpts from a speech

74 Gustave Koerner Observes the Lincoln–
Douglas Debates (1858) 362
Excerpts from a political observer's memoirs

75 John Brown's Last Speech (1859) 367
Brown's explanation to the court of his actions

76 At a Slave Auction (1859) 370
Excerpts from a newspaper article

77 Mark Twain Describes the Pony Express (1860) 377
An excerpt from *Roughing It*

78 Plantation Life During the War (1860s) 380
An excerpt from a southern woman's account

Feature: From a Confederate Receipt Book 385
Recipes for cooking with limited wartime ingredients

79 Stephen Crane Describes an Infantry Attack (1860s) 386
A chapter from *The Red Badge of Courage*

Feature: War Songs of the Blue and Gray 393
Music and lyrics of Civil War songs

80 The Poets' View of War: Whitman and Melville (1860s) 400
An excerpt from Whitman's *Speciman Days;*
poems by Whitman and Melville

81 An English War Correspondent Observes President Lincoln (1861) . . . 405
Excerpts from William Howard Russell's diary

82 Lincoln Delivers the Gettysburg Address (1863) 411
The president's speech

83 Sherman's Army Destroys a Georgia Plantation (1864) 413
Excerpts from a southern woman's diary

84 The Andersonville Trial (1865) 418
An excerpt from Saul Levitt's play about the trial

85 Proceedings of the Convention of the Colored People of Virginia (1865) . . . 430
Excerpts from the statement issued by the Convention

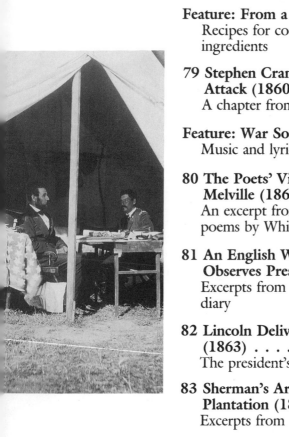

Introduction

*E*yewitnesses and Others: Readings in American History presents United States history as a collection of written evidence—primary sources—about the past. The readings in this book place you in direct contact with the people who lived and experienced history—the eyewitnesses. As you read the historical evidence they created, you enter the minds of these men and women to view the past through their eyes. Then you step aside from their points of view to make your own historical judgments about the events they describe.

This is the historian's job, and it is absolutely necessary. No two eyewitnesses ever see exactly the same thing, and eyewitness descriptions are often colored and distorted by their authors' personal involvements in the events of their times.

However, an old saying holds that if you would really understand someone you should "walk a mile in his moccasins." *Eyewitnesses and Others* invites you to step into the "moccasins" of Spanish explorers, Puritan housewives, Cherokee chiefs, runaway slaves, Civil War soldiers, and many others. Then you step into the very different shoes of the historian to try to make objective sense about what you have read.

When you read the sources in *Eyewitnesses and Others* you will at times encounter strange turns of phrase and spellings you will not find in your dictionary. This is deliberate: English vocabulary and the rules of spelling have changed over time, and the editors of *Eyewitnesses and Others* have chosen to keep the sources as true to their original language as possible. Especially difficult words or passages are explained in brackets. Only in a few particularly difficult readings has the spelling been modernized.

From *Report of the Superintendent of the U.S. Coast and Geodetic Survey.*

Columbus Discovers America (1492)

Christopher Columbus, an Italian navigator serving Spain, kept a detailed journal of his voyage to America. Although the original has been lost, many of the admiral's descriptions became part of an abridgment of the journal by Spanish historian Bartolomé de las Casas. (The portions of the following excerpts enclosed in quotation marks are Columbus' own words.) As you read this selection, try to determine for whom Columbus seems to have written his journal.

Wednesday October 10th.

He sailed west-southwest, at the rate of ten miles an hour and occasionally twelve, and at other times seven, running between day and night fifty-nine leagues [236 miles]; he told the men only forty-four [176 miles]. Here the crew could stand it no longer, they complained of the long voyage, but the Admiral encouraged them as best he could, giving them hopes of the profits that they might have. And he added that it was useless to murmur because he had come to [in quest of] the Indies, and was going to continue until he found them with God's help.

Thursday October 11th.

He sailed to the west-southwest, had a high sea, higher than hitherto. They saw pardelas and floating by the vessel a green rush. The men of the Pinta saw a reed and a stick, and got a small stick apparently cut or marked with an iron instrument, and a piece of cane, and some other grass which grows on the land, and a small board. Those of the Caravel Niña also saw other indications of land and a little stick loaded with dog roses. In view of such signs they breathed more freely and grew cheerful. They ran until sunset of that day twenty-seven leagues [about 108 miles]. After sunset he sailed on his first course to the West; they went about twelve miles an hour, and two hours after midnight they had run about ninety miles, that is twenty-two and a half leagues. . . . Two hours after midnight the land appeared, about two leagues [8 miles] off. They lowered all the sails, leaving only a storm square sail, which is the mainsail without bonnets [extra pieces of canvas attached to the bottom of a mainsail], and lay to until Friday when they reached a small island of the Lucayos, called *Guanahani* by the natives. They soon saw people naked, and the Admiral went on shore in the armed boat; also Martin Alonso Pinzon and Vincente Anes, his brother, who was commander of the Niña. . . . The Admiral . . . called them as witnesses to certify that he in the presence of them all, was taking, as he in fact took possession of said island for the King and Queen his masters, making the declarations that were required as they will be found more fully in the attestations then taken down in writing. Soon after a large crowd of natives congregated there. What follows are the Admiral's own words in his book on the first voyage and discovery of these Indies. "In order to win the friendship and affection of that people, and because I was convinced that their conversion to our Holy Faith would be better promoted through love than through force; I presented some of them with red caps and some strings of glass beads which they placed around their necks, and with other trifles of insignificant worth that delighted them and by which we have got wonderful hold on their affections. They afterwards came to the boats of the vessels swimming, bringing us parrots, cotton thread in balls, and spears, and many other things, which they bartered for others we gave them, as glass beads and little bells. Finally they received everything and gave whatever they had with good will. But I thought them to be a very poor people. . . . I saw but one very young girl, all the rest being young men, none of them being over thirty years of age; their forms being very well proportioned; their bodies graceful and their features handsome: their hair is as coarse as the hair of horse's tail and cut short: they wear their hair over their eye brows except a little behind which they wear long, and which they never cut: some of them paint themselves black, and they are of the color of the Canary islanders, neither black nor white, and some paint themselves white, and some red, and some with whatever they find, and some paint their faces, and some the whole body, and some their eyes only, and some their noses only. They do not carry arms and have no knowledge of them, for when I showed them the swords they took them by the edge, and through ignorance, cut themselves. They have no iron; their spears consist of staffs without iron, some of them having a fish's tooth at the end, and the others other things. As a body they are of good size, good demeanor, and well formed; I saw some with scars on their bodies, and to my signs asking them what these meant, they answered in the same manner, that people from neighboring islands wanted to capture them, and they had defended themselves; and I did believe, and do believe, that they came from the mainland to take them prisoners. They must be good servants and very intelligent, because I see that they repeat very quickly what I told them, and is is my conviction that they would easily become Christians, for they seem not to have any sect. If it please our Lord, I will take six of them from here to your Highnesses on my departure, that they may learn to speak. I have seen here no beasts whatever, but parrots only. . . .

       Saturday October 13th.
"At dawn many of these men came down to the shore, all are, as already, said, youths of good size and very handsome: their hair is not wooly, but loose and coarse like horse hair, they have broader

heads and foreheads than I have ever seen in any other race of men, and the eyes very beautiful not small, none of them are black, but of the complexion of the inhabitants of the Canaries, as it is to be expected, for it is east [and] west with the island of Hierro in the Canaries, in the same line [latitude]. All without exception have very straight limbs, and no bellies, and very well formed. They came to the ship in canoes, made out of trunks of trees all in one piece, and wonderfully built according to the locality, in some of them forty or forty-five men came, others were smaller, and in some but a single man came. They paddled with a peel [an oar with a wide blade] like that of a baker, and make wonderful speed; and if it capsizes all begin to swim and set it right again, and bail out the water with calabashes [gourds] which they carry. They brought balls of spun cotton, parrots, spears, and other little things which would be tedious to describe, and gave them away for anything that was given to them. I examined them closely and tried to ascertain if there was any gold, and noticed that some carried a small piece of it hanging from a little hole in their nose, and by signs I was able to understand that by going to

Christopher Columbus preferred to win over the Indians with love rather than force. In this eighteenth-century Spanish engraving, Columbus has just presented the Indians with gifts.

the south or going around the island to the south-ward, there was a king who had large gold vessels, and gold in abundance. I endeavored to persuade them to go there, and I afterwards saw that they had no wish to go. I determined to wait, until tomor-row evening, and then to sail for the southwest, for many of them told me that there was a land to the south and to the southwest and to the northwest, and that those from the northwest came frequently to fight with them, and so go to the southwest to get gold and precious stones. This island is very large and very level and has very green trees, and abundance of water, and a very large lagoon in the middle, without any mountain, and all is covered with verdure [vegetation], most pleasing to the eye; the people are remarkably gentle, and from the desire to get some of our things, and thinking that nothing will be given to them unless they give some thing, and having nothing they take what they can and swim off [to the ship]; but all that they have they give for any thing that is offered to them; so that they bought even pieces of crockery, and pieces of broken glass, and I saw sixteen balls of cotton given for three ceotis of Portugal, which is equivalent to a blanca of Castile [ceotis and blancas are ancient Spanish forms of money], and in them there must have been more than one arraba of spun cotton. I forbad this and allowed no one to take any unless I ordered it to be taken for your Highnesses should it be found in abundance. It grows in the island, although on account of the shortness of time I could not assert it positively; and likewise the gold which they carry hanging in their noses is found here; but in order to lose no time I am now going to try if I can find the island of Cipango. . . .

Sunday October 14.
"At dawn I ordered the boat of the ship and the boats of the Caravels to be got ready, and went along the island, in a north-northeasterly direction, to see the other side, which was on the other side

> This island is very large and very level and has very green trees . . .

of the east, and also to see the villages, and soon
saw two or three and their inhabitants, coming to
the shore calling us and praising God; some brought
us water, some eatables; others, when they saw that
I did not care to go on shore, plunged into the sea
swimming and came, and we understood that they
asked us if we had come down from heaven; and
one old man got into the boat, while others in a
loud voice called both men and women saying: come
and see the men from heaven: bring them food and
drink. A crowd of men and many women came,
each bringing something, giving thanks to God,
throwing themselves down, and lifting their hands
to heaven, and entreating or beseeching us to land
there: . . . the people are totally unacquainted with
arms, as your Highnesses will see by observing the
seven [earlier indicated six] which I have caused to
be taken in order to carry them to Castile to be
taught our language, and to return them unless your
Highnesses when they shall send orders may take
them all to Castile, or keep them in the same island
as captives, for with fifty men all can be kept in
subjection, and made to do whatever you desire."

REVIEWING THE READING

1. Who did Columbus expect to read his
   journal? How can you tell?

2. Why do you think Columbus told his
   crews that the fleet was covering less distance each day than it really was?

3. **Using Your Historical Imagination.** According to Columbus, what were the attributes of the native peoples he had
   encountered? Reading between the lines,
   what conclusions can you draw about
   Spanish intentions toward the natives?

2

From *History of the Indies* by Bartolomé de las Casas.

Bartolomé de las Casas Condemns Spanish Treatment of the Indians (ca. 1510)

Friar Bartolomé de las Casas came to Spain's colonies in the New World in 1502. He personally witnessed the harsh working conditions forced on many Indians by the Spanish. In his book History of the Indies *he detailed the plight of the Indians and strongly condemned Spanish labor practices. As you read this excerpt, consider what seems to have been the main use the Spanish made of the Indians.*

At first, the Indians were forced to stay six months away from home at work. Later, the time was extended to eight months and this was called a shift, at the end of which they brought all the gold for minting [making into coins]. During the minting period, the Indians were allowed to go home, a few days' journey on foot. One can imagine their state when they arrived after eight months, and those who found their wives there must have cried, lamenting their condition together. Of those who had worked in the mines, a bare 10 percent survived to start the journey home. Many Spaniards had no scruples about making them work on Sundays and holidays, if not in the mines, then on minor tasks such as building and repairing houses, carrying firewood, etc. They fed them cassava bread, which is adequate nutrition only when supplemented with meat, fish, or other more substantial food. The minero [Spaniard in charge of the mines] killed a pig once a week, but he kept more than half for himself and had the leftover cooked daily for thirty or forty Indians, which came to a bite of meat the size of a walnut, per individual. While the minero was eating, the Indians were under the table, just like dogs and cats, ready to snatch a bone. This ration applied only to mine workers; others never tasted meat in their lives and sustained themselves exclusively on cassava and other roots.

In exchange for his life of services, an Indian received 225 *maravedis*, paid them once a year as pin money or *cacona*, as Indians call it, which means bonus or reward. This sum bought a comb, a small mirror, and a string of green or blue glass beads.

I believe the above clearly demonstrates that the Indians were totally deprived of their freedom and were put in the harshest, fiercest, most horrible servitude and captivity which no one who has not seen it can understand. Even beasts enjoy more freedom when they are allowed to graze in the fields. When the Indians were allowed to go home, they often found it deserted and had no other recourse

Friar Bartolomé de las Casas toured the Spanish colonies and saw the exploitation of the Indians by their Spanish conquerors.

than to go out into the woods to find food and die. When they fell ill, which was very frequently because they are a delicate people unaccustomed to such work, the Spaniards did not believe them and pitilessly called them lazy dogs, and kicked and beat them; and when illness was apparent they sent them home as useless. I sometimes came upon dead bodies on my way, and upon others who were gasping and moaning in their death agony, repeating "Hungry, hungry." And this was the freedom, the good treatment, and the Christianity that Indians received.

Is there a single nation which would not think that the world is full of just such evildoers as the Spaniards if their first experience with that outside world was with a people who entered territories by force, killed the people, and deprived them of their rights? Just because the Spaniards told them to obey the King of Castile [Spain], supposing they understood, what obligation did they have to obey since they already had their own kings? Or rather, if they had consented, would they not be judged as ridiculously stupid for doing so? Was trying to defend oneself from Spanish cruelties such a crime? Even beasts are allowed the right of self-defense.

REVIEWING THE READING

1. According to Las Casas, what was the primary purpose for which the Spanish used the Indians?

2. What hardships did the Indians endure during their forced labor in the mines?

3. **Using Your Historical Imagination.** Why do you think the Spaniards treated the Indians as they did, and why is Las Casas, a Spaniard himself, so bitterly in disagreement with this policy?

Coronado Explores the Southwest (1541)

3

From *The Journey of Coronado, 1540–1542* by George Parker Winship.

The enormous quantities of gold discovered in Mexico and Peru led to Spanish explorations farther north. In 1540, Spanish provincial governor Franciso Coronado led an expedition to locate seven legendary cities of gold far to the north in a region known as Cibola. Months of hard travel ended in bitter disappointment in July 1540. The villages of Cibola were made of adobe bricks and their Indian inhabitants had little of value. Coronado did not give up, however. While he was at Cibola, the Indians told him of a rich city called Quivira located hundreds of miles to the east. Hoping to find the gold that had eluded him in Cibola, in the spring of 1541 he left his camp near what is now Albuquerque, New Mexico. Months later he wrote a report of his expedition to Charles I of Spain. He had explored the trackless plains of North America as far as what we know as central Kansas and had encountered several tribes of Plains Indians, but once again the legends of gold had proven false. In these excerpts from his report to the Spanish king, consider the ways in which Coronado tries to soften the bad news.

After nine days' march I reached some plains, so vast that I did not find their limit anywhere that I went, although I traveled over them for more than 300 leagues [about 1200 miles]. And I found such a quantity of cows [buffalo] in these, of the kind that I wrote Your Majesty about, which they have in this country, that it is impossible to number them, for while I was journeying through these plains,

Coronado and his men explored the plains of North America as far east as central Kansas in search of the elusive city of gold, Quivira.

until I returned to where I first found them, there was not a day that I lost sight of them. And after seventeen days' march I came to a settlement of Indians who are called Querechos, who travel around with these cows, who do not plant, and who eat the raw flesh and drink the blood of the cows they kill, and they tan the skins of the cows, with which all the people of this country dress themselves here. They have little field tents made of the hides of the cows, tanned and greased, very well made, in which they live while they travel around near the cows, moving with these. They have dogs which they load, which carry their tents and poles and belongings. These people have the best figures of any that I have seen in the Indies. They could not give me any account of the country where the guides were taking me. I traveled five days more as the guides wished to lead me, until I reached some plains, with no more landmarks than as if we had been swallowed up in the sea, where they strayed about, because there was not a stone, nor a bit of rising ground, nor a tree, nor a shrub, nor anything to go by. There is much very fine pasture land, with good grass. And while we were lost in these plains, some horsemen who went off to hunt cows fell in with some Indians who also were out hunting, who are enemies of those that I had seen in the last settlement, and of another sort of people who are called Teyas; they have their bodies and faces all painted, are a large people like the others, of a very good build; they eat the raw flesh just like the Querechos, and live and travel round with the cows in the same way as these. I obtained from these an account of the country where the guides were taking me, which was not like what they had told me, because these made out that the houses there were not built of stones, with stories, as my guides had described it, but of straw and skins, and a small supply of corn there.

This news troubled me greatly, to find myself on these limitless plains, where I was in great need of water, and often had to drink it so poor that it was more mud than water. Here the guides confessed to me that they had not told the truth in regard to the size of the houses, because these were of straw, but that they had done so regarding the large number of inhabitants and the other things about their habits. . . . It seemed to me best, in order to see if there was anything there of service to Your Majesty, to go forward with only 30 horsemen until I should be able to see the country, so as to give Your Majesty a true account of what was to be found in it. I sent all the rest of the force I had with me to this province, with Don Tristan de Arellano in command, because it would have been impossible to prevent the loss of many men, if all had gone on, owing to the lack of water and because they also had to kill

bulls and cows on which to sustain themselves. And
with only the 30 horsemen whom I took for my
escort, I traveled forty-two days after I left the force,
living all this while solely on the flesh of the bulls
and cows which we killed, at the cost of several of
our horses which they killed, because, as I wrote
Your Majesty, they are very brave and fierce animals;
and going many days without water, and cooking
the food with cow dung, because there is not any
kind of wood in all these plains, away from the
gullies and rivers, which are very few.

It was the Lord's pleasure that, after having
journeyed across these deserts seventy-seven days,
I arrived at the province they call Quivira, to which
the guides were conducting me, and where they
had described to me houses of stone, with many
stories; and not only are they not of stone, but of
straw, but the people in them are as barbarous as
all those whom I have seen and passed before this;
they do not have cloaks, nor cotton of which to
make these, but use the skins of the cattle they
kill, which they tan, because they are settled among
these on a very large river. They eat the raw flesh
like the Querechos and Teyas; they are enemies of
one another, but are all of the same sort of people,
and these at Quivira have the advantage in the houses
they build and in planting corn. In this province
of which the guides who brought me are natives,
they received me peaceably, and although they told
me when I set out for it that I could not succeed
in seeing it all in two months, there are not more
than 25 villages of straw houses there and in all
the rest of the country that I saw and learned about,
which gave their obedience to Your Majesty and
placed themselves under your royal overlordship.

The province of Quivira is 950 leagues [3,800
miles] from Mexico. Where I reached it, it is in
the fortieth degree [of latitude]. The country itself
is the best I have ever seen for producing all the
products of Spain, for besides the land itself being

very fat and black and being very well watered by
the rivulets and springs and rivers, I found prunes
like those of Spain and nuts and very good sweet
grapes and mulberries. I have treated the natives of
this province, and all the others whom I found wherever I went, as well as was possible, agreeably to
what Your Majesty had commanded, and they have
received no harm in any way from me or from those
who went in my company. . . . And what I am
sure of is that there is not any gold nor any other
metal in all that country, and the other things of
which they had told me are nothing but little villages,
and in many of these they do not plant anything
and do not have any houses except of skins and
sticks, and they wander around with the cows; so
that the account they gave me was false, because
they wanted to persuade me to go there with the
whole force, believing that as the way was through
such uninhabited deserts, and from the lack of water,
they would get us where we and our horses would
die of hunger. And the guides confessed this, and
said they had done it by the advice and orders of
the natives of these provinces.

REVIEWING THE READING

1. What excuse does Coronado make for
   his failure to find gold? How does he
   try to convince the king that his expedition was not a total failure?

2. Why might the Indians at Cibola have
   wanted to mislead Coronado with tales
   of gold far to the east?

3. **Using Your Historical Imagination.** If you
   were the king of Spain, what conclusions
   would you draw about the culture of the
   Plains Indians from Coronado's account?

4

From *The Portable North American Indian Reader*, edited by Frederick W. Turner III.

A Speech by Powhatan (1609)

For 15 years the English of Jamestown got along reasonably well with the native peoples of tidewater Virginia. These Indians called themselves the Powhatans, and their chief in 1607 was also known as Powhatan. Relationships were at times uneasy, and there were a few skirmishes between newcomers and natives, but Powhatan did not view the tiny Jamestown settlement as a serious threat. Furthermore, he was fascinated by English-made pots, pans, mirrors, axes, colored cloth, and other trade goods. In 1614, after John Rolfe married Powhatan's daughter Pocahontas, something of an alliance was formed. The following selection is from a speech made by Chief Powhatan in 1609, which was recorded by John Smith. As you read the excerpts, consider what sort of relationship Powhatan says that he wishes to establish with the English.

Why will you take by force what you may obtain by love? Why will you destroy us who supply you with food? What can you get by war? . . . We are unarmed, and willing to give you what you ask, if you come in a friendly manner. . . .

I am not so simple as not to know it is better to eat good meat, sleep comfortably, live quietly with my women and children, laugh and be merry with the English, and being their friend, trade for their copper and hatchets, than to run away from them. . . .

Take away your guns and swords, the cause of all our jealousy, or you may die in the same manner.

The English settlers of Jamestown and Chief Powhatan treated each other with respect.

REVIEWING THE READING

1. What does Powhatan say his people have been doing for the English?

2. What sort of relationship does he say that he prefers?

3. **Using Your Historical Imagination.** Can you suggest a likely reason that Chief Powhatan made this particular speech?

<table>
<tr><td>

5

From *Of Plymouth Plantation* by William Bradford.

</td><td>

Bradford Describes the Founding of Plymouth Plantation (1620)

</td></tr>
</table>

William Bradford's eyewitness account of the founding of Plymouth Colony is one of the first masterpieces of American literature. Bradford, a Pilgrim farmer from Yorkshire, became one of the leaders of the new colony. His fellow citizens elected him governor no less than thirty times.

Bradford's record, Of Plymouth Plantation, *was written between 1630 and 1647. In it he told of the hardships of the sea voyage on the Mayflower and the terrible "starving time" in the dark and cold winter of 1620 to 1621, when half the Pilgrims died of exposure, disease, and malnutrition. Bradford, like the other Pilgrims, believed that God's providence—his divine will—could be seen in day-to-day events. As you read the excerpts consider the occurrences in this account thought by Bradford to be signs of divine providence.*

September 6 [1620]

These troubles being blown over, and now all being compact together in the one ship, they put to sea again with a prosperous wind, which continued divers [many] days together, which was some encouragement unto them; yet, according to the usual manner, many were afflicted with seasickness. . . .

After they had enjoyed fair winds and weather for a season, they were encountered many times with crosswinds and met with many fierce storms, with which the ship was shroudly [wickedly] shaken

and her upper works made very leaky; and one of
the main beams in the midships was bowed and
cracked, which put them in some fear that the ship
could not be able to perform the voyage. So some
of the chief of the company, perceiving the mariners
to fear the sufficiency of the ship, as appeared by
their mutterings, they entered into serious consulta-
tion with the master and other officers of the ship,
to consider in time of the danger, and rather to
return than to cast themselves into a desperate and
inevitable peril. And truly there was great distraction
and difference of opinion amongst the mariners
themselves; fain [gladly] would they do what could
be done for their wages' sake (being now near half
the seas over), and on the other hand they were
loath [reluctant] to hazard their lives too desperately.
But in examining all opinions, the master and others
affirmed they knew the ship to be strong and firm
under water; and for the buckling of the main beam,
there was a great iron screw the passengers brought
out of Holland, which would raise the beam into
his place; the which being done, the carpenter and
master affirmed that with a post put under it, set
firm in the lower deck, and otherways bound, he
would make it sufficient. And as for the decks and
upper works, they would caulk them as well as they
could, and though with the working of the ship
they would not long keep staunch [watertight], yet
there would otherwise be no great danger, if they
did not overpress her with sails. So they committed
themselves to the will of God and resolved to
proceed.

In sundry of these storms the winds were so
fierce and the seas so high as they could not bear
a knot of sail, but were forced to hull [lay to and
drift under short sail] for divers days together. And
in one of them, as they thus lay at hull in a mighty
storm, a lusty young man called John Howland, coming upon some occasion above the gratings, was,
with a seele [roll] of the ship, thrown into sea; but

it pleased God that he caught hold of the topsail
halyards which hung overboard and ran out at length.
Yet he held his hold (though he was sundry fathoms
under water) till he was hauled up by the same
rope to the brim of the water, and then with a
boat hook and other means got into the ship again
and his life saved. And though he was something
ill with it, yet he lived many years after and became
a profitable member both in church and commonwealth. In all this voyage there died but one of
the passengers, which was William Butten, a youth,
servant to Samuel Fuller, when they drew near the
coast.

*The Pilgrims were ill
prepared for the harsh
New England winter.
More than half of them
died from the combined
effects of cold, lack of
food, and disease.*

But to omit other things (that I may be brief)
after long beating at sea they fell with that land
which is called Cape Cod; the which being made
and certainly known to be it, they were not a little
joyful. After some deliberation had amongst themselves and with the master of the ship, they tacked
about and resolved to stand for the southward (the

wind and weather being fair) to find some place about Hudson's River for their habitation. But after they had sailed that course about half the day, they fell amongst dangerous shoals and roaring breakers, and they were so far entangled therewith as they conceived themselves in great danger; and the wind shrinking upon them withal, they resolved to bear up again for the Cape and thought themselves happy to get out of those dangers before night overtook them, as by God's good Providence they did. And the next day they got into the Cape Harbor, where they rid [anchored] in safety. . . .

Being thus arrived in a good harbor, and brought safe to land, they fell upon their knees and blessed the God of Heaven who had brought them over the vast and furious ocean, and delivered them from all the perils and miseries thereof, again to set their feet on the firm and stable earth, their proper element. . . .

But here I cannot but stay and make a pause, and stand half amazed at this poor people's present condition; and so I think will the reader, too, when he well considers the same. Being thus passed the vast ocean, and a sea of troubles before in their preparation (as may be remembered by that which went before), they had now no friends to welcome them nor inns to entertain or refresh their weather-beaten bodies; no houses or much less towns to repair to, to seek for succor [aid]. It is recorded in Scripture as a mercy to the Apostle and his ship-wrecked company, that the barbarians showed them no small kindness in refreshing them, but these savage barbarians, when they met with them (as after will appear) were readier to fill their sides full of arrows than otherwise. And for the season it was winter, and they that know the winters of that country know them to be sharp and violent, and subject to cruel and fierce storms, dangerous to travel to unknown places, much more to search an unknown coast. Be-sides, what could they see but a hideous and desolate

. . . and the whole country, full of woods and thickets, represented a wild and savage hue.

wilderness, full of wild beasts and wild men—and what multitudes there might be of them they know not. Neither could they, as it were, go up to the top of Pisgah [the mountain from which Moses first viewed the land that had been promised to the Hebrews by God] to view from this wilderness a more goodly country to feed their hopes; for which way soever they turned their eyes (save upward to the heavens) they could have little solace or content in respect of any outward objects. For summer being done, all things stand upon them with a weather-beaten face, and the whole country, full of woods and thickets, represented a wild and savage hue. If they looked behind them, there was the mighty ocean which they had passed and was now as a main bar and gulf to separate them from all the civil parts of the world. . . .

What could now sustain them but the Spirit of God and His grace? May not and ought not the children of these fathers rightly say: "Our fathers were Englishmen which came over this great ocean, and were ready to perish in this wilderness; but they cried unto the Lord, and He heard their voice and looked on their adversity," etc? "Let them therefore praise the Lord, because He is good: and His mercies endure forever." "Yea, let them which have been redeemed of the Lord, shew how He hath delivered them from the hand of the oppressor. When they wandered in the desert wilderness out of the way, and found no city to dwell in, both hungry and thirsty, their soul was overwhelmed in them. Let them confess before the Lord His loving-kindness and His wonderful works before the sons of men.". . .

The Starving Time [1620–1621]
But that which was most sad and lamentable was that in two or three months' time half of their company died, especially in January and February, being the depth of winter, and wanting houses and other

comforts; being infected with the scurvy and other
diseases which this long voyage and their inaccom-
modate condition had brought upon them. So as
there died sometimes two or three of a day in the
foresaid time, that of 100 and odd persons, scarce
fifty remained. And of these, in the time of most
distress, there was but six or seven sound persons
who to their great commendations, be it spoken,
spared no pains night nor day, but with abundance
of toil and hazard of their own health, fetched them
wood, made them fires, dressed them meat, made
their beds, washed their loathsome clothes, clothed
and unclothed them: in a word, did all the homely
and necessary offices for them which dainty and
queasy stomachs cannot endure to hear named; and
all this willingly and cheerfully, without any grudging
in the least, showing herein their true love unto
their friends and brethren; a rare example and worthy
to be remembered. Two of these seven were Mr.
William Brewster, their reverend elder, and Myles
Standish, their captain and military commander, to
whom myself and many others were much beholden
in our low and sick condition. And yet the Lord
so upheld these persons as in this general calamity
they were not at all infected either with sickness
or lameness. . . .

Indian Relations
All this while the Indians came skulking about them,
and would sometimes show themselves aloof off,
but when any approached near them, they would
run away; and once they stole away their tools where
they had been at work and were gone to dinner.
But about the 16th of March, a certain Indian came
boldly amongst them and spoke to them in broken
English, which they could well understand but marveled at it. At length they understood, by discourse
with him, that he was not of these parts but belonged
to the eastern parts where some English ships came
to fish, with whom he was acquainted and could

He told them also of another Indian whose name was Squanto . . .

name sundry of them by their names, amongst whom he had got his language. He became profitable to them in acquainting them with many things concerning the state of the country in the east parts where he lived, which was afterward profitable unto them; as also of the people here, of their names, number, and strength, of their situation and distance from this place, and who was chief amongst them. His name was Samoset. He told them also of another Indian whose name was Squanto, a native of this place, who had been in England and could speak better English than himself.

Being, after some time of entertainment and gifts, dismissed, a while after he came again, and five more with him, and they brought again all the tools that were stolen away before, and made way for the coming of their great Sachem [chief], called Massasoit. Who, about four or five days after, came with the chief of his friends and other attendance, with the aforesaid Squanto. With whom, after friendly entertainment and some gifts given him, they made a peace with him (which hath now continued this 24 years) in these terms:

1. That neither he nor any of his should injure or do hurt to any of their people.
2. That if any of his did hurt to any of theirs, he should send the offender, that they might punish him.
3. That if anything were taken away from any of theirs, he should cause it to be restored; and they should do the like to his.
4. If any did unjustly war against him, they would aid him; if any did war against them, he should aid them.
5. He should send to his neighbors confederates to certify them of this, that they might not wrong them, but might be likewise comprised in the conditions of peace.

6. That when their men came to them, they should leave their bows and arrows behind them.

After these things he returned to his place, called Sowams, some 40 miles from this place, but Squanto continued with them and was their interpreter and was a special instrument sent of God for their good beyond their expectation. He directed them how to set their corn, where to take fish and to procure other commodities, and was also their pilot to bring them to unknown places for their profit, and never left them till he died. He was a native of this place, and scarce any left alive besides himself. He was carried away [earlier] with divers others by one Hunt, a master of a ship, who thought to sell them for slaves in Spain. But he got away for England and was entertained by a merchant in London, and employed to Newfoundland and other parts by one Mr. Dermer, a gentlemen employed by Sir Ferdinando Gorges and others for discovery and other design in these parts.

REVIEWING THE READING

1. What examples of the working of God's providence are suggested by Bradford?

2. Why was the Pilgrims' meeting with Samoset and Squanto a turning point in the history of Plymouth Colony?

3. **Using Your Historical Imagination.** Imagine that you are a Pilgrim settler. What would you ask Samoset and Squanto to do to help you survive and prosper?

6

From *Letter to his father and mother, March 20, April 2 and 3, 1623* by Richard Frethorne, in *The Records of the Virginia Company of London,* edited by Susan M. Kingsbury.

An Indentured Servant Writes Home (1623)

By 1618 the struggling Jamestown colony of the London Company had discovered a cash crop. Tobacco grew well in Virginia and found a ready market back home. To encourage the production of tobacco the Company offered a liberal headright system to new settlers. Persons who relocated to Virginia received 50 acres of land for each "head" transported, and this included their indentured servants as well as themselves. In return for free passage to Virginia, indentured servants contracted to serve their master for seven years. Only at the end of the seven years were they free to pursue their own fortunes in the New World.

Even in the 1620s conditions were harsh and dangerous in Virginia, and the death rate from disease and malnutrition was very high. In 1623 indentured servant Richard Frethorne wrote his mother and father complaining of the bitter hardships he was enduring in Jamestown. Frethorne's woeful letter survives in the records of the London Company, but nothing more is known of the young man or of what ultimately happened to him. The chances are high that he too perished in Virginia in 1623. As you read this excerpt, consider what Richard Frethorne was trying to accomplish with his letter home.

Loving and kind father and mother my most humble duty remembered to you hoping in God of your good health, as I myself am . . . . at the making hereof, this is to let you understand that I your Child am in a most heavy Case by reason of the nature of the Country . . . is such that it Causeth

much sickness, as the scurvy and the bloody flux,
and divers other diseases, which maketh the body
very poor, and Weak, and when we are sick there
is nothing to Comfort us; for since I came out of
the ship, I never ate anything but peas, and loblollie
(that is water gruel)[possibly made from oats] as
for deer or venison I never saw any since I came
into this land; there is indeed some fowl, but We
are not allowed to go, and get it, but must Work
hard both early, and late for a mess of water gruel,
and a mouthful of bread, and beef, a mouthful of
bread for a penny loaf must serve for 4 men which
is most pitiful . . . people cry out day, and night,
Oh that they were in England without their limbs
and would not care to lose any limb to be in England
again, yea though they beg from door to door, for
we live in fear of the Enemy every hour, yet we
have had a Combat with them on the Sunday before
Shrovetide, and we took two alive, and make slaves
of them, but it was by policy, for we are in great
danger, for our Plantation is very weak, by reason
of the death, and sickness, of our Company, for
we came but Twenty for the marchaunte [merchants],
and they are half dead Just; and we look every hour
When two more should go, yet there came some
for other men yet to live with us, of which there
is but one alive, and our Lieutenant is dead, and
his father, and his brother, I have nothing to Comfort
me, nor there is nothing to be gotten here but sickness, and death, except that one had money to lay
out in some things for profit; But I have nothing at
all, no not a shirt to my back, but two Rags nor
no Clothes, but one poor suit, nor but one pair of
shoes, but one pair of stockings, but one Cap, but
two band, my Cloak is stolen by one of my own
fellows, and to his dying hour would not tell me
what he did with it but some of my fellows saw
him have butter and beef out of a ship, which my
Cloak I doubt [fear] paid for, so that I have not a
penny, nor a [half] penny Worth to help me to

Some of the labor needed to improve the Jamestown colony was provided by indentured servants. In exchange for their passage to the New World, they agreed to work for their masters for seven years.

either spice, or sugar, or strong Waters, without the which one cannot live here, for as strong beer in England doth fatten and strengthen them so water here doth wash and weaken this here, only keep life and soul together. But I am not half a quarter so strong as I was in England, and all is for want of victuals, for I do protest unto you, that I have eaten more in [a] day at home than I have allowed me here for a Week. You have given more than my day's allowance to a beggar at the door; and if Mr. Jackson had not relieved me, I should be in a poor Case, but he like a father and she like a loving mother doth still help me, for when we go up to James Town that is 10 miles of us, there lie all the ships that Come to the land, and there they must deliver their goods, and when we went up to Town as it may be on Monday, at noon, and come there by night, then load the next day by noon, and go home in the afternoon, and unload, and then away again in the night, and be up about midnight, then if it rained, or blowed ever so hard we must lie in the boat on the water, and have nothing but a little bread, for when we go into the boat we have a loaf allowed to two men, and it is all if we stayed

there 2 days, which is hard, and must lie all that
while in the boat, but that Goodman Jackson pitied
me and made me a Cabin to lie in always when I
come up, and he would give me some poor Jacke
[a kind of fish] [to take] home with me which Com-
forted me more than peas, or water gruel. Oh they
be very godly folks, and love me very well, and
will do anything for me, and he much marveled
that you would send me a servant to the Company,
he saith I had been better knocked on the head,
and Indeed so I find it now to my great grief and
misery, and saith, that if you love me you will redeem
me suddenly, good father do not forget me, but
have mercy and pity my miserable Case. I know if
you did but see me you would weep to see me, for
I have but one suit, but it is a strange one, it is
very well guarded, wherefore for God's sake pity
me, I pray you to remember my love to all my
friends, and kindred, I hope all my Brothers and
Sisters are in good health, and as for my part I
have set down my resolution that certainly Will
be, that is, that the Answer of this letter will be
life or death to me, therefore good father send as
soon as you can.

REVIEWING THE READING

1. What seems to have been the main purpose of Frethorne's letter home?

2. Of the many hardships of life in Virginia,
   what do you think bothered him the most?

3. **Using Your Historical Imagination.** What
   does Richard Frethorne's account suggest
   about the methods by which indentured
   servants were recruited to go to Virginia?
   What does it suggest about the life of
   the poorer classes in England?

7

From *The Works of Anne Bradstreet*, edited by Jeannine Hensley.

A Poem by Anne Bradstreet (1666)

Anne Bradstreet came to Massachusetts Bay Colony at the age of 18, the wife of a young Puritan who later became governor of the colony. Educated by tutors in her native England, she was a gifted writer who created the first American poetry. Her writing was not intended for publication, but a brother-in-law took some of Bradstreet's poems to England in 1647 and published them there. The poems became popular, and Anne Bradstreet continued to write poetry until her death in 1672.

Anne Bradstreet was a religious person first and a poet second. Many of her poems, such as the one that follows, demonstrate the Puritan religious consciousness in action. The poem is based on a real event and was entitled "Here Follow Some Verses upon the Burning of Our House, July 10, 1666." Consider what Bradstreet sees as the personal lesson taught by the destruction of her home, her library, and all of her unpublished poems.

In silent night when rest I took
  For sorrow near I did not look
I wakened was with thund'ring noise
And piteous shrieks of dreadful voice.
That fearful sound of "Fire!" and "Fire!"
Let no man know is my desire.
I, starting up, the light did spy,
And to my God my heart did cry
To strengthen me in my distress
And not to leave me succorless.
Then, coming out, beheld a space
The flame consume my dwelling place.
And when I could no longer look,

I blest His name that gave and took,
That laid my goods now in the dust.
Yea, so it was, and so 'twas just.
It was His own, it was not mine,
Far be it that I should repine;
He might of all justly bereft
But yet sufficient for us left.
When by the ruins oft I past
My sorrowing eyes aside did cast,
And here and there the places spy
Where oft I sat and long did lie:
Here stood that trunk, and there that chest,
There lay that store I counted best.
My pleasant things in ashes lie,
And them behold no more shall I.
Under thy roof no guest shall sit,
Nor at thy table eat a bit.
No pleasant tale shall e'er be told,
Nor things recounted done of old.
No candle e'er shall shine in thee,

Puritans, such as Anne Bradstreet, followed a strict moral and religious code in their daily lives.

Nor bridegroom's voice e'er heard shall be.
In silence ever shall thou lie,
Adieu, Adieu, all's vanity.
Then straight I 'gin my heart to chide,
And did thy wealth on earth abide?
Didst fix thy hope on mold'ring dust?
The arm of flesh didst make thy trust?
Raise up thy thoughts above the sky
That dunghill mists away may fly.
Thou hast an house on high erect,
Framed by that mighty Architect,
With glory richly furnished,
Stands permanent though this be fled.
It's purchased and paid for too
By Him who hath enough to do.
A price so vast as is unknown
Yet by His gift is made thine own;
There's wealth enough, I need no more
Farewell, my pelf,* farewell my store.
The world no longer let me love,
My hope and treasure lies above.

*pelf: worldly goods

REVIEWING THE READING

1. What is the religious lesson Bradstreet says she learned as a result of the burning of her house?

2. How was Bradstreet awakened on the night of the fire?

3. **Using Your Historical Imagination.** What is the relationship between the religious theme expressed in Bradstreet's poem and the idea of material progress—the accumulation of property and wealth in this world?

The Importance of Indian Corn (1600s)

8

From *Home Life in Colonial Days* by Alice Morse Earle.

Although we may sometimes think of history as only a matter of great events, important leaders, politics, and war, the reality was quite different. The basic patterns of daily life in the past are also important, and of these basic patterns what could be more important than food? In these excerpts from her book Home Life in Colonial Days, *social historian Alice Morse Earle tells how Europeans learned to use the native American grain crop of the Americas—Indian corn, or maize. As you read try to determine what basic lesson Morse seems to offer for any settlers in a strange land.*

A great field of tall Indian corn waving its stately and luxuriant green blades, its graceful spindles, and glossy silk under the hot August sun, should be not only a beautiful sight to every American, but a suggestive one; one to set us thinking of all that Indian corn means to us in our history. It was a native of American soil at the settlement of this country, and under full and thoroughly intelligent cultivation by the Indians, who were also native sons of the New World. Its abundance, adaptability, and nourishing qualities not only saved the colonists' lives but altered many of their methods of living, especially their manner of cooking and their tastes in food.

One of the first things that every settler in a new land has to learn is that he must find food in that land; that he cannot trust long to any supplies of food which he has brought with him, or to any fresh supplies which he has ordered to be sent after him. He must turn at once to hunting, fishing, planting, to furnish him with food grown and found in the very place where he is.

This was quickly learned by the colonists in America, except in Virginia, where they had sad starving-times before all were convinced that corn was a better crop for settlers than silk or any of the many hoped-for productions which might be valuable in one sense but which could not be eaten. Powhatan, the father of the Indian princess Pocahontas, was one of the first to "send some of his People that they may teach the English how to sow the Grain of his Country." Captain John Smith, ever quick to learn of every one and ever practical, got two Indians, in the year 1608, to show him how to break up and plant forty acres of corn, which yielded him a good crop. A succeeding governor of Virginia, Sir Thomas Dale, equally practical, intelligent, and determined, assigned small farms to each colonist, and encouraged and enforced the growing of corn. Soon many thousand bushels were raised. There was a terrible Indian massacre in 1622, for the careless colonists, in order to be free to give their time to the raising of that new and exceedingly alluring and high-priced crop, tobacco, had given the Indians firearms to go hunting game for them; and the lesson of easy killing with powder and shot, when once learned, was turned with havoc upon the white men. The following year comparatively little corn was planted, as the luxuriant foliage made a perfect ambush for the close approach of the savages to the settlements. There was, of course, scarcity and famine as the result; and a bushel of corn-meal became worth twenty to thirty shillings, which sum had a value equal to twenty to thirty dollars to-day [the 1890s]. The planters were each compelled by the magistrates the following year to raise an ample amount of corn to supply all the families; and to save a certain amount for seed as well. There has been no lack of corn since that time in Virginia. . . .

The stores brought over by the Pilgrims were poor and inadequate enough; the beef and pork were tainted, the fish rotten, the butter and cheese corrupted. European wheat and seeds did not mature well. Soon, as Bradford says in his now famous *Log-Book*, in his picturesque and forcible English, "the grim and grizzled face of starvation stared" at them. The readiest supply to replenish the scanty larder [food stores] was fish, but the English made surprisingly bungling work over fishing, and soon the most unfailing and valuable supply was the native Indian corn, or "Guinny wheat," or "Turkie wheat," as it was called by the colonists.

. . . the most unfailing and valuable supply was the native Indian corn . . .

Famine and pestilence had left eastern Massachusetts comparatively bare of inhabitants at the time of the settlement of Plymouth; and the vacant cornfields of the dead Indian cultivators were taken and planted by the weak and emaciated Plymouth men, who never could have cleared new fields. From the teeming sea, in the April run of fish, was found the needed fertilizer. Says Governor Bradford:—

> "In April of the first year they began to plant their corne, in which service Squanto stood them in great stead, showing them both ye manner how to set it, and after, how to dress and tend it."

From this planting sprang not only the most useful food, but the first and most pregnant [significant] industry of the colonists.

The first fields and crops were communal, and the result was disastrous. The third year, at the sight of the paralyzed settlement, Governor Bradford wisely decided, as did Governor Dale of Virginia, that "they should set corne every man for his owne particuler, furnishing a portion for public officers, fishermen, etc., who could not work, and in that regard trust to themselves." Thus personal energy succeeded to communal inertia; Bradford wrote that women and children cheerfully worked in the fields to raise corn which should be their very own.

A field of corn on the coast of Massachusetts or Narragansett or by the rivers of Virginia, growing long before any white man had ever been seen on these shores, was precisely like the same field planted three hundred years later by our American farmers. There was the same planting in hills, the same number of stalks in the hill, with pumpkin vines running among the hills, and beans climbing the stalks. The hills of the Indians were a trifle nearer together than those of our own day are usually set, for the native soil was more fertile.

The Indians taught the colonists much more than the planting and raising of corn; they showed also how to grind the corn and cook it in many palatable ways. The various foods which we use to-day made from Indian corn are all cooked just as the Indians cooked them at the time of the settlement of the country; and they are still called with Indian names, such as hominy, pone, suppawn, samp, succotash.

The Indian method of preparing maize or corn was to steep or parboil it in hot water for twelve hours, then to pound the grain in a mortar or a hollowed stone in the field, till it was a coarse meal. It was then sifted in a rather closely woven basket, and the large grains which did not pass through the sieve were again pounded and sifted. . . .

Suppawn was another favorite of the settlers, and was an Indian dish made from Indian corn; it was a thick corn-meal and milk porridge. It was soon seen on every Dutch table, for the Dutch were very fond of all foods made from all kinds of grain; and it is spoken of by all travellers in early New York, and in the Southern colonies.

Samp and samp porridge were soon abundant dishes. Samp is Indian corn pounded to a coarsely ground powder. Roger Williams wrote of it:—

"Nawsamp is a kind of meal pottage un-parched. From this the English call their samp, which is the Indian corn beaten and boiled and eaten hot or cold with milk and butter, and is a diet exceedingly wholesome for English bodies."

The Swedish scientist, Professor Kalm, told that the Indians gave him "fresh maize-bread, baked in an oblong shape, mixed with dried huckleberries, which lay as close in it as raisins in a plum pudding."

Roger Williams said that sukquttahhash was "corn seethed [boiled] like beans." Our word "succotash" we now apply to corn cooked with beans. Pones were the red men's appones [baked corn cakes].

The love of the Indians for "roasting ears" was quickly shared by the white man. In Virginia a series of plantings of corn were made from the first of

In this nineteenth-century engraving Pocahontas is bringing corn to the colonists at Jamestown. The Indians also taught the colonists how to plant and raise corn, helping them to become self-sufficient.

"They lap their corn in rowles within the leaves of the corne . . ."

April to the last of June, to afford a three months' succession of roasting ears.

The traveller, Strachey, writing of the Indians in 1618, said: "They lap their corn in rowles within the leaves of the corne and so boyle yt for a dayntie." This method of cooking we have also retained to the present day.

It seemed to me very curious to read in Governor Winthrop's journal, written in Boston about 1630, that when corn was "parched," as he called it, it turned inside out and was "white and floury within"; and to think that then little English children were at that time learning what pop-corn was, and how it looked when it was parched, or popped.

Hasty pudding had been made in England of wheat-flour or oatmeal and milk, and the name was given to boiled puddings of corn-meal and water. It was not a very suitable name, for corn-meal should never be cooked hastily, but requires long boiling or baking. The hard Indian pudding slightly sweetened and boiled in a bag was everywhere made. It was told that many New England families had three hundred and sixty-five such puddings in a year. . . .

There was one way of eating corn which was spoken of by all the early writers and travellers which we should not be very well satisfied with now, but it shows us how useful and necessary corn was at that time, and how much all depended on it. This preparation of corn was called nocake or nookick. An old writer named Wood thus defined it:—

> "It is Indian corn parched in the hot ashes, the ashes being sifted from it; it is afterwards beaten to powder and put into a long leatherne bag trussed at the Indian's backe like a knapsacke, out of which they take three spoonsful a day."

It was held to be the most nourishing food known, and in the smallest and most condensed form. Both Indians and white men usually carried it in a pouch when they went on long journeys, and mixed it with snow in the winter and water in summer. Gookin says it was sweet, toothsome, and hearty. With only this nourishment the Indians could carry loads "fitter for elephants than men." Roger Williams says a spoonful of this meal and water made him many a good meal. When we read this we are not surprised that the Pilgrims could keep alive on what is said was at one time of famine their food for a day,—five kernels of corn apiece. . . .

One special use of corn should be noted. By order of the government of Massachusetts Bay in 1623, it was used as ballots in public voting. At annual elections of the governors' assistants in each town, a kernel of corn was deposited to signify a favorable vote upon the nominee, while a bean signified a negative vote; "and if any free-man shall put in more than one Indian corn or bean he shall forfeit for every such offence Ten Pounds."

REVIEWING THE READING

1. According to Earle, what is the main lesson taught by the story of the adoption of Indian corn by the colonial pioneers?

2. What was the first method used by the colonists to convert Indian corn to flour? What other power sources for accomplishing this soon came into use?

3. **Using Your Historical Imagination.** Why do you think the colonial settlers were often rather slow to adopt the cultivation of Indian corn? Why does this process seem to have gone more slowly in Virginia than in New England?

9

From *Home Life in Colonial Days* by Alice Morse Earle.

Tapping the Sugar Tree (1600s)

The English colonists in North America were a self-reliant and, in many cases, a self-sufficient group of people. The environment supplied many of their needs. The woods and forests provided game for food and wood for houses, furniture, utensils, and tools. The colonists learned that their environment could also provide foods that might be considered luxuries. The sap of maple trees, for example, was used by the colonists to make sugar.

In the following excerpt from her book on life in the colonies, social historian Alice Morse Earle describes the work involved in collecting the maple sap and turning it into sugar. As you read consider the things that made these outings especially appealing to colonial boys.

Governor Berkeley of Virginia, writing in 1706, called the maple the sugar-tree; he said:—

"The Sugar-Tree yields a kind of Sap or Juice which by boiling is made into Sugar. This Juice is drawn out, by wounding the Trunk of the Tree, and placing a Receiver under the Wound. It is said that the Indians make one Pound of Sugar out of eight Pounds of the Liquor [liquid]. It is bright and moist with a full large Grain [crystal], the Sweetness of it being like that of good Muscovada [raw or unrefined sugar made from cane]."

The sugar-making season was ever hailed with delight by the boys of the household in colonial days, who found in this work in the woods a wonderful outlet for the love of wild life which was strong in them. It had in truth a touch of going a-gypsying, if any work as hard as sugaring-off could have anything common with gypsy life. The maple-trees were tapped as soon as the sap began to run in the trunk and showed at the end of the twigs; this was in late winter if mild, or in the earliest spring. A notch was cut in the trunk of the tree at a convenient height from the ground, usually four or five feet, and the running sap was guided by setting in the notch a semicircular basswood spout cut and set with a special tool called a tapping-gauge. In earlier days the trees were "boxed," that is, a great gash cut across the side and scooped out and down to gather the sap. This often proved fatal to the trees, and was abandoned. A trough, usually made of a butternut log about three feet long, was dug out, Indian fashion, and placed under the end of the spout. These troughs were made deep enough to hold about ten quarts. In later years a hole was bored in the tree with an augur; and sap-buckets were used instead of troughs.

Sometimes these troughs were left in distant sugar-camps from year to year, turned bottom side up, through the summer and winter. It was more thrifty and tidy, however, to carry them home and store them. When this was done, the men and boys began work by drawing the troughs and spouts and provisions to the woods on hand-sleds. Sometimes a mighty man took in a load on his back. It is told of John Alexander of Brattleboro, Vermont, that he once went into camp *upon snowshoes* carrying for three miles one five-pail iron kettle, two sap-buckets, an axe and trappings, a knapsack, four days' provisions, and a gun and ammunition.

The master of ceremonies—the owner of the camp—selected the trees and drove the spouts, while the boys placed the troughs. Then the snow had to be shovelled away on a level spot about eighteen or twenty feet square, in which strong forked sticks were set twelve feet apart. Or the ground was chosen so that two small low-spreading and strong trees could be trimmed and used as forks. A heavy green

Cooking with Maple Syrup

The recipes on these pages are for foods that might have been made in a colonial kitchen after maple sugaring time. They appeared in the magazine *Early American Life*.

Maple Bran Muffins

2 cups all-purpose flour
2 tablespoons brown sugar
1/4 teaspoon salt
1 1/4 teaspoons soda
2 tablespoons grated orange rind
1 1/2 cups bran
2 cups buttermilk
1 beaten egg
1/2 cup maple syrup
4 tablespoons melted butter
1/2 cup chopped nuts
1/2 cup raisins

Sift flour, sugar, salt, and soda together.
Add orange rind and set aside.
Mix buttermilk and bran and let stand ten minutes.
Add egg, maple syrup, and butter.
Mix wet and dry ingredients together.
Add nuts and raisins.
Bake in greased muffin tins in a 350-degree-Fahrenheit oven for 30 minutes.
Makes about two dozen small or one dozen custard-cup-sized muffins. Be sure not to over-mix. Especially good served with cranberry preserves.

This nineteenth-century engraving shows the party atmosphere that characterized maple-sugaring season. The tapped maple trees can be seen in the background.

stick was placed across from fork to fork, and the sugaring-off kettles, sometimes five in number, hung on it. Then dry wood had to be gathered for the fires; hard work it was to keep them constantly supplied. It was often cut a year in advance. As the sap collected in the troughs it was gathered in pails or buckets which, hung on a sap-yoke across the neck, were brought to the kettles and the sap set a-boiling down. When there was a "good run of sap," it was usually necessary to stay in the camp over night. Many times the campers stayed several nights. As the "good run" meant milder weather, a night or two was not a bitter experience; indeed, I have never heard any one speak nor seen any account of a night spent in a sugar-camp except with keen expressions of delight. If possible, the time was chosen during a term of moonlight; the snow still covered the fields and its pure shining white light could be seen through the trees.

"God makes sech nights, so white and still
Fer's you can look and listen.
Moonlight an' snow, on field and hill,
All silence and all glisten."

The great silence, broken only by [the] steady dropping of the sap, the crackle of blazing brush, and the occasional hooting of startled owls; the stars seen singly overhead through the openings of the trees, shining down the dark tunnel as bright as though there were no moon; above all, the clearness and sweetness of the first atmosphere of spring,— gave an exaltation of the senses and spirit which the country boy felt without understanding, and indeed without any formulated consciousness. If the camp were near enough to any group of farmhouses to have visitors, the last afternoon and evening in camp was made a country frolic. Great sled-loads of girls came out to taste the new sugar, to drop it into the snow to candy, and to have an evening of fun.

REVIEWING THE READING

1. Why did colonial boys look forward to the hard work of the sugar-making season?

2. How did the colonists know when the sap was ready to be collected, and what time of year did this usually occur?

3. **Using Your Historical Imagination.** In addition to learning and practicing skills associated with sap collecting and sugar making, what values or character traits do you think colonial boys might have developed on such an outing?

Grandmother's Maple Cake
2 1/4 cups cake flour
3 teaspoons baking powder
1/4 teaspoon salt
1/3 cup butter
1/2 cup sugar
3/4 cup maple syrup
1/3 cup milk
3 egg whites (room temperature)
Sift flour, baking powder, and salt together. Set aside.
Cream butter and sugar until light and fluffy.
Mix milk and maple syrup together.
Add to butter-sugar mixture alternately with dry ingredients.
Beat egg whites until they stand in soft peaks.
Fold into batter.
Pour into greased nine-inch square pan or into greased cupcake pans.
Bake in 350-degree-Fahrenheit oven (25 minutes for cupcakes, 30 minutes or longer for large cake) until cake shrinks from side of pan and cake tester comes out clean.
Frost with Maple Snow Frosting (recipe below).

Maple Snow Frosting
Cook 1 cup maple syrup to 238 degrees on candy thermometer, removing crystals that form on side of pan as it cooks.
Strain through cheesecloth. While maple syrup is cooking, beat 2 room-temperature egg whites until stiff.
Dribble hot maple syrup into egg whites slowly and continue to beat until frosting holds shape. Pile on cake.

<table>
<tr><td>

10

</td></tr>
</table>

From "The Journal of Madame Knight" by Sarah Kemble Knight, in *Early American Life,* Volume VIII.

Madam Knight Travels by Horseback (1704)

Sarah Kemble Knight was a schoolteacher and a recorder of public documents. In her later years she ran an inn near New London, Connecticut. Perhaps her venture into innkeeping was prompted by her experiences on her horseback trip from Boston to New York when she was 38 years old. Except for a post rider (mail carrier) or guides hired by the day, Madam Knight traveled alone. She wrote about the people she met, the inns she stayed in, and the countryside she rode through in a journal that was published nearly one hundred years after her death.

The excerpts that follow cover the first two days of Madam Knight's journey—her departure from Boston to her arrival in present-day southern Rhode Island. As you read note the dangers or hardships that Madam Knight encountered on her journey.

Monday, October 2, 1704

About three o'clock afternoon, I begun my journey from Boston to New Haven, being about two-hundred miles. My kinsman, Capt. Robert Luist, waited on me [went with me] as far as Dedham, where I was to meet the western post [mail carrier].

I visited the Reverend Mr. Belcher, the minister of the town, and tarried there till evening in hopes the post would come along.

(When the post failed to materialize, Madam Knight, after much dickering over price, engaged a guide to accompany her twelve miles to Billings's Tavern, where the post rider was known to lodge.)

I paid honest John with money and dram [drink] according to contract, and dismissed him, and pray'd Miss to show me where I must lodge. She conducted me to a parlor in a little back lean-to [wing or room added to the house], which was almost filled with the bedstead, which was so high that I was forced to climb on a chair to get up to the writched bed that lay on it; stretched my tired limbs, and lay'd my head on the sad-colored pillow, I began to think on the transactions of the past day.

Tuesday, October 3

About eight in the morning, I with the post proceeded forward without observing anything remarkable. About two, afternoon, arrived at the post's second stage [station or resting place], where the western post met him and exchanged letters. Here, having called for something to eat, the woman brought in a twisted thing like a cable, but somewhat whiter, and laying it on the board, tugg'd for life to bring it to a capacity to spread [Knight is sarcastically referring to a rumpled tablecloth], which having with great pains accomplished, she served us a dish of pork and cabbage, I suppose the remains of dinner. The sauce was deep purple, which I tho't was boil'd in her dye kettle; the bread was Indian, and everything on the table service agreeable to these. I, being hungry got a little down; but my stomach was soon cloy'd [disgusted by excess] and what cabbage I swallowed serv'd for a cud the whole day after.

Having discharged the Ordinary [paid the bill at the inn] for self and guide (as I understood was the custom), about three, afternoon, went on with the third guide, who rode very hard; and having crossed Providence Ferry, we came to a river, which they generally ride through. But I dared not venture, so the post got a lad and a canoe to carry me to t'other side, and he rid through and led my horse. The canoe was very small and shallow, so that when we were in she seem'd ready to take in water, which greatly terrified me, and caused me to become very circumspect, sitting with my hands fast on each side, my eyes steady, not daring so much as to lodge my tongue more on one side of my mouth than t'other, nor so much as think on Lott's wife [who was turned into a pillar of salt for disobeying God's orders], for a wry thought would have overset our boat: But was soon put out of this pain, by feeling the canoe on shore, which I as soon almost saluted with my feet; and rewarding my sculler [rower], again mounted and made the best of our way forwards. The road here was very even and the day pleasant, it being now near sunset. But the post told me we had near fourteen miles to ride to the next stage, where we were to lodge.

(Much of the fourteen-mile ride was in darkness, with Madam Knight imagining enemies behind every tree and dreading the "hazzardos" river the post rider had told her they must cross.)

I knew by the going of the horse that we had entered the water. . . . Riding up close by my side, my guide bid me not to fear—we should be over immediately. I now rallied all the courage I was mistress of, knowing I must either venture my fate of drowning or be left like the Children in the wood. So, as the post bid me, I gave reins to my nag and, sitting as steady as just before in the canoe, in a few minutes was safe to the other side, which he told me was Narragansett County. . . .

I was roused by . . . the Post's sounding his horn, which assured me he was arrived at the Stage where we were to lodge, and the music was then most musical and agreeable to me.

Being come to Mr. Havens's, I was very civilly received and courteously entertained in a clean comfortable house; and the good woman was very active in helping off my riding clothes, and then ask't what I would eat. I told her I had some chocolate if she would prepare it, which with the help of some milk

and a little clean brass kettle she soon effected to my satisfaction. I then betook me to my apartment, which was a little room parted from the kitchen by a single board partition where, after I had noted the occurances of the past day, I went to bed, which tho' pretty hard, was neat and handsome. But I could get no sleep because of the clamor of some of the town toper-ers [drunkards] in next room, who were entered into a strong debate concerning the significance of the name of their County, Narraganset. . . . I heartily fretted, and wish't 'um tongue tied, but with little success. . . . I set my candle on a chest by the bedside, and setting up, fell to my old way of composing my resentments, in the following manner:

Inns such as the one shown in this engraving from the nineteenth century provided early travelers with much-welcomed lodging and food on their long and often uncomfortable journeys.

I ask thy Aid, O Potent Rum!
To charm these wrangling Topers Dum.
Thou has their Giddy Brains possest—
The man confounded with the Beast—
And I, poor I, can get no rest.
Intoxicate them with thy fumes:
O still their Tongues till morning comes!

And I know not but my wishes took effect, for the dispute soon ended with t'other Dram; and so Good night!

REVIEWING THE READING

1. What did Madam Knight seem to fear most on her journey? What do you think might account for this?

2. How do you know that Madam Knight favored the third inn (Mr. Havens'), over the first inn (Billings' Tavern), or the second, unnamed inn?

3. **Using Your Historical Imagination.** Based on the reading, write a brief paragraph describing the chief characteristics of Knight's personality.

The Secret Diary of William Byrd II (1709)

From *The Secret Diary of William Byrd of Westover, 1709–1712*, edited by Louis B. Wright and Marion Tinling.

William Byrd II was the son of an Englishman who had become a successful planter and was a member of the early colonial elite. Educated in England, William Byrd was well prepared to follow his father and assume a position of leadership among the Virginia planters. He kept a secret personal journal written in a kind of antique shorthand, which scholars have now deciphered. The following selection contains excerpts from that diary. As you read these entries, take note of what Byrd mentions as being part of his everyday personal routine.

August 1—I rose at break of day and drank some warm milk and rode to Mr. Harrison's, where I got a permit to load tobacco on board my sloop [a sailing vessel]. . . . I ate some watermelon and stayed till about 9 o'clock, when I returned and read a chapter [probably of the Bible] in Hebrew and some Greek in Josephus. I said my prayers and went to see old Ben [probably a Negro slave] and found him much better. I read some geometry. I ate fish for dinner. In the afternoon the Doctor and my wife played at piquet [a card game]. Joe Wilkinson [a nearby landowner] came and gave me an account of the tobacco that he raised this year and I agreed [to hire him as] my overseer at Burkland [one of Byrd's plantations] the next year. I read some Greek in Homer and took a walk about the plantation. I neglected to say my prayers. I had good health, good thoughts, and good humor, thanks be to God Almighty.

August 2—I rose at 5 o'clock and read two chapters in Hebrew and some Greek in Josephus. I said my prayers and drank whey [the watery liquid left after milk has coagulated] for breakfast. It was terribly hot. I wrote a letter to the Governor of Barbados [in the West Indies], to whom I intend to consign my sloop and cargo. Old Ben was still better and began to complain he was hungry. I ate chicken for my dinner. In the afternoon my wife and the Doctor played at piquet and the Doctor was beat. My neighbor Harrison had the ague [chills and fever] but was somewhat better this day. I wrote more letters to Barbados. I walked about the plantation. . . . I said a short prayer. It rained a little. I had good health, good thoughts, and good humor, thanks be to God Almighty.

August 8—I rose at 5 o'clock and read a chapter in Hebrew and some Greek in Josephus. My sloop sailed this morning for Barbados, God send her a good and expeditious [speedy] voyage. I was angry with B-l-n-m and he ran away. I likewise [punished] Tom [probably a slave]. I said my prayers and ate milk for breakfast. I walked out to see my people at work at the ditch. I read a little geometry. I ate mutton [sheep] for dinner. In the evening I took a little nap, ... I walked to the ditch again. In the evening I said my prayers. My man Jack was lame again. I had good health, good thoughts, and good humor, thanks be to God Almighty.

August 13—I rose at 5 o'clock and read a chapter in Hebrew and some Greek in Josephus. I said my prayers and ate bread and butter for breakfast. Twelve Pamunkey Indians came over. We gave them some victuals [food] and some rum and put them over the river. I danced my dance [probably a group of exercises]. I removed more books into the library. I read some geometry and walked to see the people at work. I ate fish for dinner. I was almost the whole afternoon in putting up my books. In the evening John Blackman came from the Falls [one of Byrd's

In addition to keeping a diary that has proven of great historical value, William Byrd II assembled the largest library in colonial America.

plantations] and brought me word that some of my people were sick and that my coaler was sick at the coal mine. I scolded with him about the little work he had done this summer. I took a walk about the plantation. I had a little scold with the Doctor about his boy. I said my prayers and had good health, good thoughts, and good humor, thanks be to God Almighty.

(The stock phrases with which Byrd opened and closed his diary entries have been eliminated from the remainder of the excerpt.)

August 14—I sent away my sloop which came yesterday to Falling Creek. John Blackman returned to the Falls. The old man grew better in his lameness and the [slave] boy who broke his leg was much better, thanks be to God. I ate boiled mutton for dinner. In the afternoon I took a nap. My cousin Betty Harrison came over and stayed till the evening.

I took a walk about the plantation with my wife who has not quarreled with me in a great while. . . .

September 2—It rained again this day, thanks be to God for his great goodness, who sent us rain almost all day and all the night following. I read some geometry. Notwithstanding the rain Mrs. Ware came to [ask] me to take tobacco for her debt to me, but I refused because tobacco was good for nothing [the price of tobacco was low]. I ate hashed pork for dinner. In the afternoon Mr. Taylor came from Surry [county] about his bill of exchange [a written order to pay a certain amount of money to a specified person]. He told me there was news by way of Barbados that the peace [between the English and the French and Spanish, who were fighting in the West Indies] was expected there to be already concluded. The rain kept him here all night but Mrs. Ware went away.

September 3—I said my prayers and ate chocolate with Mr. Taylor for breakfast. Then he went away. I read some geometry. We had no court [the county court that tried local cases] this day. My wife was indisposed [Mrs. Bryd was pregnant] again but not to much purpose. I ate roast chicken for dinner. In the afternoon I beat Jenny [a house servant and probably a Negro slave] for throwing water on the couch. I took a walk to Mr. Harrison's who told me he heard the peace was concluded in the last month. After I had been courteously entertained with wine and cake I returned home, where I found all well, thank God.

September 5—My wife was much out of order and had frequent returns of her pains. I read some geometry. I ate roast mutton for dinner. In the afternoon I wrote a letter to England and I read some Greek in Homer. Then in the evening I took a walk about the plantation and when I returned I found my wife very bad. I sent for Mrs. Hamlin and my cousin Harrison about 9 o'clock and I said my prayers heartily for my wife's happy delivery [of the baby], and had good health, good thoughts, and good humor, thanks be to God Almighty. I went to bed about 10 o'clock and left the women full of expectation with my wife.

September 6—About one o'clock this morning my wife was happily delivered of a son [named Parke, who died July 3, 1710], thanks be to God Almighty. I was awake in a blink and rose and my cousin Harrison met me on the stairs and told me it was a boy. We drank some French wine and went to bed again and rose at 7 o'clock. I read a chapter in Hebrew and then drank chocolate with the women for breakfast. I returned God humble thanks for so great a blessing and recommended my young son to His divine protection. My cousin Harrison and Mrs. Hamlin went away about 9 o'clock and I [rewarded] them for that kindness. I sent Peter [a servant] away who brought me a summons to the Council. I read some geometry. The Doctor brought me two letters from England . . . I ate roast mutton for dinner. In the afternoon I wrote a letter to England and took a walk about the plantation.

September 11—My wife and child were extremely well, thanks to God Almighty, who I hope will please to keep them so. I recommended my family to the divine protection and passed over the creek and then rode to my brother Duke's whom I found just recovered of the ague by means of my physic [medicine]. Here I ate some roast beef for dinner, and then proceeded to Colonel Duke's, whom I found indisposed.

September 12—I rose at 5 o'clock and said my prayers and then the Colonel and I [talked] about his debt to Mr. Perry in which I promised to be the mediator. . . . Then I met Colonel Bassett and with him rode to Williamsburg [the colonial capital]. . . . Then I went to Mr. President's, where I found several of the Council. The President persuaded me to be sworn, which I agreed to, and accordingly went to Council where I was sworn a

. . . I read a chapter in Hebrew and then drank chocolate with the women for breakfast.

member of the Council. God grant I may distinguish myself with honor and good conscience. We dined together and I ate beef for dinner. In the evening we went to the President's where I drank too much French wine and played at cards and I lost 20 shillings. . . .

September 13—I rose at 5 o'clock and read some Greek in Lucian and a little Latin in Terence. I neglected to say my prayers and ate rice milk for breakfast. Several people came to see me and Mr. Commissary desired me to frame a letter to the Lord Treasurer which I did and then went to the meeting of the College [of William and Mary, then still a grammar school] where after some debate the majority were for building the new college on the old wall; I was against this and was for a new one for several reasons. . . . I received some protested bills [checks or bills of exchange upon which payment had been refused] and then we went to the President's and played at cards and I lost £4 about 10 o'clock and went home.

REVIEWING THE READING

1. How would you describe Byrd's personal eating, exercise, and sleeping habits. What conclusion could you draw about his physical health?

2. What kinds of books did Byrd read? What does this tell you about his intellect and education?

3. **Using Your Historical Imagination.** What kind of legislator do you think Byrd made for Virginia? Give evidence to support your view.

Slavery in Virginia (1720s)

12

From *Journal & Letters of Philip Vickers Fithian, 1773–1774: A Plantation Tutor of the Old Dominion*, edited by Hunter Dickinson Farish; and *Laws of Virginia, 1619–1792*, edited by William Waller Hening.

The English who settled in North America had no previous experience with lifelong, hereditary slavery. Therefore, the first Africans brought to the colonies in the 1600s served as indentured servants. But even as paid servants they were usually considered inferior. Gradually, as tobacco became the main crop of Virginia, even the labor of indentured servants was too costly, and the indentured servitude of blacks evolved into legal slavery.

This reading consists of two excerpts. The first is from the journal of Philip Fithian, a tutor on the Virginia plantation owned by a Mr. Carter. The second excerpt is a portion of the laws passed in Virginia to govern the slaves. Compare Fithian's attitude toward the treatment of the slaves with the attitudes expressed in the Virginia laws.

From Philip Fithian's Journal

Thursday 23.

I then asked the young man [a slave of Mr. Carter] what their allowance is? He told me that excepting some favourites about the table, their weekly allowance is a peck of Corn, & a pound of Meat a Head [each]!—And Mr. Carter is allow'd by all, & from what I have already seen of others, I make no Doubt at all but he is, by far the most humane to his Slaves of any in these parts! Good God! are these Christians?—When I am on the Subject, I will relate further, what I heard Mr. George Lee's Overseer, one Morgan, say the other day that he himself had often done to Negroes, and found it useful; He said that whipping of any kind does them no good, for they will laugh at your greatest Severity;

But he told us he had invented two things, and by several experiments had proved their success.—For Sulleness, Obstinacy, or Idleness, says he, Take a Negro, strip him, tie him fast to a post; take then a sharp Curry-Comb [a metallic-toothed comb used to groom horses], & curry [beat] him severely till he is well scrap'd; & call a Boy with some dry Hay, and make the Boy rub him down for several Minutes, then salt him, & unlose him. He will attend to his Business, (said the inhuman Infidel) afterwards!—But savage Cruelty does not exceed His next diabolical Invention—To get a Secret from a Negro, says he, take the following Method—Lay upon your Floor a large thick plank, having a peg about eighteen Inches long, of hard wood, & very Sharp, on the upper end, fixed fast in the plank—then strip the Negro, tie the Cord to a staple in the Ceiling, so as that his foot may just rest on the sharpened Peg, then turn him briskly round, and you would laugh (said our informer) at the Dexterity of the Negro, while he was releiving [lifting in relief] his Feet on the sharpen'd Peg!—I need say nothing of these seeing there is a righteous God, who will take vengeance on such Inventions!

From the Law Codes of Virginia
ACT X.
An act for preventing Negroes Insurrections.

WHEREAS the frequent meeting of considerable numbers of negroe slaves under pretence of feasts and burialls is judged of dangerous consequence; for prevention whereof for the future, *Bee it enacted by the kings most excellent majestie by and with the consent of the generall assembly, and it is hereby enacted by the authority aforesaid,* that from and after the publication of this law, it shall not be lawfull for any negroe or other slave to carry or arme himselfe with any club, staffe, gunn, sword or any other weapon of defence or offence, nor to goe or depart from of his masters ground without a certificate from his

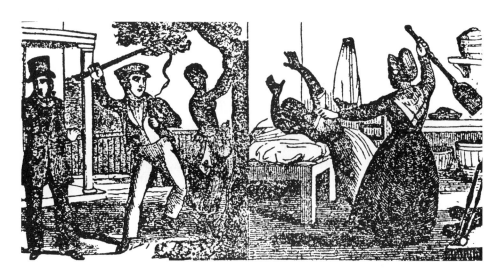

master, mistris or overseer, and such permission not to be granted but upon perticuler and necessary occasions; and every negroe or slave soe offending not haveing a certificate as aforesaid shalbe sent to the next constable [law officer], who is hereby enjoyned and required to give the said negroe twenty lashes on his bare back well layd on, and soe sent home to his said master, mistris or overseer. *And it is further enacted by the authority aforesaid* that if any negroe or other slave shall presume to lift up his hand in opposition against any christian, shall for every such offence, upon due proofe made thereof by the oath of the party before a magistrate [judge], have and receive thirty lashes on his bare back well laid on. . . .

1705

Slave owners punished their slaves in many ways. These engravings are from the 1840 Anti-Slavery Almanac.

CHAP. XLIX
. . . IV. *And also be it enacted, by the authority aforesaid, and it is hereby enacted,* That all servants imported and brought into this country, by sea or land, who were not christians in their native country, (except Turks and Moors in amity with her majesty, and others that can make due proof of their being free in England, or any other christian country, before

they were shipped, in order to transportation hither) shall be accounted and be slaves, and as such be here bought and sold notwithstanding a conversion to christianity afterwards. . . .

XXXIV. And if any slave resist his master, or owner, or other person, by his or her order, correcting such slave, and shall happen to be killed in such correction, it shall not be accounted felony; but the master, owner, and every such other person so giving correction, shall be free and acquit of all punishment and accusation for the same, as if such accident had never happened: And also, if any negro, mulatto, or Indian, bond or free, shall at any time, lift his or her hand, in opposition against any christian, not being negro, mulatto, or Indian, he or she so offending, shall, for every such offence, proved by the oath of the party, receive on his or her bare back, thirty lashes, well laid on; cognizable [determined] by a justice of the peace for that county wherein such offence shall be committed.

XXXV. *And also be it enacted, by the authority aforesaid, and it is hereby enacted,* That no slave go armed with gun, sword, club, staff, or other weapon, nor go from off the plantation and seat of land where such slave shall be appointed to live, without a certificate of leave in writing, for so doing, from his or her master, mistress, or overseer: And if any slave shall be found offending herein, it shall be lawful for any person or persons to apprehend and deliver such slave to the next constable or head-borough [town official], who is hereby enjoined and required, without further order or warrant, to give such slave twenty lashes on his or her bare back, well laid on, and so send him or her home: And all horses, cattle, and hogs, now belonging, or that hereafter shall belong to any slave, or of any slaves mark in this her majesty's colony and dominion, shall be seised and sold by the church-wardens of the parish, wherein such horses, cattle, or hogs shall be, and the profit thereof applied to the use of the poor of the said parish.

XXXVI. *And also it is hereby enacted and declared,* That baptism of slaves doth not exempt them from bondage; and that all children shall be bond or free, according to the condition of their mothers, and the particular directions of this act.

REVIEWING THE READING

1. How does the attitude of Philip Fithian toward the treatment of slaves differ from attitudes represented in the Virginia laws governing slaves?

2. Under what conditions could a slave leave the plantation grounds?

3. **Using Your Historical Imagination.** Imagine that you are a slave on a Virginia plantation. Do you think you would try to run away? If not, how would you endure your situation?

13

From *A Brief Narrative of the Case and Tryal of John Peter Zenger, Printer of the New-York Weekly Journal.*

Publisher John Peter Zenger's Trial in Colonial New York (1738)

Before the American Revolution, the British government held tight control over some of the American colonies, sometimes even restricting freedom of expression. The British allowed the colonists very little participation in government, which caused resentment that was expressed from time to time. In his newspaper, the New York Weekly Journal, *John Peter Zenger published articles that criticized the crown-appointed governor of New York. He was arrested and brought to trial before a jury, which heard Philadelphia lawyer Andrew Hamilton defend the truth of Zenger's assertions and his right to publish whatever can be shown to be accurate and true. The excerpt below is adapted from Zenger's own written account of the trial. These court proceedings reveal the differences in attitude between the colonists and the British authorities. The verdict of the jury in this trial was a landmark in the history of the press and freedom of speech in America. Notice how the opposing sides differ in their definitions of the term "seditious libel."*

CLERK OF COURT: The people will rise for the Chief Justice. (Pause) The Court of our Lord the King for the Colony of New York is now in session.

MR. RICHARD BRADLEY: I now open the case against John Peter Zenger, until recently of the City of

New York, Printer. Mr. Zenger has a reputation as a printer and publisher of false news that wickedly and maliciously criticize the government of our said Lord the King and that of the Colony of New York. On the twenty-eighth day of January, in 1735, Mr. Zenger did falsely, seditiously [encouraging rebellion], and scandalously print and publish, and cause to be printed and published, a certain false, malicious, seditious, scandalous libel [false statement injuring someone's reputation] in the newspaper entitled the *New York Weekly Journal.*

This libel says, and let me read it to you: "The People of this City and Colony of New York think as matters now stand, that their LIBERTIES AND PROPERTIES are endangered, and that SLAVERY is likely to be forced on them and their descendants, if some current governmental practices are not changed. WE SEE MEN'S DEED DESTROYED, JUDGES UNJUSTLY DISPLACED, NEW COURTS SET UP, WITHOUT CONSENT OF THE LEGISLATURE. TRIALS BY JURIES ARE TAKEN AWAY WHEN A GOVERNOR PLEASES, MEN OF PROPERTY DENIED THEIR VOTES. Who can then call anything his own, or enjoy any liberty longer than those in power will yield to let them do it, for which reason I have left the Colony of New York for New Jersey, as I believe more will."

Sir, this kind of writing is a disturbance of the peace and a great scandal on the King, and of all others concerned in the administration of the government. Therefore I bring the charge of seditious libel [writing that creates discontent with the government or resistance to it by making fun of government officials] against John Peter Zenger.

CLERK OF COURT: How does the defendant plead to these charges?

. . . To this charge I plead not guilty, and I am ready to prove it.

PETER ZENGER: To this charge I plead Not Guilty, and I am ready to prove it.

MR. ANDREW HAMILTON: May it please your honour; I am involved in this case on the part of Mr. Zenger the defendant. The charge against my client was sent to me, a few days before I left home, with some instructions to let me know how far I might rely upon the truth of the article in the paper that has just been set forth before you which are said to be libelous. I do not think it proper for me to deny the publication of complaints, which I think, is the right of every free-born subject to make, when the matters so published can be supported with truth. Therefore I'll save Mr. Bradley some trouble and for my client confess, that he both printed and published the newspaper set forth in the charge, and I hope in so doing he has committed no crime.

MR. BRADLEY: The case before the Court is, whether Mr. Zenger is guilty of libelling the Governor of New York, and indeed the whole government. Mr. Hamilton has confessed the printing and publishing of the article by Mr. Zenger, and I think nothing is plainer, than that the words in the charge are scandalous, seditious, and tend to disturb the minds of the people of this Colony.

MR. HAMILTON: May it please your honor; I cannot agree with Mr. Bradley: For though I freely acknowledge, that there are such things as libels, yet I must insist at the same time, that what my client is charged with, is not a libel. And I observed just now, that Mr. Bradley in defining a libel, made use of the words scandalous, seditious, and tend to disturb the people. But he omitted the word "false."

MR. BRADLEY: I think I did not omit the word false. But it has been said already, that it may be a libel regardless of whether it is true or not.

MR. HAMILTON: In this I must still differ with Mr. Bradley. We are to be tried upon the charge now before the Court and jury, and to which we have pleaded Not Guilty. And by it we are charged with printing and publishing, a certain false, malicious, seditious, scandalous libel. This word false must have some meaning, or else how came it to be there?

MR. CHIEF JUSTICE: Mr. Hamilton, a libel is nevertheless a libel whether it is true or not.

MR. HAMILTON: I thank your honor. Then, gentlemen of the jury, it is to you we must now appeal, for the truth of the facts we have offered. You are citizens of New York. You are really what the law supposes you to be, honest and lawful men. The facts which we offer to prove were not committed in a corner. They are known to be true, and therefore in your justice lies our safety.

I hope to be pardoned, sir, for my zeal upon this occasion. It is an old and wise caution, that when our neighbor's house is on fire, we ought to take care of our own. I live in a government in the Colony of Pennsylvania where liberty is well understood, and freely enjoyed. Yet experience has shown us all (I'm sure it has to me) that a bad example of rule in one government, is soon set up as an example in another. Therefore I cannot but think it mine, and every honest man's duty, that while we pay all

The acquittal of John Peter Zenger at his trial for seditious libel was fundamental to the establishment of freedom of the press in the United States.

Men who oppress the people under their government force them to cry out and complain . . .

due obedience to men in authority we ought at the same time to be upon our guard against how they use that power.

Men who oppress the people under their government force them to cry out and complain and then make that very complaint the foundation for new oppressions, and prosecutions. I wish I could say there were no instances of this kind. But, to conclude; the question before the Court and you, gentlemen of the jury, is not of small nor private concern. It is not the cause of a poor printer, nor of New York alone, which you are now trying. No! It may in its results affect every freeman that lives under a British government on the mainland of America. It is the best cause. It is the cause of liberty. I make no doubt that your upright conduct, this day, will not only entitle you to the love and esteem of your fellow-citizens, but that every man, who prefers freedom to a life of slavery, will bless and honour you as men who have halted an attempt of tyranny. And by your verdict, you will have laid a noble foundation for securing to ourselves, our descendants and our neighbors, the liberty both of exposing and opposing tyrannical power by speaking and writing truth.

MR. CHIEF JUSTICE: Gentlemen of the jury. Mr. Hamilton has taken great pains to show how little regard juries are to pay to the opinion of the judges. This is done, no doubt, with the intention that you should take but very little notice of what I may say upon this occasion. I shall therefore only observe to you that, as Mr. Zenger has confessed to publishing those words, the only thing that can come in question before you is, whether the words, as set forth in the newspaper, make a libel. I shall trouble you no further with anything more of my own, but read to you the words of a learned and upright judge in a case very much like this one.

"It is necessary for all governments that the people should have a good opinion of it. And nothing can be worse to any government than to have people attempt to create distrust and dislike of the management of it. This has always been looked upon as a crime, and no government can be safe without punishing those who attempt to create distrust or dislike of it."

Now you are to consider whether these words I have read to you do not tend to create a bad opinion of our government?

CLERK OF COURT: The Court will rise. The jury may withdraw. (A short time later)

CLERK OF COURT: The Court will rise for the Chief Justice. (Pause) Has the jury agreed on their verdict? Is John Peter Zenger guilty of printing and publishing the libels mentioned?

FOREMAN OF THE JURY: Not Guilty!

Upon which there were three cheers in the hall which was crowded with people, and the next day John Peter Zenger was released from prison.

REVIEWING THE READING

1. What exactly was John Peter Zenger accused of in Mr. Bradley's opening remarks to the court?

2. In Mr. Hamilton's closing remarks, what does he say that the trial is really all about?

3. **Using Your Historical Imagination.** When Hamilton says ". . . that when our neighbor's house is on fire, we ought to take care of our own," what kind of political comparison do you think he is making?

14

From *Documents relating to the Colonial History of the State of New Jersey,* edited by William Nelson.

A Collection of Runaways (1740s)

People in the colonies often ran advertisements in the newspapers. In some ways, certain ads were similar to the "Lost and Found" advertisements that appear in modern newspapers. As you read the following advertisements written during the 1740s, consider the kinds of "lost items" the colonists advertised for.

Run away from *Marten Ryerson,* of *Readingtown,* in the Country of *Hunterdon* a Young Servant Man named *William Hains* small Stature Ruddy Complexion, big Nose, big Blew Eyes, Pock-Broken, had no Hair, Branded on the Brawn of his Thumb, of the Left Hand, had on when he Run away a white Shirt, and a Saylors Frock [outer shirt], pair of Trousers, but has since got a Greek Vestment; it's probable that he has chang'd his Name, for he has already pass'd by the Name of *Thomson* and *Robinson.* Whoever takes up the said Servant, and Secures him so that his said Master may have him again shall have *Five Pounds* Reward besides all Reasonable Charges paid by

Marten Ryerson.

—*The New-York Weekly Journal,* June 15, 1741.

Deserted from his Majesty's Service out of the American Regiment of Foot, commanded by Col. William Gooch, and lately inlisted in West-Jersey, by Lieutenant Anthony Palmer, the following Soldier, . . .

Thomas Fury, a Labourer, Born in the North of Ireland, about 21 years of Age, 5 Foot 10 Inches high, well-set, fair complexioned, with very fair Eye Brows, grey Eyes, and much Pockfretten [pock-marked or pitted]: Had on when he went away, a greyish homespun Coat, with brass Buttons, the lowermost but one having the Top broke off and in

other Places some off. Linnen Trowsers, and a pair
of new Shoes. He worked some time since as a
Labourer in Maryland in Chester County, but lately
in Trenton: Whoever secures the said Deserter so
as his Officer may have him again, Shall receive
Three Pounds Reward, and all reasonable Charges:
or if any one will inform the said Officer, by whom
he is conceal'd, so that it may be prov'd, shall receive
Five Pounds Sterling, paid by

                                        Anthony Palmer.

    N.B. If the said Deserter will return, he shall
be kindly received by his Officer, and not prosecu-
ted.—*The Pennsylvania Gazette*, July 22, 1742. . . .

    There was lately committed to the Goal [jail]
of Sussex County, upon Delaware, two Men, sus-
pected to be Servants, . . . John Williams, a West-
Countryman, aged about 32 Years, says he came
into the Western Part of Virginia with one Capt.
Taylor, from Bristol; He is a lusty Man, wears his
own Hair, ozenbrigs Shirt, yarn Stockings, old brown
Coat, very much patch'd, an old felt Hat, leather
Breeches, white homespun twiled Jacket, metal But-
tons of several Sorts upon all his Cloathing. And
Thomas Rogers. . . . They say they came in Freemen.
The Owners (if any they have) are desired to come
or send for them, in one Month's Time after this
Date, otherwise they will be discharged paying their
Fees.

                                    Peter Hall, Sheriff.
                        Lewistown, March 9, 1742.
    —*The Pennsylvania Gazette*, March 17, 1742. . . .

    Run away on the 3d of August from Benjamin
Thomson, of Cohansie, the two following Servants, . . .

    One John Hacket, this Country-born, short and
thick, aged about 28 Years: Had on an old felt Hat,
two Shirts, one tow the other ozenbrigs, old patch'd
Jacket, lightish colour'd Great Coat, ozenbrigs Trowsers, good Shoes, and a Pair of Shoe-Packs.

The other named Richard Lane, this Country-born. . . . Whoever secures the said Servants, so that their Master may have them again, shall have Four Pounds Reward, and reasonable Charges, paid by

Benjamin Thomson.

N.B. They took with them two Guns, one long the other short, and a middle-siz'd Dog, that goes by the Name of Gunner, and when he's travelling paces. —*The Pennsylvania Gazette*, Sept. 8, 1743. . . .

Taken up, about 6 Months ago, as a Runaway, and now is in *Trenton* Goal, one *John Parra*, a well set Fellow, about 24 Years of Age, and pretends to know something of the Hatter's Trade. If no Person claims him before the first Day of May next, he will be sold for defraying his Charges. *By Order of the Court.*

William Brown, Under Sheriff.
—*The Pennsylvania Gazette*, April 4, 1745. . . .

This nineteenth-century engraving shows a runaway slave hunt through a canebrake in the American South.

Broke out of Trenton Goal, on Saturday Night last, one James Johnston, a lusty, strong built Man, about six Foot high, of a fresh Complexion, and fair insinuating Speech: He is an Irishman, and his right Name is White; he lately ran from his Bail, and entered on Board the Dreadnought, Capt. Cunningham, who upon Application caused him to be set on Shore at Newcastle, and committed to Goal there, from whence he was brought last Thursday. Whoever shall apprehend the said Johnston and secure him, shall have Five Pounds Proclamation Money as a Reward.   William Brown, Under Sheriff.
    —*The Pennsylvania Gazette,* Nov. 7, 1745. . . .

Run away from Samuel Lippincott of Northampton in the county of Burlington, an Irish servant Maid, named Mary Muckleroy, of a middle Stature: Had on when she went away, a blue and white striped gown, of large and small stripes, cuffed with blue, a white muslin handkerchief, an old blue quilt, a new Persian black bonnet, a new pair of calf-skin shoes, a fine Holland cap, with a cambrick border, an old black short cloak lined with Bengal, blue worsted stockings, with white clocks, a very good fine shirt, and a very good white apron. She took with her a sorrel horse, about 14 hands [4 feet 6 inches] high, shod before, and paces very well. It is supposed there is an Irishman gone with her. Whoever takes up and secures the said woman and horse, so that they may be had again, shall have Three Pounds reward, and reasonable charges paid by
                        Samuel Lippincott.
    —*The Pennsylvania Gazette,* April 16, 1748. . . .

Run away the 7th of this instant July, from Matthew Forsyth, of Chesterfield, Burlington county, an apprentice lad, named Elisha Bullingham, by trade a house-carpenter, about 16 years of age: Had on, or took with him, a half worn felt hat, old brown drugget [wool] coat, one pair leather breeches, two ozenbrigs shirts, and two pair of ozenbrigs trousers; his hair is newly cut off, and he has his indentures [papers identifying him as an indentured servant] with him. Whoever takes up and secures said apprentice, so that his master may have him again, shall have *Forty Shillings* reward, and reasonable charges, paid by me

Matthew Forsyth.

N.B. He is supposed to be going towards New-England; wherefore all masters of vessels, or others, are forbid to carry him off at their peril.

—*The Pennsylvania Gazette*, July 13, 1749. . . .

Whereas Margaret Simkins, wife of Daniel Simkins, of Stow creek, in the county of Cumberland, and province of West-Jersey, hath, and doth elope [run away] from time to time from her said husband, to his great damage; these are to forewarn, all persons from trusting said Margaret on his account, for he will pay no debts of her contracting from the date hereof.

Daniel Simkins.
—*The Pennsylvania Gazette*, Feb. 6, 1749.

REVIEWING THE READING

1. What kinds of runaways are described in the newspaper advertisements?

2. Why do you think owners offered higher rewards for indentured servants than for slaves?

3. **Using Your Historical Imagination.** Why do you think an indentured servant, who usually had to remain in servitude only for a period of seven years, would run away?

Jonathan Edwards Describes the Peace of Christ (1741)

15

From *Jonathan Edwards, Representative Selections,* edited by Clarence H. Faust and Thomas H. Johnson.

Jonathan Edwards succeeded his grandfather as pastor of the Congregational Church in Northampton, Massachusetts. His brilliant sermons and strong personality helped bring about the Great Awakening of the 1740s. Edwards and other preachers delivered "fire and brimstone" sermons designed to spread religious feelings and encourage listeners to confess their sins and be "born again."

The following excerpt is taken from Edwards' famous sermon "The Peace Which Christ Gives His True Followers"—one of the best-known sermons of the Great Awakening. As you read this excerpt from the sermon given in 1841, consider what Edwards believes to be the difference between Christian peace and worldly peace.

John XIV. 27.—Peace I leave with you, my peace I give unto you: not as the world giveth, give I unto you.

III. This legacy of Christ to his true disciples is very diverse from all that the men of this world ever leave to their children when they die. The men of this world, many of them, when they come to die, have great estates to bequeath to their children, an abundance of the good things of this world, large tracts of ground, perhaps in a fruitful soil, covered with flocks and herds. They sometimes leave to their children stately mansions, and vast treasures of silver, gold, jewels, and precious things, fetched from both the Indies, and from every side of the globe of the earth. They leave them wherewith to live in much state and magnificence, and make a great show among men, to fare very sumptuously [magnificantly], and swim in worldly pleasures. Some have crowns, sceptres, and palaces, and great monarchies to leave to their heirs. But none of these things are to be compared to that blessed peace of Christ which he has bequeathed to his true followers. These things are such as God commonly, in his providence, gives his worst enemies, those whom he hates and despises most. But Christ's peace is a precious benefit, which he reserves for his peculiar favorites. These worldly things, even the best of them, that the men and princes of the world leave for their children, are things which God in his providence throws out to those whom he looks on as dogs; but Christ's peace is the bread of his children. All these earthly things are but empty shadows, which, however men set their hearts upon them, are not bread, and can never satisfy their souls; but this peace of Christ is a truly substantial, satisfying food, Isai. iv. 2. None of those things, if men have them to the best advantage, and in ever so great abundance, can give true peace and rest to the soul, as is abundantly manifest not only in reason, but experience; it being found in all ages, that those who have the most of them, having commonly the least quietness of mind. It is true, there may be a kind of quietness, a false peace they may have in their enjoyment of worldly things; men may bless their soul, and think themselves the only happy persons, and despise others; may say to their souls, as the rich man did, Luke xii. 19, "soul, thou hast much goods laid up for many years, take thine ease, eat, drink, and be merry." But Christ's peace, which he gives to his true disciples, vastly differs from this peace that men have in the enjoyments of the world, in the following respects:

1. Christ's peace is a reasonable peace and rest of soul; it is what has its foundation in light and knowledge, in the proper exercises of reason, and a right view of things; whereas the peace of the

world is founded in blindness and delusion [mistaken belief]. The peace that the people of Christ have, arises from their having their eyes open, and seeing things as they be. The more they consider, and the more they know of the truth and reality of things, the more they know what is true concerning themselves, the state and condition they are in; the more they know of God, and the more certain they are that there is a God, and the more they know what manner of being he is, the more certain they are of another world and future judgment, and of the truth of God's threatenings and promises; the more their consciences are awakened and enlightened, and the brighter and the more searching the light is that they see things in, the more is their peace established; whereas, on the contrary, the peace that the men of the world have in their worldly enjoyments can subsist no otherwise than by their being kept in ignorance. They must be blindfolded and deceived, otherwise they can have no peace: do but let light in upon their consciences, so that they may look about them and see what they are, and what circumstances they are in, and it will at once destroy all their quietness and comfort. Their peace can live nowhere but in the dark. Light turns their ease into torment. The more they know what is true concerning God and concerning themselves, the more they are sensible of the truth concerning those enjoyments which they possess; and the more they are sensible what things now are, and what things are like to be hereafter, the more will their calm be turned into a storm. The worldly man's peace cannot be maintained but by avoiding consideration and reflection. If he allows himself to think, and properly exercise his reason, it destroys his quietness and comfort. If he would establish his carnal [worldly] peace, it concerns him to put out the light of his mind, and turn beast as fast as he can. The faculty of reason, if at liberty, proves a mortal enemy to his peace. It concerns him if he would keep alive

> . . . but let light in upon their consciences, so that they may look upon them and see what they are . . .

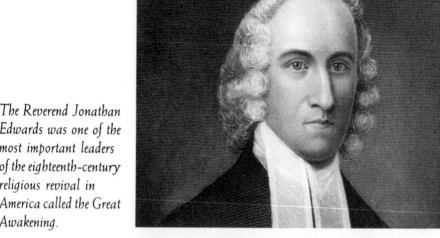

The Reverend Jonathan Edwards was one of the most important leaders of the eighteenth-century religious revival in America called the Great Awakening.

his peace, to contrive all ways that may be, to stupify his mind and deceive himself, and to imagine things to be otherwise than they be. But with respect to the peace which Christ gives, reason is its great friend. The more this faculty is exercised, the more it is established. The more they consider and view things with truth and exactness, the firmer is their comfort, and the higher their joy. How vast a difference is there between the peace of a Christian and the worldling! How miserable are they who cannot enjoy peace any otherwise than by hiding their eyes from the light, and confining themselves to darkness; whose peace is properly stupidity; as the ease that a man has who has taken a dose of stupifying poison, and the ease and pleasure that a drunkard may have in a house on fire over his head, or the joy of a distracted man in thinking that he is a king, though a miserable wretch confined in bedlam [a home for the insane]: whereas, the peace which Christ gives his true disciples, is the light of life, something of the tranquillity of heaven, the peace of the celestial paradise, that has the glory of God to lighten it.

2. Christ's peace is a virtuous and holy peace. The peace that the men of the world enjoy is vicious; it is a vile stupidity, that depraves [corrupts] and

debases the mind, and makes men brutish. But the peace that the saints enjoy in Christ, is not only their comfort, but it is a part of their beauty and dignity. The Christian tranquillity, rest, and joy of real saints, are not only unspeakable privileges, but they are virtues and graces of God's Spirit, wherein the image of God in them does partly consist. This peace has its source in those principles that are in the highest degree virtuous and amiable, such as poverty of spirit, holy resignation, trust in God, divine love, meekness, and charity; the exercise of such blessed fruits of the Spirit as are spoken of, Gal. 22,23.

3. This peace greatly differs from that which is enjoyed by the men of the world, with regard to its exquisite sweetness. It is a peace that passes all that natural men enjoy in worldly things so much, that it passes their understandings and conception, Phil. iv. 7. It is exquisitely sweet, because it has so firm a foundation as the everlasting rock that never can be moved. It is sweet, because perfectly agreeable to reason. It is sweet, because it rises from holy and divine principles, that as they are the virtue, so they are the proper happiness of men.

> . . . it has so firm a foundation as the everlasting rock . . .

It is exquisitely sweet, because of the greatness of the objective good that the saints enjoy, and have peace and rest in, being no other than the infinite bounty and fulness of that God who is the fountain of all good. It is sweet, on account of the fulness and perfection of that provision that is made for it in Christ and the new covenant, where there is a foundation laid for the saints' perfect peace; and hereafter they shall actually enjoy perfect peace; and though their peace is not now perfect, it is not owing to any defect in the provision made, but in their own imperfection and misery, sin and darkness; and because as yet they do partly cleave [attach themselves] to the world and seek peace from thence, and do not perfectly cleave to Christ. But the more they do so, and the more they see of the provision

there is made, and accept of it, and cleave to that alone, the nearer are they brought to perfect tranquillity, Isaiah xxvi. 5.

4. The peace of the Christian infinitely differs from that of the worldling, in that it is unfailing and eternal peace. That peace which carnal men have in the things of the world, is, according to the foundation that it is built upon, of short continuance; like the comfort of a dream, I John ii. 17, I Cor. vii. 31. These things, the best and most durable of them, are like bubbles on the face of the water; they vanish in a moment, Hos. x. 7.

But the foundation of the Christian's peace is everlasting; it is what no time, no change, can destroy. It will remain when the body dies; it will remain when the mountains depart and the hills shall be removed, and when the heavens shall be rolled together as a scroll. The fountain of his comfort shall never be diminished, and the stream shall never be dried. His comfort and joy is a living spring in the soul, a well of water springing up to everlasting life.

REVIEWING THE READING

1. According to Edwards, what does God give "his worst enemies, those whom he hates and despises most"?

2. What is the difference between worldly peace and Christian peace, according to Edwards?

3. **Using Your Historical Imagination.** Imagine you are a wealthy property owner in Edwards' congregation listening to this sermon. What would you think about the sermon? What questions would you like to ask your minister after it was over?

A Slave's Story (ca. 1750)

16

From *The Interesting Narrative of the Life of Olaudah Equiano or Gustavus Vassa, the African* by Olaudah Equiano.

Until recent times slavery was fairly common. Enslaved people, with the exception of American slaves, usually resulted from conquest. In the southern English colonies, the demand for agricultural labor sustained slavery for several hundred years.

The following reading consists of excerpts from a book written by a former slave. It tells the story of Olaudah Equiano, a member of the Ibo tribe in Benin (present-day Nigeria), who was sold into slavery at the age of eleven. For about seven months, before he was shipped to the colonies, he served as a slave for different masters in Africa. As you read note how the treatment of slaves by other Africans differed from their treatment by whites.

Capture in Africa

One day, when all our people were gone out to their work as usual, and only I and my dear sister were left to mind the house, two men and a woman got over our walls, and in a moment seized us both; and, without giving us time to cry out, or make resistance, they stopped our mouths, and ran off with us into the nearest wood. . . .

The next day proved a day of greater sorrow than I had yet experienced; for my sister and I were then separated, while we lay clasped in each other's arms; it was in vain that we besought them not to part us; she was torn from me, and immediately carried away, while I was left in a state of distraction not to be described. . . .

A Slave in Africa

At length, after many days traveling, during which I had often changed masters, I got into the hands

of a chieftain, in a very pleasant country. This man had two wives and some children; and they all used me extremely well, and did all they could to comfort me; particularly the first wife, who was something like my mother. Although I was a great many days' journey from my father's house, yet these people spoke exactly the same language with us. This first master of mine, as I may call him, was a smith, and my principal employment was working his bellows. . . . I was there I suppose about a month, and they at last used to trust me some little distance from the house. This liberty I used in embracing every opportunity to inquire the way to my own home. . . . I had also remarked where the sun rose in the morning, and set in the evening, as I had traveled along; and I observed that my father's house was towards the rising of the sun. . . .

(Equiano accidently killed one of the chickens he was tending and fearing a beating from the old woman slave he assisted, he escaped to the woods. But hunger, fatigue, the great distance back to his father's house, and the hopelessness of his situation soon made him return to his master's house.)

She was very much surprised to see me, and could scarcely believe her own eyes. She now promised to intercede for me, and went for her master, who soon after came, and, having slightly reprimanded me, ordered me to be taken care of, and not ill treated. . . .

(His master sold Equiano. Equiano changed masters several more times before reaching the sea coast.)

The Middle Passage
The first object which saluted my eyes when I arrived on the coast was the sea, and a slave ship, which was then riding at anchor, and waiting for its cargo. These filled me with astonishment, which was soon converted into terror, which I am yet at a loss to describe; . . . I was immediately handled, and tossed up to see if I was sound, by some of the crew; and

This engraving shows the hold of the slave ship Gloria *during the terrible "middle passage" from Africa to the United States.*

I was now persuaded that I had got into a world of bad spirits, and that they were going to kill me. . . . I now saw myself deprived of all chance of returning to my native country, or even the least glimpse of hope of gaining the shore, which I now considered as friendly; and I even wished for my former slavery in preference to my present situation, which was filled with horrors of every kind, ... I was soon put down under the decks, and there I received such a salutation in my nostrils, as I had never experienced in my life; so that, with the loathsomeness of the stench, and crying together, I became so sick and low that I was not able to eat,

nor had I the least desire to taste any thing. I now
wished for the last friend, death, to relieve me; but
soon, to my grief, two of the white men offered
me edibles; and, on my refusing to eat, one of them
held me fast by the hands, and laid me across, I
think the windlass [a machine for hoisting or haul-
ing], and tied my feet, while the other flogged me
severely. . . .

I feared I should be put to death, the white
people looked and acted as I thought, in so savage
a manner; for I had never seen among any people
such instances of brutal cruelty; and this not only
shown towards us blacks, but also to some of the
whites themselves. . . .

The stench of the hold while we were on the
coast was so intolerably loathsome, that it was dangerous to remain there for any time, and some of
us had been permitted to stay on the deck for the
fresh air; but now that the whole ship's cargo were
confined together, it became absolutely pestilential
[deadly]. The closeness of the place, and the heat
of the climate, added to the number in the ship,
which was so crowded that each had scarcely room
to turn himself, almost suffocated us. This produced
copious perspirations, so that the air soon became
unfit for respiration, from a variety of loathsome
smells, and brought on a sickness among the slaves,
of which many died, thus falling victims to the impro-
vident avarice [greed], as I may call it, of their purchasers. This wretched situation was again aggra-
vated by the galling [irritation] of the chains, now
become insupportable [unbearable]; and the filth of
the necessary tubs, into which the children often
fell, and were almost suffocated. The shrieks of the
women, and the groans of the dying, rendered the
whole a scene of horror almost inconceivable. . . .

One day, when we had a smooth sea and moderate wind, two of my wearied countrymen who were
chained together (I was near them at the time), pre-
ferring death to such a life of misery, somehow made

through the nettings and jumped into the sea; immediately another quite dejected fellow, who on account of his illness, was suffered to be out of irons, also followed their example; and I believe many more would very soon have done the same if they had not been prevented by the ship's crew, who were instantly alarmed. Those of us that were the most active were in a moment put down under the deck, and there was such a noise and confusion amongst the people of the ship as I never heard before, to stop her, and get the boat out to go after the slaves. However two of the wretches were drowned, but they got the other, and afterwards flogged him unmercifully for thus attempting to prefer death to slavery. . . .

Many a time we were near suffocation from the want of fresh air, which we were often without for whole days together. This, and the stench . . . carried off [killed] many. . . .

Barbados and the Slave Market

We were conducted immediately to the merchant's yard, where we were all pent up together like so many sheep in a fold, without regard to sex or age. . . . We were not many days in the merchant's custody before we were sold after their usual manner which is this:—On a signal given, (as the beat of a drum), the buyers rush at once into the yard where the slaves are confined, and make choice of that parcel they like best. The noise and clamor with which this is attended, and the eagerness visible in the countenances [faces] of the buyers, serve not a little to increase the apprehension of the terrified Africans, who may well be supposed to consider them as the ministers of that destruction to which they think themselves devoted. In this manner, without scruple, are relations and friends separated, most of them never to see each other again. I remember in the vessel in which I was brought over, in the men's apartment, there were several brothers, who

Many a time we were near suffocation from the want of fresh air . . .

in the sale, were sold in different lots; and it was very moving on this occasion to see and hear their cries at parting. O, ye nominal Christians [Christians in name only]! might not an African ask you, learned you this from your God, who says unto you, Do unto all men as you would men should do unto you? Is it not enough that we are torn from our country and friends to toil for your luxury and lust of gain? Must every tender feeling be likewise sacrificed to your avarice? Are the dearest friends and relations, now rendered more dear by their separation from their kindred, still to be parted from each other, and thus prevented from cheering the gloom of slavery with the small comfort of being together and mingling their sufferings and sorrows? Why are parents to lose their children, brothers their sisters, or husbands their wives? Surely this is a new refinement [improvement] in cruelty, which, while it has no advantage to atone for it, thus aggravates distress, and adds fresh horrors even to the wretchedness of slavery.

REVIEWING THE READING

1. How did Equiano's treatment as a slave in Africa differ from his later treatment during the Middle Passage and the arrival in the colony of Barbados?

2. How did Equiano characterize the white slavers and slave buyers? What opinion did he have of them?

3. **Using Your Historical Imagination.** Imagine that you were one of Equiano's African masters. What reaction do you think you might have if you knew what kind of slavery the Africans would be subjected to after they left Africa?

Novelist James Fenimore Cooper Writes of the Frontier (1750s)

From *The Last of the Mohicans* by James Fenimore Cooper.

The Last of the Mohicans, *first published in 1826, was written by one of the very first American novelists, James Fenimore Cooper. An energetic writer with many interests, Cooper wrote books on a variety of subjects, but he is best known for his series of frontier novels.*

The following excerpt from Chapter 3 shows how Cooper gives his Indian characters qualities not usually attributed to them at the time he was writing—in the early 1800s. The novel is set in the forests of New York state during the time of the French and Indian War. In this portion of the book, the white woodsman Hawkeye and his Indian companion, Chingachgook, discuss the meeting of the Mohican Indians and the first European settlers. As you read notice what Chingachgook says about the other Indian tribes that had encountered the Mohicans before the arrival of the white man.

The vast canopy of woods spread itself to the margin of the river overhanging the water, and shadowing its dark current with a deeper hue. The rays of the sun were beginning to grow less fierce, and the intense heat of the day was lessened, as the cooler vapors of the springs and fountains rose above their leafy beds, and rested in the atmosphere. Still that breathing silence, which marks the drowsy sultriness of an American landscape in July, pervaded the secluded spot, interrupted only by the low voices

of the men, the occasional and lazy tap of a wood-
pecker, the discordant cry of some gaudy jay, or a
swelling on the ear, from the dull roar of a distant
waterfall.

These feeble and broken sounds were, however,
too familiar to the foresters, to draw their attention
from the more interesting matter of their dialogue.
While one of the loiterers showed the red skin and
wild accoutrements [clothing or equipment] of a
native of the woods, the other exhibited, through
the mask of his rude and nearly savage equipments,
the brighter, though sunburnt and long-faded complexion of one who might claim descent from a
European parentage. The former was seated on the
end of a mossy log, in a posture that permitted
him to heighten the effect of his earnest language,
by the calm but expressive gestures of an Indian
engaged in debate. His body, which was nearly
naked, presented a terrific emblem [symbol] of death,
drawn in intermingled colors of white and black.
His closely shaved head, on which no other hair
than the well known and chivalrous scalping tuft
[a small bunch of hair left on the top of the head,
which enabled enemy warriors to take the scalp and
gain honor without having to kill the enemy] was
preserved, was without ornament of any kind, with
the exception of a solitary eagle's plume, that crossed
his crown, and depended over the left shoulder. A
tomahawk and scalping-knife, of English manufacture, were in his girdle [belt]; while a short military
rifle, of that sort with which the policy of the whites
armed their savage allies, lay carelessly across his
bare and sinewy knee. The expanded chest, full
formed limbs, and grave countenance of this warrior,
would denote that he had reached the vigor of his
days, though no symptoms of decay appeared to
have yet weakened his manhood.

The frame of the white man, judging by such
parts as were not concealed by his clothes, was like
that of one who had known hardships and exertion

from his earliest youth. His person, though muscular, was rather attenuated [thin] than full; but every nerve and muscle appeared strung and indurated [hardened] by unremitted exposure and toil. He wore a hunting-shirt of forest green, fringed with faded yellow, and a summer cap of skins which had been shorn of their fur. He also bore a knife in a girdle of wampum [sash of beaded shells], like that which confined the scanty garments of the Indian, but no tomahawk. His moccasins were ornamented after the gay fashion of the natives, while the only part of his under-dress which appeared below the hunting-frock, was a pair of buckskin leggings, that laced at the sides, and which were gartered above the knees with the sinews of a deer. A pouch and horn completed his personal accoutrements, though a rifle of great length [hunting rifle], which the theory of the more ingenious whites had taught them was the most dangerous of all fire-arms, leaned against a neighboring sapling. The eye of the hunter, or scout, whichever he might be, was small, quick, keen, and restless, roving while he spoke, on every side of him, as if in quest of game, or distrusting the sudden approach of some lurking enemy. Notwithstanding the symptoms of habitual suspicion, his countenance was not only without guile, but at the moment at which he is introduced, it was charged with an expression of sturdy honesty.

> The eye of the hunter . . . was small, quick, keen, and restless . . .

"Even your traditions make the case in my favor, Chingachgook," he said, speaking in the tongue which was known to all the natives who formerly inhabited the country between the Hudson and the Potomac, and of which we shall give a free translation for the benefit of the reader; endeavoring, at the same time, to preserve some of the peculiarities, both of the individual and of the language. "Your fathers came from the setting sun, crossed the big river [Mississippi], fought the people of the country, and took the land; and mine came from the red sky of the morning, over the salt lake, and did their work much after the fashion that had been set by yours; then let God judge the matter between us, and friends spare their words!"

"My fathers fought with the naked redmen!" returned the Indian sternly, in the same language. "Is there no difference, Hawkeye, between the stone-headed arrow of the warrior, and the leaden bullet with which you kill?"

"There is reason in an Indian, though nature has made him with a red skin!" said the white man, shaking his head like one on whom such an appeal to his justice was not thrown away. For a moment he appeared to be conscious of having the worst of the argument, then, rallying again, he answered the objection of his antagonist in the best manner his limited information would allow: "I am no scholar, and I care not who knows it; but judging from what I have seen, at deer chases and squirrel hunts, of the sparks below, I should think a rifle in the hands of their grandfathers was not so dangerous as a hickory bow and a good flint-head might be, if drawn with Indian judgment, and sent by an Indian eye."

"You have the story told by your fathers," returned the other, coldly waving his hand. "What say your old men? Do they tell the young warriors, that the pale-faces met the redmen, painted for war and armed with the stone hatchet and wooden gun?"

"I am not a prejudiced man, nor one who vaunts [prides] himself on his natural privileges, though the worst enemy I have on earth, and he is an Iroquois, daren't deny that I am genuine white," the scout replied, surveying, with secret fashion, the faded color of his bony and sinewy hand: "and I am willing to own that my people have many ways, of which, as an honest man, I can't approve. It is one of their customs to write in books what they have done and seen, instead of telling them in their villages, where the lie can be given to the face of a cowardly boaster, and the brave soldier can call on his comrades to witness for the truth of his words.

In consequence of this bad fashion, a man who is
too conscientious to misspend his days among the
women, in learning the names of black marks may
never hear of the deeds of his fathers, nor feel a
pride in striving to outdo them. For myself, I conclude
the Bumppos could shoot, for I have a natural turn
with a rifle, which must have been handed down
from generation to generation, as, our holy com-
mandments tell us, all good and evil gifts are be-
stowed; though I should be loth to answer for other
people in such a matter. But every story has its two
sides; so I ask you, Chingachgook, what passed,
according to the traditions of the redmen, when
our fathers first met?"

A silence of a minute succeeded, during which
the Indian sat mute; then, full of the dignity of his
office, he commenced his brief tale, with a solemnity
that served to heighten its appearance of truth.

"Listen, Hawkeye, and your ear shall drink no
lie. 'Tis what my fathers have said, and what the
Mohicans have done." He hesitated a single instant,
and bending a cautious glance toward his companion,
he continued, in a manner that was divided between
interrogation and assertion, "Does not this stream
at our feet run towards the summer, until its waters
grow salt, and the current flows upward?"

> . . . Listen, Hawkeye, and your ear shall drink no lie.

"It can't be denied that your traditions tell you
true in both these matters," said the white man;
"for I have been there, and have seen them; though,
why water, which is so sweet in the shade, should
become bitter in the sun, is an alteration for which
I have never been able to account."

"And the current!" demanded the Indian, who
expected his reply with that sort of interest that a
man feels in the confirmation of testimony, at which
he marvels even while he respects it; "the fathers
of Chingachgook have not lied!"

"The Holy Bible is not more true, and that is
the truest thing in nature. They call this up-stream
current the tide, which is a thing soon explained,

This is an illustration from an early edition of James Fenimore Cooper's novel The Last of the Mohicans.

and clear enough. Six hours the waters run in, and six hours they run out, and the reason is this: when there is higher water in the sea than in the river, they run in, until the river gets to be highest, and then it runs out again."

"The waters in the woods, and on the great lakes, run downward until they lie like my hand," said the Indian, stretching the limb horizontally before him, "and then they run no more."

"No honest man will deny it," said the scout, a little nettled at the implied distrust of his explanation of the mystery of the tides: "and I grant that it is true on the small scale, and where the land is level. But everything depends on what scale you look at things. Now, on the small scale, the 'arth [earth] is level; but on the large scale it is round. In this manner, pools and ponds, and even the great fresh-water lake, may be stagnant, as you and I both know they are, having seen them; but when you come to spread water over a great tract, like the sea, where the earth is round, how in reason can the water be quiet? You might as well expect the river to lie still on the brink of those black rocks a mile above us, though your own ears tell you that it is tumbling over them, at this very moment!"

If unsatisfied by the philosophy of his companion, the Indian was far too dignified to betray his unbelief. He listened like one who was convinced, and resumed his narrative in his former solemn manner.

"We came from the place where the sun is hid at night, over great plains where the buffaloes live, until we reached the big river. There we fought the Alligewi till the ground was red with their blood. From the banks of the big river to the shores of the salt lake, there was none to meet us. The Maquas followed at a distance. We said the country should be ours from the place where the water runs up no longer on this stream, to a river twenty suns' journey toward the summer. The land we had taken like warriors, we kept like men. We drove the Maquas into the woods with the bears. They only tasted salt at the licks: they drew no fish from the great lake; we threw them the bones."

"All this I have heard and believe," said the white man, observing that the Indian paused: "but it was long before the English came into the country."

"A pine grew then where this chestnut now stands. The first pale-faces who came among us spoke no English. They came in a large canoe, when my

. . . we were one people, and we were happy.

fathers had buried the tomahawk [made peace] with the redmen around them. Then, Hawkeye," he continued, betraying his deep emotion only by permitting his voice to fall to those low, guttural tones, which rendered his language, as spoken at times, so very musical: "then, Hawkeye, we were one people, and we were happy. The salt lake gave us its fish, the wood its deer, and the air its birds. We took wives who bore us children; we worshipped the Great Spirit; and we kept the Maquas beyond the sound of our songs of triumph!"

"Know you anything of your own family at that time?" demanded the white. "But you are a just man, for an Indian! and, as I suppose you hold their gifts, your fathers must have been brave warriors, and wise men at the council fire."

"My tribe is the grandfather of nations, but I am an unmixed man. The blood of chiefs is in my veins, where it must stay forever. The Dutch landed, and gave my people the fire-water [alcoholic beverages]; they drank until the heavens and the earth seemed to meet, and they foolishly thought they had found the Great Spirit. Then they parted with their land. Foot by foot, they were driven back from the shores, until I, that am a chief and a sagamore [a lesser chief of the Algonquians], have never seen the sun shine but through the trees, and have never visited the graves of my fathers!"

"Graves bring solemn feelings over the mind," returned the scout, a good deal touched at the calm suffering of his companion; "and they often aid a man in his good intentions; though, for myself, I expect to leave my own bones unburied, to bleach in the woods, or to be torn asunder by the wolves. But where are to be found those of your race who came to their kin in the Delaware country, so many summers since?"

"Where are the blossoms of those summers!— fallen, one by one; so all of my family departed, each in his turn, to the land of spirits. I am on the hill-top, and must go down into the valley; and when Uncas follows in my footsteps, there will no longer be any of the blood of the sagamores, for my boy is the last of the Mohicans."

REVIEWING THE READING

1. Who were the Alligewi and the Maquas? What became of them?

2. How does Chingachgook describe his tribe before and after the arrival of the Dutch?

3. **Using Your Historical Imagination.** Put into you own words the arguments on both sides of this dialogue—Chingachgook's assertions about what the Europeans did to his people and the scout's defense of the actions of the whites.

18

From *Myths of the Cherokee, 19th Annual Report of the Bureau of American Ethnology, 1987–98.*

A Cherokee Legend: How the World Was Made (ca. 1750)

The Cherokee, who called themselves Yunwiya, the "real people," originally occupied about 40,000 square miles of the Appalachian region of North America. The Cherokee may have numbered well over 20,000 before their population was drastically reduced by wars, European diseases, and forced removal by the United States government. Like many Native American peoples, the Cherokee created a rich oral literature of myth and legend to explain the origins of the landscape, animals, plants, and human beings. As you read the following Cherokee myth, recorded in the late 1890s, consider what creature the Cherokee believed created the earth.

T he earth is a great island floating in a sea of water, and suspended at each of the four cardinal points by a cord hanging down from the sky vault, which is of solid rock. When the world grows old and worn out, the people will die and the cords will break and let the earth sink down into the ocean, and all will be water again. The Indians are afraid of this.

When all was water, the animals were above in Gălûñ'lătĭ, beyond the arch; but it was very much crowded, and they were wanting more room. They wondered what was below the water, and at last Dâyuni'sĭ, "Beaver's Grandchild," the little Water-beetle, offered to go and see if it could learn. It darted in every direction over the surface of the water, but could find no firm place to rest. Then it dived to the bottom and came up with some soft mud, which began to grow and spread on every side until it became the island which we call the earth. It was afterward fastened to the sky with four cords, but no one remembers who did this.

At first the earth was flat and very soft and wet. The animals were anxious to get down, and sent out different birds to see if it was yet dry, but they found no place to alight and came back again to Gălûñ′lătĭ. At last it seemed to be time, and they sent out the Buzzard and told him to go and make ready for them. This was the Great Buzzard, the father of all the buzzards we see now. He flew all over the earth, low down near the ground, and it was still soft. When he reached the Cherokee country, he was very tired, and his wings began to flap and strike the ground, and wherever they struck the earth there was a valley, and where they turned up again there was a mountain. When the animals above saw this, they were afraid that the whole world would be mountains, so they called him back,

This engraving from the eighteenth century shows Cherokee Indians during a visit to London.

but the Cherokee country remains full of mountains to this day.

When the earth was dry and the animals came down, it was still dark, so they got the sun and set it in a track to go every day across the island from east to west, just overhead. It was too hot this way, and Tsiska'gĭlĭ', the Red Crawfish, had his shell scorched to a bright red, so that his meat was spoiled; and the Cherokee do not eat it. The conjurers [magicians] put the sun another handbreadth higher in the air, but it was still too hot. They raised it another time, and another, until it was seven handbreadths high and just under the sky arch. Then it was right, and they left it so. This is why the conjurers call the highest place Gûlkwâ'gine Di'gălûñ'lătiyûñ', "the seventh height," because it is seven handbreadths above the earth. Every day the sun goes along under this arch, and returns at night on the upper side to the starting place.

There is another world under this, and it is like ours in everything—animals, plants, and people—save that the seasons are different. The streams that come down from the mountains are the trails by which we reach this underworld, and the springs at their heads are the doorways by which we enter it, but to do this one must fast [go without food] and go to water and have one of the underground people for a guide. We know that the seasons in the underworld are different from ours, because the water in the springs is always warmer in winter and cooler in summer than the outer air.

When the animals and plants were first made— we do not know by whom—they were told to watch and keep awake for seven nights, just as young men now fast and keep awake when they pray to their medicine. They tried to do this, and nearly all were awake through the first night, but the next night several dropped off to sleep, and the third night others were asleep, and then others, until, on the seventh night, of all the animals only the owl, the panther, and one or two more were still awake. To these were given the power to see and to go about in the dark, and to make prey of the birds and animals which must sleep at night. Of the trees only the cedar, the pine, the spruce, the holly, and the laurel were awake to the end, and to them it was given to be always green and to be greatest for medicine, but to the others it was said: "Because you have not endured to the end you shall lose your hair every winter."

Men came after the animals and plants. At first there were only a brother and sister until he struck her with a fish and told her to multiply, and so it was. In seven days a child was born to her, and thereafter every seven days another, and they increased very fast until there was danger that the world could not keep them. Then it was made that a woman should have only one child in a year, and it has been so ever since.

REVIEWING THE READING

1. What being formed the earth?

2. Where did the Cherokee believe the sun went at night?

3. **Using Your Historical Imagination.** What do you think is the purpose of a creation myth like that of the Cherokee?

19

From *Travels* by Andrew Burnaby.

Andrew Burnaby Forecasts the American Future (1760)

Andrew Burnaby was a knowledgeable Englishman with wide experience of the American colonies. In London in 1775 he published a popular account of his life in America. Toward the end of his detailed description of the colonies, he analyzed American weaknesses. Burnaby's predictions about the ultimate future of America have proven very wrong. But as you read the following excerpt from his book, note what Burnaby says are the weaknesses of the southern and northern colonies.

Having travelled over so large a tract of this vast continent, before I bid a final farewell to it, I must beg the reader's indulgence, while I stop for a moment, and as it were from the top of a high eminence, take one general retrospective look at the whole.—An idea, strange as it is visionary, has entered into the minds of the generality of mankind, that empire is travelling westward; and every one is looking forward with eager and impatient expectation to that destined moment, when America is to give law to the rest of the world. But if ever an idea was illusory and fallacious [misleading], I will venture to predict, that this will be so.

America is formed for happiness, but not for empire: in a course of 1200 miles I did not see a single object that solicited charity [showed a need for outside help]; but I saw insuperable [not to be overcome] causes of weakness, which will necessarily prevent its being a potent state.

Our colonies may be distinguished into the southern and northern; separated from each other by the Susquehannah [River] and that imaginary line which divides Maryland from Pensylvania.

The southern colonies have so many inherent causes of weakness, that they can never possess any real strength.—The climate operates very powerfully upon them, and renders them indolent, inactive, and unenterprizing; this is visible in every line of their character. I myself have been a spectator, and it is not an uncommon sight, of a man in the vigour of life, lying upon a couch, and a female slave standing over him, wafting off the flies, and fanning him, while he took his repose.

The southern colonies (Maryland, which is the smallest and most inconsiderable, alone excepted) will never be thickly seated [populated]: for as they are not confined within determinate limits, but extend to the westward indefinitely, men, sooner than apply to laborious occupations, occupations militating [having influence] with their dispositions, and generally considered too as the inheritance and badge of slavery, will gradually retire westward, and settle upon fresh lands, which are said also to be more fertile; where, by the servitude of a Negro or two, they may enjoy all the satisfaction of an easy and indolent independency: hence the lands upon the coast will of course remain thin of inhabitants.

The mode of cultivation [farming] by slavery, is another insurmountable cause of weakness. The number of Negroes in the southern colonies is upon the whole nearly equal, if not superior, to that of the white men; and they propagate and increase even faster.—Their condition is truly pitiable; their labour excessively hard, their diet poor and scanty, their treatment cruel and oppressive: they cannot therefore but be a subject of terror to those who so inhumanly tyrannize over them.

The Indians near the frontiers are a still further formidable cause of subjection. The southern Indians

. . . **The mode of cultivation by slavery, is another insurmountable cause of weakness.**

According to Andrew Burnaby, the use of slave labor, such as that depicted here, was a weakness of the American colonies.

are numerous, and are governed by a sounder policy than formerly: experience has taught them wisdom. They never make war with the colonists without carrying terror and devastation along with them. They sometimes break up intire counties together.— Such is the state of the southern colonies.—

The northern colonies are of stronger stamina, but they have other difficulties and disadvantages to struggle with, not less arduous, or more easy to be surmounted, than what have been already mentioned. Their limits being defined, they will undoubtedly become exceedingly populous: for though men will readily retire back towards the frontiers of their own colony, yet they will not so easily be induced to settled beyond them, where different laws and policies prevail, and where, in short, they are a different people: but in proportion to want of territory, if we consider the proposition in a general and abstract light, will be want of power.—But the northern colonies have still more positive and real disadvantages to contend with. They are composed of people of different nations, different manners, different religions, and different languages. They have a mutual jealousy of each other, fomented [promoted] by considerations of interest, power, and ascendency. Religious zeal too, like a smothered fire, is secretly burning in the hearts of the different sectaries [members] that inhabit them, and were it not restrained by laws and superior authority, would soon burst out into a flame of universal persecution. Even the peaceable Quakers struggle hard for preeminence, and evince in a very striking manner, that the passions of mankind are much stronger than any principles of religion.

The colonies, therefore, separately considered, are internally weak; but it may be supposed, that, by an union or coalition, they would become strong and formidable: but an union seems almost impossible: one founded in dominion or power is morally so: for, were not England to interfere, the colonies themselves so well understand the policy of preserving a balance, that, I think, they would not be idle spectators, were any one of them to endeavour to subjugate [conquer and subdue] its next neighbour. Indeed, it appears to me a very doubtful point, even supposing all the colonies of America to be united under one head, whether it would be possible to keep in due order and government so wide and extended an empire; the difficulties of communication, of intercourse [interaction], of correspondence, and all other circumstances considered.

REVIEWING THE READING

1. What does Burnaby mean by the statement "America is formed for happiness, but not for empire"?

2. Compare the weaknesses of the southern and northern colonies as they were viewed by Burnaby.

3. **Using Your Historical Imagination.** Which of the various obstacles Burnaby identifies as standing in the way of the formation of an American nation seem to have been truly significant? How can you explain the fact that a nation formed despite these obstacles?

20

From *Liberty's Daughters: The Revolutionary Experience of American Women, 1750–1800*, by Mary Beth Norton.

Women Fight for Liberty (1760s)

The American protest against British taxation and British rule was fueled by the economic contributions of women in the colonies. During the 1760s many colonial women assisted in the boycott of British goods by starting "home industries." By making their own goods in their own homes, colonial women furthered the fight for American economic independence. In the following excerpts from her book Liberty's Daughters, *historian Mary Beth Norton looks back at a group of colonial women who were actively involved in this effort. As you read the selection, note the importance of the spinning bee to American economic independence.*

Women could hardly have remained aloof from the events of the 1760s and early 1770s even had they so desired, for, like male Americans, they witnessed the escalating violence of the prerevolutionary decade. . . .

The male leaders of the boycott movement needed feminine cooperation, but they wanted to set the limits on women's activism. They did not expect, or approve, signs of feminine autonomy [self-direction].

. . . [and they] failed to come to terms with the implications of the issues raised by the growing interest in politics among colonial women.

American men's inability to perceive the alterations that were occurring in their womenfolk's self-conceptions was undoubtedly heightened by the superficially [seemingly] conventional character of feminine contributions to the protest movement. Women participating in the boycott simply made different decisions about what items to purchase and consume; they did not move beyond the boundaries of the feminine sphere. Likewise, when colonial leaders began to emphasize the importance of producing homespun as a substitute for English cloth, they did not ask women to take on an "unfeminine" task: quite the contrary, for spinning was the very role symbolic of femininity itself. . . .

Initially, the authors of newspaper articles recommending an expansion of home manufactures did not single out women for special attention. . . .

But this neglect did not continue beyond the end of 1768, for, as a writer in the *Providence Gazette* had noted late the previous year, "[W]e must after all our efforts depend greatly upon the female sex for the introduction of economy among us." The first months of 1769 brought an explosion in the newspaper coverage of women's activities, especially in New England. Stories about spinning bees . . . became numerous and prominently featured. . . .

It is impossible to know whether the increased coverage of spinning bees in 1769 indicated that women's activities expanded at precisely that time,

Many colonial women fought for the Revolution by spinning yarn so that the colonies did not have to import English cloth.

or whether the more lengthy, detailed, and numerous stories merely represented the printers' new interest in such efforts. But one fact is unquestionable: the ritualized gatherings attended by women often termed Daughters of Liberty carried vital symbolic meaning both to the participants and to the editors. . . .

The meetings, or at least the descriptions of them, fell into a uniform pattern. Early in the morning, a group of eminently respectable young ladies (sometimes as many as one hundred, but normally twenty to forty), all of them dressed in homespun, would meet at the home of the local minister. There they would spend the day at their wheels, all the while engaging in enlightening conversation. . . . At nightfall, they would present their output to the clergyman, who might then deliver a sermon on an appropriate theme. For example, . . . the Reverend John Cleveland of Ipswich told the seventy-six spinners gathered at his house, "[T]he women might recover to this country the full and free enjoyment of all our rights, properties and privileges (which is more than the men have been able to do)" by consuming only American produce and manufacturing their own clothes.

REVIEWING THE READING

1. According to Norton, what activity symbolized femininity among the colonists?

2. Who were the Daughters of Liberty? Where would they meet, and how did they spend their day?

3. **Using Your Historical Imagination.** What "symbolic meaning" do you think there was in the ritualized gatherings of the Daughters of Liberty?

Patrick Henry Takes a Stand (1775)

21

From Patrick Henry's Speech Before the Virginia Convention.

After serving as one of Virginia's delegates to the First Continental Congress, Patrick Henry returned to his home state convinced that the colonies could not avoid war with England. Henry supported forming a Virginia militia to oppose the British. Other Virginians disagreed. Henry forcefully expressed his views in a speech delivered to the Virginia Convention. As you read the following excerpt from his speech, consider the reasons Henry presents for taking immediate action.

March 23, 1775

Mr. President: No man thinks more highly than I do of the patriotism, as well as abilities, of the very worthy gentlemen who have just addressed the House. But different men often see the same subjects in different lights; and, therefore, I hope that it will not be thought disrespectful to those gentlemen if, entertaining as I do, opinions of a character very opposite to theirs, I shall speak forth my sentiments freely and without reserve. This is no time for ceremony. The question before the House is one of awful moment [importance] to this country. For my own part I consider it as nothing less than a question of freedom or slavery; and in proportion to the magnitude of the subject ought to be the freedom of the debate. It is only in this way that we can hope to arrive at truth, and fulfill the great responsibility which we hold to God and our country. Should I keep back my opinions at such a time, through fear of giving offense, I should consider myself as guilty of treason toward my country, and of an act of disloyalty toward the majesty of heaven, which I revere above all earthly kings.

Mr. President, it is natural to man to indulge in the illusions of hope. We are apt to shut our eyes against a painful truth, and listen to the song of that siren till she transforms us into beasts [refers to mythological creature who lured sailors to their death or transformation]. Is this the part of wise men, engaged in a great and arduous [difficult] struggle for liberty? Are we disposed to be of the number of those who, having eyes, see not, and having ears, hear not the things which so nearly concern their temporal [earthly] salvation? For my part, whatever anguish of spirit it may cost, I am willing to know the whole truth; to know the worst and to provide for it.

I have but one lamp by which my feet are guided . . .

I have but one lamp by which my feet are guided, and that is the lamp of experience. I know of no way of judging of the future but by the past. And judging by the past, I wish to know what there has been in the conduct of the British ministry for the last ten years to justify those hopes with which gentlemen have been pleased to solace [comfort] themselves and the House [convention]? Is it that insidious [treacherous] smile with which our petition has been lately received? Trust it not, sir; it will prove a snare to your feet. Suffer not yourselves to be betrayed with a kiss. Ask yourselves how this gracious reception of our petition comports [agrees] with those warlike preparations which cover our waters and darken our land. Are fleets and armies necessary to a work of love and reconciliation? Have we shown ourselves so unwilling to be reconciled that force must be called in to win back our love? Let us not deceive ourselves, sir. These are the implements of war and subjugation [slavery], the last arguments to which kings resort.

I ask, gentlemen, sir, what means this martial array [military display] if its purpose be not to force us to submission? . . . They are meant for us; they can be meant for no other. They are sent over to bind and rivet upon us those chains which the British

ministry [has] been so long forging. And what have we to oppose to them? Shall we try argument? Sir, we have been trying that for the last ten years. Have we anything new to offer on the subject? Nothing . . . Sir, we have done everything that could be done to avert [prevent] the storm which is now coming on. We have petitioned, we have remonstrated [pleaded], we have supplicated [humbly asked], we have prostrated ourselves [thrown ourselves down] before the throne, and have implored its interposition [intervention] to arrest the tyrannical hands of the ministry and parliament. Our petitions have been slighted; our remonstrances have produced additional violence and insult; our supplications have been disregarded; and we have been spurned, with contempt, from the foot of the throne. In vain, after these things, may we indulge the fond hope of peace and reconciliation. There is no longer any room for hope. If we wish to be free, if we

Patrick Henry addresses the Virginia Assembly.

mean to preserve inviolate [pure] those inestimable
[valuable] privileges for which we have been so long
contending, if we mean not basely to abandon the
noble struggle in which we have been so long engaged and which we have pledged ourselves never
to abandon until the glorious object of our contest
shall be obtained, we must fight! I repeat it, sir—
we must fight! . . .

They tell us, sir, that we are weak, unable to
cope with so formidable an adversary. But when
shall we be stronger? Will it be the next week or
the next year? Will it be when we are totally disarmed
and when a British guard shall be stationed in every
house? Shall we gather strength by irresolution [hesi-
tation] and inaction? Shall we acquire the means
of effectual [effective] resistance by lying supinely
[quietly] on our backs and hugging the delusive phan-
tom of hope until our enemies shall have bound us
hand and foot? Sir, we are not weak, if we make a
proper use of those means which the God of nature
hath placed in our power. Three millions of people
armed in the holy cause of liberty and in such a
country as that which we possess are invincible by
any force which our enemy can send against us.
Besides, sir, we shall not fight our battles alone.
There is a just God who presides over the destinies
of nations and who will raise friends to fight our
battles for us. The battle, sir, is not to the strong
alone. It is to the vigilant, the active, the brave.
Besides, sir, we have no election [choice]. If we
were base [mean] enough to desire it, it is now
too late to retire from the contest. There is no retreat
but in submission and slavery! Our chains are forged.
Their clanking may be heard on the plains of Boston!
The war is inevitable—and let it come! I repeat it,
sir—let it come!

It is in vain, sir, to extenuate [prolong] the
matter. Gentlemen may cry peace, peace. But there
is no peace. The war is actually begun! The next
gale that sweeps from the north will bring to our

ears the clash of resounding arms! Our brethren are already in the field! Why stand we here idle? What is it that gentlemen wish? What would they have? Is life so dear, or peace so sweet, as to be purchased at the price of chains and slavery? Forbid it, Almighty God! I know not what course others may take; but as for me, give me liberty or give me death!

REVIEWING THE READING

1. Why is Patrick Henry convinced that the British mean to wage war on the colonies?

2. What action does Henry urge his fellow Virginians to take?

3. **Using Your Historical Imagination.** If you were a member of the Virginia Convention, how do you think you might be affected by Patrick Henry's speech? Would you agree or disagree with him? Give reasons for your answer.

22

From "The Crisis" by Thomas Paine, in *Thomas Paine*, edited by Harry Hayden Clark.

Thomas Paine's "The Crisis" (1776)

Thomas Paine came to the colonies from England in 1774, on the advice of his friend Benjamin Franklin. His writings greatly influenced the leaders of the American Revolution.

The jubilant celebrations that accompanied the adoption of the Declaration of Independence in July gave way to despair as winter approached. Washington's ragged army, reduced to about 5,000 men, was camped on the west bank of the Delaware River in December 1776. The colonial cause seemed doomed. This desperate situation prompted Thomas Paine to write "The Crisis." When Washington had "The Crisis" read to his cold, hungry troops, their spirits revived. Their victories at Trenton and Princeton a few days later were turning points in the war.

The following selection is excerpted from "The Crisis." As you read this selection, think about how Thomas Paine's words could inspire the soldiers of the Continental Army.

These are the times that try men's souls. The summer soldier and the sunshine patriot will, in this crisis, shrink from the service of his country; but he that stands it *now*, deserves the love and thanks of man and woman. Tyranny, like hell, is not easily conquered; yet we have this consolation with us, that the harder the conflict, the more glorious the triumph. What we obtain too cheap, we esteem too lightly; it is dearness [costliness] only that gives everything its value. Heaven knows how to put a proper price upon its goods; and it would be strange indeed if so celestial [heavenly] an article as FREEDOM should not be highly rated. Britain, with an army

This contemporary portrait of essayist Thomas Paine shows the writer with two of his most important political titles, The Rights of Man *and* Common Sense.

to enforce her tyranny, has declared that she has a right (*not only to* TAX) but "to BIND *us in* ALL CASES WHATSOEVER"; and if being *bound in that manner* is not slavery, then is there not such a thing as slavery upon earth. Even the expression is impious [disrespectful]; for so unlimited a power can belong only to God. . . .

I have as little superstition in me as any man living; but my secret opinion has ever been, and still is, that God Almighty will not give up a people to military destruction, or leave them unsupportedly to perish, who have so earnestly and so repeatedly sought to avoid the calamities of war, by every decent method which wisdom could invent. Neither have I so much of the infidel [non-Christian] in me as to suppose that he has relinquished [given up] the government of the world, and given us up to the care of devils; and as I do not, I cannot see on what grounds the king of Britain can look up to heaven for help against us: a common murderer, a highwayman, or a housebreaker, has as good a pretense as he. . . .

I shall conclude this paper with some miscellaneous remarks on the state of our affairs; and shall begin with asking the following question, Why is it that the enemy have left the New England provinces, and made these middle ones the seat of war? The answer is easy: New England is not infested with tories, and we are. I have been tender [careful] in raising the cry against these men, and used numberless arguments to show them their danger, but it will not do to sacrifice a world either to their folly [foolishness] or their baseness [treachery]. The period is now arrived in which either they or we must change our sentiments, or one or both must fall. And what is a tory? Good God! what is he? I should not be afraid to go with a hundred Whigs against a thousand tories, were they to attempt to get into arms. Every tory is a coward; for servile [submissive], slavish, self-interested fear is the foundation of toryism; and a man under such influence, though he may be cruel, never can be brave. . . .

Not a place upon earth might be so happy as America. Her situation is remote from all the wrangling world, and she has nothing to do but trade with them. A man can distinguish himself between temper and principle; and I am as confident as I am that God governs the world, that America will never be happy till she gets clear of foreign dominion. Wars, without ceasing, will break out till that period arrives, and the continent must in the end be conqueror; for though the flame of liberty may sometimes cease to shine, the coal can never expire. . . .

Quitting this class of men [Tories], I turn with the warm ardor of a friend to those who have nobly stood, and are yet determined to stand the matter out: I call not upon a few, but upon all: not on *this*

State or *that* State, but on *every* State: up and help us; lay your shoulders to the wheel; better have too much force than too little, when so great an object is at stake. Let it be told to the future world, that in the depth of winter, when nothing but hope and virtue could survive, that the city and the country, alarmed at one common danger, came forth to meet and to repulse it. Say not that thousands are gone—[but] turn out your tens of thousands; throw not the burden of the day upon Providence, but *"show your faith by your works,"* that God may bless you. It matters not where you live, or what rank of life you hold, the evil or the blessing will reach you all. The far and the near, the home counties and the back, the rich and the poor, will suffer or rejoice alike. The heart that feels not now is dead; the blood of his children will curse his cowardice who shrinks back at a time when a little might have saved the whole and made *them* happy. I love the man that can smile in trouble, that can gather strength from distress and grow brave by reflection. It is the business of little minds to shrink; but he whose heart is firm, and whose conscience approves his conduct, will pursue his principles unto death. My own line of reasoning is to myself as straight and clear as a ray of light. Not all the treasures of the world, so far as I believe, could have induced me to support an offensive war, for I think it murder; but if a thief breaks into my house, burns and destroys my property, and kills or threatens to kill me or those that are in it, and to *"bind me in all cases whatsoever"* to his absolute will, am I to suffer it? What signifies it to me whether he who does it is a king or a common man; my countryman or not my countryman; whether it be done by an individual villain, or an army of them? . . .

> **I love the man that can smile in trouble . . .**

There are cases which cannot be overdone by language, and this is one. There are persons, too, who see not the full extent of the evil which threatens them: they solace [comfort] themselves with hopes that the enemy, if he succeed, will be merciful. It is the madness of folly, to expect mercy from those who have refused to do justice; and even mercy, where conquest is the object, is only a trick of war. The cunning of the fox is as murderous as the violence of the wolf, and we ought to guard equally against both. . . .

I thank God that I fear not. I see no real cause for fear. I know our situation well, and can see the way out of it. . . . Once more we are again collected and collecting, our new army at both ends of the continent is recruiting fast, and we shall be able to open the next campaign with sixty thousand men, well-armed and clothed. This is our situation, and who will may know it. By perseverance [devotion] and fortitude [courage] we have the prospect of a glorious issue [final outcome]; by cowardice and sub-mission, the sad choice of a variety of evils: a ravaged country—a depopulated city—habitations [homes] without safety, and slavery without hope. . . . Look on this picture and weep over it! and if there yet remains one thoughtless wretch who believes it not, let him suffer it unlamented.

REVIEWING THE READING

1. What does Thomas Paine mean by "sum-mer soldier" and "sunshine patriot"?

2. How does Paine characterize the Tories?

3. **Using Your Historical Imagination.** Imagine that you are a soldier in Washing-ton's army and have listened to a reading of "The Crisis." What do you find in Paine's article that justifies the cause for which you are fighting? Explain your an-swer.

Mercy Otis Warren Ridicules British and Tories (1776)

23

From *The Plays and Poems of Mercy Otis Warren* by Mercy Otis Warren.

Mercy Otis Warren, the wife of American general James Warren, became an important political dramatist and propagandist during the Revolutionary War. She wrote several anonymous propaganda plays that were published during the war years. Her writings gained the admiration of George Washington, John Adams, and many other prominent Americans.

The Blockheads: or, the Affrighted Officers was written to ridicule the British troops and American Tories trapped in Boston by the rebel army. In this, as in her other political plays, Warren's theme is American virtue and British incompetence. As you read this excerpt from the first act of The Blockheads, *consider Warren's description of Tory motives for supporting the British.*

Act 1. Scene 1
A Room with the [British] Officers, etc.

PUFF: Well, gentlemen, a pretty state for British generals and British troops—the terror of the world become mere scarecrows to themselves. We came to America, flushed with high expectations of conquest, and curbing these sons of riot. We toured . . . as if our success was certain; as if we had only to curb a few licentious [morally unrestrained] villains, or hang them as spectacles for their brethren. But how are we deceived? Instead of this agreeable employ, we are shamefully confined within the bounds of three miles, wrangling and starving among ourselves.

SHALLOW: Cursed alternative, either to be murdered without, or starved within. These Yankee dogs treat

A group of boys pokes fun at a Tory, a common occurrence during the Revolutionary War period.

us like a parcel of poltroons [cowards]; they divert themselves by firing at us, as at a flock of partridges. A man can scarcely put his nose over the intrenchments without losing it; another loses his eyes only looking through the ambuseirs [openings to shoot through]. They have a set of fellows called riflers; they would shoot the very devil if he was to come within a league of them.

Capt. Basbaw: Gentlemen, it will not do to set groaning here; let us determine upon some plan quickly to be done, otherwise I shall bid you farewell, and you may follow after as well as you are able. You find every night brings them nearer and nearer; they raise a hill and fortify it in 6 hours. I expect soon to see a fortification grown out of the channel, and our ships of war to be blown up by some damned machine. Such devils are capable of anything; the power of miracles is put into their hands, and they improve the patent to admiration. You must do something to dispossess them of those fortifications, otherwise we shall not only be starved, but absolutely murdered.

Lord Dapper: Starved or murdered are trifles, compared to being taken prisoners, to be dragged before their congresses, committees, etc. A pack of mutton-headed fellows, with their rusty muskets, are more dread visitors than a tribe of furies [angry spirits], just arrived from hell; therefore let us do something in earnest, or perhaps we shall be too late for relief.

Puff: The eminence [fortification] on Dorchester hill, which they began last night, they must at all hazards be dispossessed of; we must rally our weak numbers, and drive them if possible; but such is our situation, our men are become mere skeletons; their present diet renders them more capable of terrifying their enemies, than fighting of them: They will think the ghosts of their forefathers are coming to battle against them. Poor devils! I pity their miserable state, but so the fates have ordered it, we can only laugh or pity each other.

LORD DAPPER: Cursed cruel fate that we should thus be penned up! Churchill's description of Scotland is but a shadow to it; if that great genius was now alive, we should soon have a new edition with amendments. He represents their flies and spiders, etc. as starving, but here they are absolutely starved. Poor innocent insects, I forgive ye your former tormenting of my legs; ye sucked till you could find no nourishment, and then fell at my feet and died. Thousands have lain gasping within the small circle of my chair; their case was truly deplorable. I felt their state by experience. My case is somewhat parallel to the prodigal son. I may well adopt his words, "how many hired servants of my father's have bread enough and to spare, while I perish with hunger."

SHALLOW: We shall all be obliged to follow his example; I never thought to make an improvement of a parable, but our case is now so truly deplorable that necessity prompts me to it. Hard crusts and rusty bones have never till now become my diet; they do not suit my digestion. My teeth are worn to stumps and my lips are swelled like a blubber-mouth . . . by thumping hard bones against them; my jaw bone has been set a dozen times, dislocated by chewing hard pork, as tough as an old swine's [rump].
PUFF: Well gentlemen, we are all acquainted with each other's circumstances, but however, we cannot mend them by recounting them. Let us rally our men and drive those rebels from their fortifications, or else we may soon expect to be introduced to their honors Adams and Hancock, with sundry other gentlemen of distinction. My Lord Dapper must have the command, and I doubt not we shall be able to dispossess them. Let us keep up our spirits, for we have nothing else to feed on, though it is a poor dish for a greedy appetite.

LORD DAPPER: Some pretence must be made, as our honor is at stake.

Act 1 Scene 2
A room with [Tory] refugees, and friends to government.

Nothing can be more wretched than our state . . .

SURLY: Nothing can be more wretched than our state, vagabonds and outcasts in the world! Here we are, friends we have none, we fled here for protection, but how are we disappointed! Those on whom we depended, are as miserable as ourselves! We have been cajoled into all this by that cursed H——n. He pleased us with pensions, posts of honor, and profit, but the villain has fled, and left us to shirk for ourselves. My dwellings I have forsaken, my family are left to feed on the charity of friends, if they can find any; while I, poor wretch, have thrown myself upon the mercy of those who are unable to help me. My money I have let out on government security—and poor security too, I am afraid. From affluence and splendor, I am reduced to wretchedness and misery, and skulk about the streets like a dog that has lost one ear. Oh cursed ambition! Much better had it been if I had stayed among my country-men, and partook quietly of the produce of my farm. Why need I have meddled in politics, or burnt my fingers dabbling in this sea of fire. My tenants and my oxen would have been much more agreeable companions than these herd of stalking poltroons, swaggering with their swords at their rump and afraid to draw them from the scabbard.

SIMPLE: We have reason to blame ourselves. We have brought affairs to the present state. We were fond of the titles of Colonel, Esquire, etc.—a gewgaw [trinket] of a commission was sufficient to render us enemies to our country. We contrived a thousand tricks to make ourselves obnoxious to our country-men, that we might be noticed as friends of govern-ment; we thought this would recommend us to some lucrative post; We embraced the shadow of grandeur, but the substance has fled. A bow from a general or an officer is all the satisfaction we have for our loyalty. I am become almost ashamed of my company; a pack of strutting pedantics [people who show off what they know], looking like elopers [runaways] from the grave, "grinning horribly their ghastly smiles;" gallanting their drosly nymphs, haggared with constant use. Sometimes I am ready to heave myself upon the mercy of my injured country, but the awful ideas of committees, courts of inquiry, etc. terrify me from this expedient: Besides, shall we stoop to submission to these miscreants? We, Col's., Esq'rs., Judges, etc. bow to the lordly sway of these vile villains? I would rather perish than do it.

REVIEWING THE READING

1. What were the motives of the Americans who sided with the British—the Tories or "friends to government"—according to Mrs. Warren? Do you think this is entirely fair?

2. What was the situation of the British troops in Boston?

3. **Using Your Historical Imagination.** How are the enemies of the American Revolution—British army officers and Tories—depicted in Mrs. Warren's propaganda play? How does this compare with examples of twentieth century propaganda you have seen.

24

From *Diary of Surgeon Albigence Waldo of the Connecticut Line.*

A Surgeon's Diary of Valley Forge (1777–1778)

Among those who served with Washington and suffered the harsh conditions at Valley Forge during the winter of 1777 and 1778 was a surgeon named Albigence Waldo. In January 1777, Dr. Waldo, a Connecticut native, was appointed surgeon of the First Connecticut Infantry Regiment of the Line. In the spring of 1777, the regiment was ordered by Washington to join the army in Pennsylvania.

The following selection consists of excerpts from Dr. Waldo's diary of his days at Valley Forge. As you read the selection, note how the wretched conditions at Valley Forge affected the soldiers, officers, and surgeons.

December 14.—Prisoners & Deserters are continually coming in. The Army which has been surprisingly healthy hitherto, now begins to grow sickly from the continued fatigues they have suffered this Campaign. Yet they still show a spirit of Alacrity [cheerful readiness] & Contentment not to be expected from so young Troops. I am Sick—discontented—and out of humour. Poor food—hard lodging—Cold Weather—fatigue— Nasty Cloaths—nasty Cookery—Vomit half my time— smoak'd out of my senses [by the smoke created by the guns]—the Devil's in't—I can't Endure it— Why are we sent here to starve and Freeze—What sweet Felicities have I left at home; A charming Wife—pretty Children—Good Beds—good food— good Cookery—all agreeable—all harmonious. Here all Confusion—smoke & Cold—hunger & filthyness—A pox on my bad luck. There comes a bowl

of beef soup—full of burnt leaves and dirt. . . .
Away with it Boys—I'll live like the Chameleon upon
Air. Poh! Poh! cries Patience within me—you talk
like a fool. Your being sick Covers your mind with
a Melanchollic [depressed] Gloom, which makes everything about you appear gloomy. See the poor
Soldier, when in health—with what cheerfulness he
meets his foes and encounters every hardship—if
barefoot, he labours thro' the Mud & Cold with a
Song in his mouth extolling [praising] War & Washington—if his food be bad, he eats it notwithstanding
with seeming content—blesses God for a good Stomach and Whistles it into digestion. But harkee Patience, a moment—There comes a Soldier, his bare
feet are seen thro' his worn out Shoes, his legs nearly
naked from the tatter'd remains of an only pair of
stockings, his Breeches not sufficient to cover his
nakedness, his Shirt hanging in Strings, his hair dis-
hevell'd, his face meagre; his whole appearance pictures a person forsaken & discouraged. He comes,
and crys with an air of wretchedness & despair, I
am Sick, my feet lame, my legs are sore, my body
cover'd with this tormenting Itch—my Cloaths are
worn out, my Constitution [health] is broken, my
former Activity is exhausted by fatigue, hunger &
Cold, I fail fast I shall soon be no more! and all
the reward I shall get will be—"Poor Will is dead."
People who live at home in Luxury and Ease, quietly
possessing their habitations, Enjoying their Wives
& families in peace, have but a very faint Idea of
the unpleasing sensations, and continual Anxiety the
Man endures who is in a Camp, and is the husband
and parent of an agreeable family. These same People
are willing we should suffer every thing for their
Benefit & advantage, and yet are the first to Condemn
us for not doing more!! . . .

    December 18.—Universal Thanksgiving—a
Roasted pig at Night. God be thanked for my health
which I have pretty well recovered. How much better
should I feel, were I assured my family were in health.

American troops try to keep warm at Valley Forge during the terrible winter of 1777-1778.

But the same good Being who graciously preserves me, is able to preserve them & bring me to the ardently wish'd for enjoyment of them again.

Rank & Precedence [the commissioned officers] make a good deal of disturbance & confusion in the American Army. The Army are poorly supplied with Provision, occasioned it is said by the Neglect of the Commissary of Purchases. Much talk among Officers about discharges. Money has become of too little consequence. The Congress have not made their Commissions valuable Enough. Heaven avert the bad consequences of these things!! . . .

December 21.—[Valley Forge.] Preparations made for hutts. Provisions Scarce. Mr. Ellis went homeward—sent a Letter to my Wife. Heartily wish myself at home, my Skin & eyes are almost spoil'd with continual smoke. A general cry thro' the Camp this Evening among the Soldiers, "No Meat! No Meat!"— the Distant vales [valleys] Echo'd back the melancholly sound—"No Meat! No Meat!" Immitating the noise of Crows & Owls, also, made a part of the confused Musick.

What have you for your Dinners Boys? "Nothing but Fire Cake & Water, Sir." At night, "Gentlemen the Supper is ready." What is your Supper Lads? "Fire Cake & Water, Sir." Very poor beef has been drawn in our Camp the greater part of this season. A Butcher bringing a Quarter of this kind of Beef into Camp one day who had white Buttons on the knees of his breeches, a Soldier cries out—"There, there Tom is some more of your fat Beef, by my soul I can see the Butcher's breeches buttons through it."

December 22.—. . . Our Division are under Marching Orders this morning. I am ashamed to say it, but I am tempted to steal Fowls if I could find them, or even a whole Hog, for I feel as if I could eat one. But the Impoverish'd Country about us, affords but little matter to employ a Thief, or keep a Clever Fellow in good humour. But why do I talk of hunger & hard usage, when so many in the World have not even fire Cake & Water to eat. . . .

January 3.—. . . To day his Excellency in Orders acquainted the Troops of the Congress's high approbation [praise] of their spirited perseverance and good Conduct this Campaign, that Rations should be raised monthly in proportion to the rise of the Articles of life, that the Congress were exerting themselves to supply the Commissary, the Cloathiers Departments, with a greater quantity of better Stores, than hitherto, that the Troops may be Supply'd with a greater quantity of Provision than they have been of late; and that a Month's Wages extraordinary shall be given to every Officer & Soldier who shall live in Hutts this Winter.

Good encouragement this, and we think ourselves deserving of it, for the hunger, Thirst, Cold & fatigue we have suffer'd this Campaign, altho' we have not fought much, yet the oldest Soldiers among us have called the Campaign a very severe & hard one.

REVIEWING THE READING

1. According to Dr. Waldo, what conditions caused the soldiers' mood to change from cheerful to discouraged?

2. Who does Dr. Waldo appear to blame for the wretched conditions in camp? Why?

3. **Using Your Historical Imagination.** Do you think Dr. Waldo was justified in his criticism of "People who live at home in Luxury and Ease?" Do you think the people at home knew about the conditions at Valley Forge? Do you think most people had the attitude of those criticized by Dr. Waldo? Give reasons for your answers.

The British Surrender at Yorktown (1781)

25

From *A Military Journal*
by James Thacher.

In the final land battle of the Revolution, the American and British troops faced each other at Yorktown, Virginia, southeast of Richmond, between the York and James rivers. On October 17, following two weeks of fierce fighting, British commander Cornwallis realized his situation was hopeless and asked for terms of surrender. The surrender took place on October 19, 1781.

The following selection is an excerpt from an eyewitness account of the surrender by an American surgeon, Dr. James Thacher. As you read the selection, carefully study Dr. Thacher's observations of the troops and individuals.

At about twelve o'clock, the combined army was arranged and drawn up in a line extending more than a mile in length. The Americans were drawn up in a line on the right side of the road, and the French occupied the left. At the head of the former the great American commander [Washington], mounted on his noble courser, took his station, attended by his aids. At the head of the latter was posted the excellent Count Rochambeau and his suite [personal staff]. The French troops, in complete uniform, displayed a martial and noble appearance, their band of music, of which the timbral [tambourine] formed a part, is a delightful novelty, and produced while marching to the ground, a most enchanting effect. The Americans though not all in uniform nor their dress so neat, yet exhibited an erect soldierly air, and every countenance beamed with satisfaction and joy. The concourse [gathering] of spectators from the country was prodigious [huge], in point of numbers probably equal to the military, but universal silence and order prevailed. It was about two o'clock when the captive army advanced through the line formed for their reception. Every eye was prepared to gaze on Lord Cornwallis, the object of peculiar interest and solicitude; but he disappointed our anxious expectations; pretending indisposition [slight illness], he made General O'Harra his substitute as the leader of his army. This officer was followed by the conquered troops in a slow and solemn step, with shouldered arms, colors cased and drums beating a British march. Having arrived at the head of the line, General O'Harra, elegantly mounted, advanced to his Excellency the Commander in Chief, taking off his hat, and apologized for the non appearance of Earl Cornwallis. With his usual dignity and politeness his Excellency pointed to Major General Lincoln for directions, by whom the British army was conducted into a

British general Cornwallis surrenders to General Washington at Yorktown, October 19, 1781.

spacious field where it was intended they should ground their arms [surrender their weapons]. The royal troops, while marching through the line formed by the allied army, exhibited a decent and neat appearance, as respects arms and clothing, for their

commander opened his store and directed every soldier to be furnished with a new suit complete, prior to the capitulation [surrender]. But in their line of march we remarked a disorderly and unsoldierly conduct, their step was irregular, and their ranks frequently broken. But it was in the field when they came to the last act of the drama, that the spirit and pride of the British soldier was put to the severest test, here their mortification [humiliation] could not be concealed. Some of the platoon officers appeared to be exceedingly chagrined [humiliated] when giving the word *"ground arms,"* and I am a witness that they performed this duty in a very unofficer like manner, and that many of the soldiers manifested a *sullen temper*, throwing their arms on the pile with violence, as if determined to render them useless. This irregularity, however, was checked by the authority of General Lincoln. After having grounded their arms and divested [ridded] themselves of their accoutrements [military equipment], the captive troops were conducted back to Yorktown and guarded by our troops till they could be removed to the place of their destination.

REVIEWING THE READING

1. According to Dr. Thacher, in regard to appearance, how did the American troops compare to the French and British troops at Yorktown?

2. What opinion do you think Dr. Thacher held of George Washington? Explain your answer.

3. **Using Your Historical Imagination.** Why do you think Cornwallis failed to appear at the surrender? If you had been Cornwallis, would you have chosen to appear in person? Give reasons for your answers.

26

From *A Loyalist's Account of Certain Occurrences in Philadelphia after Cornwallis's Surrender at Yorktown* by Anna Rawle.

Harassment of Tories After the British Surrender (1781)

Although the surrender at Yorktown took place on October 19, 1781, word did not reach some cities until several days later. American officials in Philadelphia postponed celebrations until official word of the American victory reached them on October 24.

The following selection is excerpted from the diary of Miss Anna Rawle, a Loyalist staying with her grandmother in Philadelphia at the time of the surrender. As you read this selection, think about the fear most Loyalists must have experienced following the defeat of the British by the Americans.

*O*ctober 22, 1781.—Second day. The first thing I heard this morning was that Lord Cornwallis had surrendered to the French and Americans—intelligence as surprizing as vexatious [distressing]. People who are so stupidly regardless of their own interests are undeserving of compassion, but one cannot help lamenting that the fate of so many worthy persons should be connected with the failure or success of the British army. Uncle Howell came in soon after breakfast, and tho' he is neither Whig nor Tory, looked as if he had sat up all night; he was glad to see all here so cheerful, he said. When he was gone Ben Shoemaker arrived; he was told it as he came along, and was astonished. However, as there is no letter from Washington, we flatter ourselves that it is not true. . . .

October 24.—Fourth day. I feel in a most unsettled humour. I can neither read, work or give my

attention one moment to anything. It is too true
that Cornwallis is taken. Tilghman is just arrived
with dispatches from Washington which confirm
it. B.S. came here and shewed us some papers; long
conversations we often have together on the melancholy situation of things.

October 25.—Fifth day. I suppose, dear Mammy,
thee would not have imagined this house to be illuminated [showing lights] last night, but it was. A mob
surrounded it, broke the shutters and the glass of
the windows, and were coming in, none but forlorn
women here. We for a time listened for their attacks
in fear and trembling until, finding them grow more
loud and violent, not knowing what to do, we ran
into the yard. Warm [angry] Whigs of one side,
and Hartley's of the other (who were treated even
worse than we), rendered it impossible for us to
escape that way. We had not been there many minutes before we were drove back by the sight of
two men climbing the fence. We thought the mob
were coming in thro' there, but it proved to be
Coburn and Bob. Shewell, who called to us not to
be frightened, and fixed lights up at the windows,
which pacified the mob, and after three huzzas they
moved off. A number of men came in afterwards
to see us. French and J.B. nailed boards up at the
broken pannels, or it would not have been safe to
have gone to bed. Coburn and Shewell were really
very kind; had it not been for them I really believe
the house would have been pulled down. Even the
firm Uncle Fisher was obliged to submit to have
his windows illuminated, for they had pickaxes and
iron bars with which they had done considerable
injury to his house, and would soon have demolished
it had not some of the Hodges and other people
got in back and acted as they pleased. All Uncle's
sons were out, but Sammy, and if they had been
at home it was in vain to oppose them. In short it
was the most alarming scene I ever remember. For
two hours we had the disagreeable noise of stones

. . . **had it not
been for them I
really believe the
house would
have been pulled
down.**

Patriots ride a Tory out of town on a rail during the American Revolution.

banging about, glass crashing, and the tumultuous voices of a large body of men, as they were a long time at the different houses in the neighbourhood. At last they were victorious, and it was one general illumination throughout the town. As we had not the pleasure of seeing any of the gentlemen in the house, nor the furniture cut up, and goods stolen, nor been beat, nor pistols pointed at our breasts, we may count our sufferings slight compared to many others. Mr. Gibbs was obliged to make his escape over a fence, and while his wife was endeavouring to shield him from the rage of one of the men, she received a violent bruise in the breast, and a blow in the face which made her nose bleed. Ben Shoemaker was here this morning; tho' exceedingly threatened, he says he came off with the loss of four panes of glass. Some Whig friends put candles in the windows which made peace with the mob, and they retired. John Drinker has lost half the goods out of his shop and been beaten by them; in short the sufferings of those they pleased to style Tories would fill a volume and shake the credulity of those who were not here on that memorable night, and to-day Philadelphia makes an uncommon appearance, which ought to cover the Whigs with eternal confusion. A neighbour of ours had the effrontery [boldness] to tell Mrs. G. that he was sorry for her furniture, but not for her windows—a ridiculous distinction that many of them make. J. Head has nothing left whole in his parlour. Uncle Penington lost a good deal of window-glass. Aunt Burge preserved hers thro' the care of some of her neighbours. The Drinkers and Walns make heavy complaints of the Carolinians in their neighbourhood. Walns' pickles were thrown about the streets and barrells of sugar stolen. Grandmammy was the most composed of anybody here.

REVIEWING THE READING

1. Why did the author and other Loyalists fail to believe the first news of Cornwallis' defeat?

2. What did the mobs in Philadelphia do to the Loyalists there?

3. **Using Your Historical Imagination.** Why do you think the mob wanted Loyalists to illuminate their windows? The author states that doing so seemed to pacify the mob. Why do you think this was so?

27

From *An Account of a Visit Made to Washington at Mount Vernon, by an English Gentleman, in 1785* by John Hunter.

An Englishman Visits Washington After the War (1785)

After the war George Washington once again retired to his plantation at Mount Vernon to live the life of a gentleman farmer. He seemed happy and contented with this peaceful existence, but he was a marked man—the famous military leader of the Revolutionary War—and his peaceful life at Mount Vernon was not to last. In 1787 he would be chosen presiding officer of the Constitutional Convention at Philadelphia. In 1788 the political process set up by the Constitution of the new government would elect him president.

During his brief years at Mount Vernon Washington entertained many visitors. In 1785 he was visited by an English admirer named John Hunter, who wrote the portrait of Washington as gentleman farmer that is excerpted below. Hunter was an admirer of George Washington, and his description of the great man is highly flattering. As you read look for mention of personal characteristics of Washington that might help to explain his effectiveness as a military leader.

*W*ednesday 16th. of Nov'r. 1785.—After breakfast I waited on Colonel Fitzgerald. A fire that had broke out in the town hindered us from getting off so soon as we intended. However, after some trouble it was extinguished and at half past eleven we left Alexandria with Mr. Lee, the President of Congress, his son and the servants. You have a fine view of the Potomac till you enter a wood. A small

Rivulet here divides the General's Estate from the
neighbouring farmers. His seat [home] breaks out
beautifully upon you when you little expect, being
situated upon a most elegant rising ground on the
banks of the Potomac, ten miles from Alexandria.
We arrived at Mount Vernon by one o'clock—so-
called by the General's eldest brother, who lived
there before him, after the Admiral of that name.
When Colonel Fitzgerald introduced me to the General I was struck with his noble and venerable appearance. It immediately brought to my mind the great
part he had acted in the late war. The General is
about six feet high, perfectly straight and well made;
rather inclined to be lusty [sturdy]. His eyes are
full and blue and seem to express an air of gravity.
His nose inclines to the aquiline [curved like an
eagle's beak]; his mouth small; his teeth are yet good
and his cheeks indicate perfect health. His forehead
is a noble one and he wears his hair turned back,
without curls and quite in the officer's style, and
tied in a long queue behind. Altogether he makes
a most noble, respectable appearance, and I really
think him the first man in the world. After having
had the management and care of the whole Continental army, he has now retired without receiving
any pay for his trouble, and though solicited by
the King of France and some of the first characters
in the world to visit Europe, he has denied them
all and knows how to prefer solid happiness in his
retirement to all the luxuries and flattering speeches
of European Courts. The General was born and educated near Fredericksburg [Virginia] on the Rappahannock [River]. He must be a man of great abilities
and a strong natural genius, as his master never taught
him anything but writing and arithmetic. People
come to see him here from all parts of the world—
hardly a day passes without; but the General seldom
makes his appearance before dinner; employing the
morning to write his letters and superintend his farm,
and allotting the afternoon to company; but even

> . . . he makes a
> most noble,
> respectable
> appearance . . .

This 1798 painting by George Parkyns shows a view of Mount Vernon, the residence of George Washington.

then he generally retires for two hours between tea and supper to his study to write. . . .

At three, dinner was on table, and we were shewn by the General into another room, where everything was set off with a peculiar taste, and at the same time very neat and plain. The General sent the bottle about pretty freely after dinner, and gave success to the navigation of the Potomac for his toasts, which he has very much at heart, and when finished will I suppose be the first river in the world. He never undertakes anything without having first well considered of it and consulted different people, but when once he has begun anything, no obstacle or difficulty can come in his way, but what he is determined to surmount [overcome]. The General's character seems to be a prudent, but a very persevering one. He is quite pleased at the idea of the Baltimore Merchants laughing at him, and saying it was a ridiculous plan and would never succeed. They begin now, says the General, to look a little serious about the matter, as they know it must hurt their commerce amazingly. . . .

We had a very elegant supper about [nine o'clock]. The General with a few glasses of champagne got quite merry, and being with his intimate friends laughed and talked a good deal. Before strangers he is generally very reserved, and seldom says a word. I was fortunate in being in his company with his particular acquaintances. I am told during the war he was never seen to smile. The care indeed of such an army was almost enough to make anybody thoughtful and grave. No man but the General could have kept the army together without victuals or clothes; they placed a confidence in him that they would have had in no other person. His being a man of great fortune and having no children shewed them it was quite a disinterested part that he was acting with regard to money making and that he had only the good of his country at heart. The soldiers, tho' starving at times, in a manner adored him.

We had a great deal of conversation about the slippery ground (as the General said) that Franklin was on, and also about Congress, the Potomac, improving their roads, etc. At 12 I had the honor of being lighted [guided by candlelight] up to my bedroom by the General himself.

Thursday 17th. November.—I rose early and took a walk about the General's grounds—which are really beautifully laid out. He has about 4000 acres well cultivated and superintends the whole himself. Indeed his greatest pride now is, to be thought the first farmer in America. He is quite a Cincinnatus [a legendary Roman leader who was also a farmer], and often works with his men himself—strips off his coat and labors like a common man. The General has a great turn for mechanics. It's astonishing with

The style of his house is very elegant . . .

what niceness he directs everything in the building way, condescending even to measure the things himself, that all may be perfectly uniform. The style of his house is very elegant, something like the Prince de Conde's at Chantille, near Paris, only not quite so large: but it's a pity he did not build a new one at once, as it has cost him nearly as much repairing his old one. His improvements I'm told are very great within the last year. He is making a most delightful bowling green before the house and cutting a new road through the woods to Alexandria. It would be endless to attempt describing his house and grounds—I must content myself with having seen them. The situation is a heavenly one, upon one of the finest rivers in the world. I suppose I saw thousands of wild ducks upon it, all within gun shot. There are also plenty of blackbirds and wild geese and turkies. After breakfast I went with Shaw to see his famous race-horse Magnolia—a most beautiful creature. A whole length [portrait] of him was taken a little while ago, (mounted on Magnolia) by a famous man from Europe in copper—and his bust in marble—one by order of Congress to be kept wherever they sit, and the other by the State of Virginia, to stand in the House of Assembly. They will cost about 6000 sterling Shaw says. He also showed me an elegant State Carriage, with beautiful emblematical figures on it, made him a present of by the State of Pennsylvania. I afterwards went into his stables, where among an amazing number of horses, I saw old Nelson, now 22 years of age, that carried the General almost always during the war: Blueskin, another fine old horse next to him, now and then had that honor. Shaw also shewed me his old servant, that was reported to have been taken, with a number of the General's papers about him. They have heard the roaring of many a cannon in their time. Blueskin was not the favorite, on account of his not standing fire so well as venerable old Nelson. The General makes no manner of use of them now; he keeps them in a nice stable where they feed away at their ease for their past services. There is a horse of Major Washington's there that was reckoned the finest figure in the American Army. It's astonishing what a number of small houses the General has upon his Estate for his different Workmen and Negroes to live in. He has everything within himself—Carpenters, Bricklayers, Brewers, Blacksmiths, Bakers, etc., etc. and even has a well assorted Store for the use of his family and servants.

When the General takes his coach out he always drives six horses; to his chariot he only puts four. The General has some fine deer, which he is going to enclose a park for—also some remarkable large fox hounds, made him a present of from England, as he is fond of hunting, and there are great plenty of foxes in this country.

REVIEWING THE READING

1. As described by Hunter, what characteristics of Washington would help to explain his proven effectiveness as a military leader?

2. In what way did Washington's plantation resemble a small town more than a modern agricultural estate?

3. **Using Your Historical Imagination.** John Hunter is an admirer of the famous American general and presents a highly flattering account of his personality and character. However, is there anything in his description that suggests negative factors that might limit Washington's effectiveness as a national political leader?

28

From *The Papers of James Madison*, edited by Henry D. Gilpin.

Benjamin Franklin Urges the Adoption of the Constitution (1787)

By September 17, 1787, the members of the Constitutional Convention at Philadelphia had brought their proposed draft of the Constitution to its final form. For five months heated debates had been waged over the plan for the new government, and the compromise document that was in hand still displeased many. The new Constitution now required final approval by the members of the convention. It was at this point that Benjamin Franklin rose to plead for its acceptance. Franklin admitted that he was one of those members who disliked certain aspects of the document, but he felt it the best they were likely to get. Some of those dissatisfied with the draft of the Constitution believed that it gave too many powers to the central government. Others believed it established a government still too weak to function well. Franklin's speech and the comments of James Madison that follow it are excerpted from Madison's description of the scene, which was published in The Papers of James Madison. *As you read the speech, look for evidence that reveals the opinion held by Benjamin Franklin.*

Mr. President:
I confess that there are several parts of this Constitution which I do not at present approve, but I am not sure I shall never approve them. For having lived long, I have experienced many instances of being obliged by better information, or fuller consideration, to change opinions even on important

subjects, which I once thought right, but found to be otherwise. It is therefore that, the older I grow, the more apt I am to doubt my own judgment, and to pay more respect to the judgment of others. Most men, indeed, as well as most sects in religion, think themselves in possession of all truth, and that where-ever others differ from them, it is so far error. Steele, a Protestant, in a dedication, tells the Pope, that the only difference between our churches, in their opinions of the certainty of their doctrines, is, "the Church of Rome is infallible, and the Church of England is never in the wrong." But though many private persons think almost as highly of their own infallibility as of that of their sect, few express it so naturally as a certain French lady, who, in a dispute with her sister, said, "I don't know how it happens, sister, but I meet with nobody but myself that is always in the right—*il n y a que moi qui a toujours raison.*"

In these sentiments, sir, I agree to this Constitution, with all its faults, if they are such; because I think a General Government necessary for us, and there is no form of government, but what may be a blessing to the people if well administered; and believe further, that this is likely to be well adminis-tered for a course of years, and can only end in despotism [one-person rule], as other forms have done before it, when the people shall become so corrupted as to need despotic government, being incapable of any other. I doubt, too, whether any other Convention we can obtain may be able to make a better Constitution. For when you assemble a number of men to have the advantage of their joint wisdom, you inevitably assemble with those men all their prejudices, their passions, their errors of opinion, their local interests and their selfish views. From such an assembly can a perfect production be expected? It therefore astonishes me, sir, to find this system approaching so near to perfection as it does; and I think it will astonish our enemies, who

> . . . I doubt, too, whether any other Convention we can obtain may be able to make a better Constitution.

are waiting with confidence to hear that our councils are confounded, like those of the builders of Babel; and that our States are on the point of separation, only to meet hereafter for the purpose of cutting one another's throats. Thus I consent, sir, to this Constitution, because I expect no better, and because I am not sure, that it is not the best. The opinions I have had of its errors I sacrifice to the public good. I have never whispered a syllable of them abroad. Within these walls they were born, and here they shall die. If every one of us, in returning to our constituents, were to report the objections he has had to it, and endeavour to gain partizans in support of them, we might prevent its being generally received, and thereby lose all the salutary [favorable] effects and great advantages resulting naturally in our favor among foreign nations as well as among ourselves, from our real or apparent unanimity. Much of the strength and efficiency of any government, in procuring and securing happiness to the people, depends on opinion—on the general opinion of the goodness of the government, as well as of the wisdom and integrity of its governors. I hope, therefore, that for our own sakes, as a part of the people, and for the sake of posterity, we shall act heartily and unanimously in recommending this Constitution (if approved by Congress and confirmed by the Conventions) wherever our influence may extend, and turn our future thoughts and endeavours to the means of having it well administered.

On the whole, sir, I cannot help expressing a wish that every member of the Convention, who may still have objections to it, would with me, on this occasion, doubt a little of his own infallibility, and to make manifest our unanimity, put his name to this instrument.

[Madison's account continues]. . . . The members then proceeded to sign the Constitution, as finally amended, as follows:

We, the people of the United States, in order to form a more perfect union, establish justice, insure domestic tranquillity, provide for the common defence, promote the general welfare, and secure the blessings of liberty to ourselves and our posterity, do ordain and establish this Constitution for the United States of America. . . .

Whilst the last members were signing, Doctor Franklin, looking towards the President's chair, at the back of which a rising sun happened to be painted, observed to a few members near him, that painters had found it difficult to distinguish in their art, a rising, from a setting, sun. "I have, said he, often and often, in the course of the session, and the vicissitudes of my hopes and fears as to its issue, looked at that behind the President, without being

Benjamin Franklin addresses the Constitutional Convention in Philadelphia, 1787.

able to tell whether it was rising or setting: but now at length, I have the happiness to know, that it is a rising, and not a setting sun."

REVIEWING THE READING

1. Does Franklin seem to believe that the government set up by the proposed Constitution will be too strong or too weak?

2. What message does Franklin wish to convey with his story about the "Church of England and the Church of Rome"?

3. **Using Your Historical Imagination.** What arguments does Franklin present for the adoption of the new Constitution? What is your opinion about the probable effects of these arguments on the members of the Constitutional Convention?

Patrick Henry on the Constitution (1788)

29

From *The Debates in the Several State Conventions on the Adoption of the Federal Constitution,* Volume III, edited by Jonathan Elliot.

Despite the persuasive arguments of Benjamin Franklin for acceptance of the new Constitution, many delegates returned home to lead a fight against ratification in their state conventions. One of these was Patrick Henry, who delivered speeches urging rejection of the Constitution during the Virginia ratification debates. As you read the following excerpts, note why Henry was particularly angered by the now-famous phrase "We, the people . . ."

Mr. Henry. . . . And here I would make this inquiry of those worthy characters who composed a part of the late federal Convention. I am sure they were fully impressed with the necessity of forming a great consolidated government, instead of a confederation. That this is a consolidated government is demonstrably clear; and the danger of such a government is, to my mind, very striking. I have the highest veneration [regard] for those gentlemen; but, sir, give me leave to demand. What right had they to say, *We, the people?* My political curiosity, exclusive of my anxious solicitude [concern] for the public welfare, leads me to ask, Who authorized them to speak the language of *We, the people,* instead of, *We, the states?* States are the characteristics and the soul of a confederation. . . . The federal Convention ought to have amended the old system [Articles of Confederation]; for this purpose they were solely delegated; the object of their mission extended to no other consideration. You must, therefore, forgive the solicitation of one unworthy member to know what danger could have arisen under the present Confederation, and what are the causes of this proposal to change our government. . . .

This Constitution is said to have beautiful features; but when I come to examine these features, sir, they appear to me horribly frightful. Among other deformities, it has an awful squinting; it squints towards monarchy; and does not this raise indignation in the breast of every true American?

Your President may easily become king. Your Senate is so imperfectly constructed that your dearest rights may be sacrificed by what may be a small minority; and a very small minority may continue forever unchangeably this government, although horridly defective. Where are your checks in this government? Your strongholds will be in the hands of your enemies. It is on a supposition that your American governors shall be honest, that all the good qualities of this government are founded; but its defective and imperfect construction puts it in their power to perpetrate the worst of mischiefs,

Patrick Henry, statesman and patriot, had reservations about the proposed Constitution.

should they be bad men; and, sir, would not all the world, from the eastern to the western hemisphere, blame our distracted folly in resting our rights upon the contingency of our rulers being good or bad? Show me that age and country where the rights and liberties of the people were placed on the sole chance of their rulers being good men, without a consequent loss of liberty! I say that the loss of the dearest privilege has ever followed, with absolute certainty, every such mad attempt.

If your American chief be a man of ambition and abilities, how easy is it for him to render himself absolute! The army is in his hands, and if he be a man of address [one who is confident and convincing], it will be attached to him, and it will be the subject of long meditation with him to seize the first auspicious [good] moment to accomplish his design; and, sir, will the American spirit solely relieve you when this happens? I would rather infinitely—and I am sure most of this Convention are of the same opinion—have a king, lords, and commons, than a government so replete [filled] with such insupportable evils.

REVIEWING THE READING

1. What is the reason for Patrick Henry's criticism of the constitutional phrase "We, the people. . ."?

2. What does Henry believe to be the most basic problem with the new Constitution?

3. **Using Your Historical Imagination.** Henry believes it is important to have a system of checks and balances built into the Constitution. In what way does his criticism on this issue reveal a lack of understanding of the document?

From *Debates and Proceedings of the Commonwealth of Massachusetts, Held in the Year 1788*; and *The Debates, Resolutions, and Other Proceedings in Convention, on the Adoption of the Federal Constitution.*

30

A Debate on the Constitution (1788)

The debate over ratification of the new Constitution went on at the grass-roots level in every state ratification convention. Those who spoke for or against the Constitution were often average farmers or small businesspeople, rather than intellectuals and people of education, like Hamilton and Richard Lee. In the excerpts that follow from three speeches made at the Massachusetts convention in 1788, consider which side seems to make the strongest arguments.

Amos Singletary, Worcester County . . . We [fought] with Great Britain, some said, for a three-penny duty on tea; but it was not that—it was because they claimed a right to tax us and bind us in all cases whatever. And does not this Constitution do the same? Does it not take away all we have, all our property? Does it not lay *all* taxes, duties, imposts and excises? And what more have we to give? They tell us Congress [will be able to] collect all the money they want by impost [tax on imports]. I say there has always been a difficulty about impost. Whenever the [state legislature] was agoing to lay an impost, they would tell us it was more than trade could bear, and that it hurt the fair trader, and encouraged smuggling; and there will always be the same objection—they won't be able to raise money enough by impost, and then they will lay it on the land, and take all we have got. These lawyers, and men of learning, and moneyed men, that talk so finely and gloss over matters so smoothly, to make us, poor illiterate people, swallow down the pill, expect to get into Congress themselves; they expect to be the managers of this Constitution, and get all the power and all the money into their own hands, and then they will swallow up all us little folks, like the great leviathan [sea monster], Mr. President; yes, just as the whale swallowed up Jonah. This is what I am afraid of.

General Thompson, Lincoln County —Sir, the question is, whether congress shall have power . . . ["to provide for the common defense, promote the general welfare"]. . . . I look upon [this section as] big with mischiefs. Congress will have power to keep standing armies. The great Mr. Pitt [a British statesman] says, standing armies are dangerous. . . . We are able to stand our own ground against a foreign power—they cannot starve us out, they cannot bring their ships on the land; we are a nation of healthy and strong men—our land is fertile, and we are increasing in numbers. . . . Let us amend the old confederation. Why not give congress power only to regulate trade? . . . [Where] is the bill of rights which shall check the power of this congress, which shall say, *thus far shall ye come, and no farther.* The safety of the people depends on a bill of rights. . . . There are some parts of this constitution which I cannot digest; and, sir, shall we swallow a large bone for the sake of a little meat? Some say swallow the whole now, and pick out the bone afterwards. But I say, let us pick off the meat, and throw the bone away.

This 1788 cartoon depicts the states as pillars supporting the arches of government. The nine upright pillars represent the first states that ratified the Constitution.

The Ninth PILLAR erected !

"The Ratification of the Conventions of nine States, shall be sufficient for the establishment of this Constitution, between the States so ratifying the same." *Art.* vii.

INCIPIENT MAGNI PROCEDERE MENSES.

If it is not up it will rise.

The Attraction must be irresistible

DEL. PEN. N. JER. GEOR. CON. MASSA. MARY. S° CARO. N. HAMP. VIRG. N. YORK

Jonathan Smith, Berkshire County . . . I am a plain man and get my living by the plough. I am not used to speak in public, but I beg your leave to say a few words to my brother plough-joggers in this house. . . .

We are by this Constitution allowed to send ten members to Congress. Have we not more than that number fit to go? I dare say, if we pick out ten, we shall have another ten left, and I hope ten times ten—and will not these be a check upon those that go? Will they go to Congress and abuse their power, and do mischief, when they know that they must return and look the other ten in the face, and be called to account for their conduct? Some gentlemen think that our liberty and property are not safe in the hands of moneyed men, and men of learning. I am not of that mind.

Brother farmer, let us suppose a case now: Suppose you had a farm of fifty acres, and your [ownership of that land] was disputed, and there was a farm of five thousand acres joined to you, that belonged to a man of learning, and his [right to ownership] was involved in the same difficulty; would you not be glad to have him for your friend, rather than to stand alone in the dispute? Well, the case is the same; these lawyers, these moneyed men, these men of learning, are all embarked in the same cause with us, and we must all swim or sink together; and shall we throw the Constitution overboard because it does not please us alike? Suppose two or three of you had been at the pains to break up a piece of rough land, and sow it with wheat; would you let it lie waste because you could not agree what sort of a fence to make? Would it not be better to put up a fence that did not please everyone's fancy, rather than not fence it at all, or keep disputing about it until the wild beasts came in and devoured it. Some gentlemen say—don't be in a hurry, take time to consider and don't take a leap in the dark. I say— take things in time, gather fruit when it is ripe.

. . . shall we throw the Constitution overboard because it does not please us alike?

There is a time to sow and a time to reap. We sowed our seed when we sent men to the [Constitutional] Convention; now is the harvest, now is the time to reap the fruit of our labor, and if we don't do it now, I am afraid we never shall have another opportunity.

REVIEWING THE READING

1. What criticisms of the proposed Constitution are expressed by Singletary and Thompson?

2. Comparing ratification of the Constitution to the operation of a farm, what three arguments for the Constitution does Smith make?

3. **Using Your Historical Imagination.** Based on a careful reading of the speeches of Singletary and Smith, what conclusion might you draw about the significance of social classes in America in 1788 compared to the present day?

31

From *Dissertations on the English Language: With Notes Historical and Critical* by Noah Webster.

Noah Webster Argues for a National Language (1789)

Noah Webster was a famous American journalist and educator. He graduated from Yale and practiced law for a time. He then turned to teaching and compiled an elementary spelling book, a grammar book, and a reader for schoolchildren. Webster's speller helped to standardize spelling and punctuation throughout the country.

Webster was an active Federalist and published many political pamphlets. He later became the editor of two Federalist newspapers. In 1806 Webster published his great dictionary, An American Dictionary of the English Language, *which eventually contained 12,000 words and 40,000 definitions. The following selection is excerpted from one of Webster's books, in which he argues for a national language in America. What are Webster's concerns, in regard to the English language in the colonies?*

The United States were settled by emigrants from different parts of Europe. But their descendants mostly speak the same tongue; and the intercourse [communication] among the learned of the different States, which the revolution has begun, and an American Court will perpetuate [make lasting], must gradually destroy the differences of dialect [variety of languages] which our ancestors brought from their native countries. This approximation [drawing together] of dialects will be certain; but without the operation of other causes than an intercourse at Court, it will be slow and partial. The body of the people, governed by habit, will still retain their respective peculiarities of speaking; and for want of schools and proper books, fall into many inaccuracies, which, incorporating [blending] with the language of the state where they live, may imperceptibly corrupt [spoil] the national language. Nothing but the establishment of schools and some uniformity in the use of books, can annihilate [destroy] differences in speaking and preserve the purity of the American tongue. A sameness of pronunciation is of considerable consequence in a political view; for provincial [unsophisticated] accents are disagreeable to strangers and sometimes have an unhappy effect upon the social affections. . . .

These remarks hold equally true, with respect to individuals, to small societies and to large communities. Small causes, such as a nickname, or a vulgar tone in speaking, have actually created a dissocial [unfriendly] spirit between the inhabitants of the different states, which is often discoverable in private business and public deliberations. Our political harmony is therefore concerned in a uniformity of language.

As an independent nation, our honor requires us to have a system of our own in language as well as government. Great Britain, whose children we are, and whose language we speak, should no longer be *our* standard; for the taste of her writers is already corrupted, and her language on the decline. But if it were not so, she is at too great a distance to be our model, and to instruct us in the principles of our own tongue.

It must be considered further, that the English is the common root or stock from which our national language will be derived. All others will gradually waste away—and within a century and a half, North America will be peopled with a hundred millions of men, *all speaking the same language.* . . .

A
DICTIONARY
of the
ENGLISH LANGUAGE.

BY NOAH WEBSTER, L L.D.

SPRINGFIELD, MASS.
PUBLISHED BY G. & C. MERRIAM, STATE STREET.

The title page of a nineteenth-century edition of Webster's Dictionary shows the author at work.

Numerous local causes, such as a new country, new associations of people, new combinations of ideas in arts and science, and some intercourse with tribes wholly unknown in Europe, will introduce new words into the American tongue. These causes will produce, in a course of time, a language in North America, as different from the future language of England, as the modern Dutch, Danish, and Swedish are from the German, or from one another. . . .

The Authors, who have attempted to give us a standard, make the practice of the court and stage in London, the sole criterion [standard] of propriety [what is acceptable] in speaking. An attempt to establish a standard on this foundation is both *unjust* and *idle*. . . .

We have therefore the fairest opportunity of establishing a national language, and of giving it uniformity and perspicuity [understanding], in North America, that ever presented itself to mankind. Now is the time to begin the plan. The minds of the Americans are roused by the events of a revolution; the necessity of organizing the political body and of forming constitutions of government that shall secure freedom and property, has called all the faculties of the mind into exertion; and the danger of losing the benefits of independence, has disposed [influenced] every man to embrace any scheme that shall tend, in its future operation, to reconcile the people of America to each other, and weaken the prejudices which oppose a cordial union.

On examining the language, and comparing the practice of speaking among the yeomanry [small landowners] of this country, with the stile of Shakespear and Addison, I am constrained [forced] to declare that the people of America, in particular the English descendants, speak the most *pure English* now known in the world. There is hardly a foreign idiom [expression] in their language; by which I mean, a *phrase* that has not been used by the best English writers from the time of Chaucer. . . .

The yeomanry of this country consists of substantial independent freeholders, masters of their own persons and lords of their own soil. These men have considerable education. They not only learn to read, write and keep accounts; but a vast proportion of them read newspapers every week, and besides the Bible, which is found in all families, they read the best English sermons and treatises upon religion, ethics, geography and history; . . . The people of distant counties in England can hardly understand one another, so various are their dialects; but in the extent of twelve hundred miles in America, there are very few, I question whether a hundred words, except such as are used in employments wholly local, which are not universally intelligible. . . .

The result of the whole is, that we should adhere to our own practice and general customs, unless it can be made very obvious that such practice is wrong, and that a change will produce some considerable advantage.

REVIEWING THE READING

1. What two ways did Webster suggest for helping to establish a national language?

2. Why did Webster reject Great Britain as a suitable model for the English language in America?

3. **Using Your Historical Imagination.** Webster believed that a national language was important and necessary to bind the American people together, weakening the prejudices that prevent people from living together in harmony. Do you agree or disagree with Webster's argument? Do you think there is a standard "American language" today? Explain your answers.

Thomas Jefferson Describes Washington's Character (1790s)

32

From *The Works of Thomas Jefferson*, Volume XI, edited by Paul Leicester Ford.

A few years after George Washington's death, his former secretary of state, Thomas Jefferson, was asked to describe President Washington's personal character. Dr. Walter Jones, who was preparing a book about the career of the late general, wanted to include in it Jefferson's candid opinions. Jefferson responded to Jones' request with a letter. As you read the following excerpts from that letter, note Jefferson's opinions about the strengths and weaknesses of Washington as a leader.

I think I knew General Washington intimately and thoroughly; and were I called on to delineate his character, it should be in terms like these.

His mind was great and powerful, without being of the very first order; his penetration strong, though not so acute as that of a Newton, Bacon, or Locke; and as far as he saw, no judgment was ever sounder. It was slow in operation, being little aided by invention or imagination, but sure in conclusion. Hence the common remark of his officers, of the advantage he derived from councils of war, where hearing all suggestions, he selected whatever was best; and certainly no General ever planned his battles more judiciously. But if deranged during the course of the action, if any member of his plan was dislocated by sudden circumstances, he was slow in re-adjustment. The consequence was, that he often failed in the field, and rarely against an enemy in station, as at Boston and York. He was incapable of fear,

meeting personal dangers with the calmest uncon-
cern. Perhaps the strongest feature in his character
was prudence, never acting until every circumstance,
every consideration, was maturely weighed; refrain-
ing if he saw a doubt, but, when once decided,
going through with his purpose, whatever obstacles
opposed. His integrity was most pure, his justice
the most inflexible I have ever known, no motives
of interest or consanguinity, of friendship or hatred,
being able to bias his decision. He was, indeed, in
every sense of the words, a wise, a good, and a
great man. His temper was naturally high toned;
but reflection and resolution had obtained a firm
and habitual ascendency over it. If ever, however,
it broke its bonds, he was most tremendous in his
wrath. In his expenses he was honorable, but exact;
liberal in contributions to whatever promised utility;
but frowning and unyielding on all visionary projects
and all unworthy calls on his charity. His heart was
not warm in its affections; but he exactly calculated
every man's value, and gave him a solid esteem proportioned to it. His person, you know, was fine,
his stature exactly what one would wish, his deport-

. . . the best horseman of his age . . .

ment easy, erect and noble; the best horseman of
his age, and the most graceful figure that could be
seen on horseback. Although in the circle of his
friends, where he might be unreserved with safety,
he took a free share in conversation, his colloquial
talents [abilities in informal discussion] were not
above mediocrity, possessing neither copiousness of
ideas, nor fluency of words. In public, when called
on for a sudden opinion, he was unready, short and
embarrassed. Yet he wrote readily, rather diffusely,
in an easy and correct style. This he had acquired
by conversation with the world, for his education
was merely reading, writing and common arithmetic,
to which he added surveying at a later day. His
time was employed in action chiefly, reading little,
and that only in agriculture and English history.
His correspondence became necessarily extensive,

and, with journalizing his agricultural proceedings, occupied most of his leisure hours within doors.

On the whole, his character was, in its mass, perfect, in nothing bad, in few points indifferent; and it may truly be said, that never did nature and fortune combine more perfectly to make a man great, and to place him in the same constellation with whatever worthies have merited from man an everlasting remembrance. For his was the singular destiny and merit, of leading the armies of his country successfully through an arduous war, for the establishment of its independence; of conducting its councils through the birth of a government, new in its forms and principles, until it had settled down into a quiet and orderly train; and of scrupulously obeying the laws through the whole of his career, civil and military, of which the history of the world furnishes no other example.

. . . I am satisfied the great body of republicans think of him as I do. We were, indeed, dissatisfied with him on his ratification of the British treaty. But this was short lived. We knew his honesty, the wiles with which he was encompassed, and that age had already begun to relax the firmness of his purposes; and I am convinced he is more deeply seated

This engraving of George Washington's Cabinet shows (from left to right) Washington, Henry Knox, Alexander Hamilton, Thomas Jefferson, and Edmund Randolph.

. . . he considered our new constitution as an experiment . . .

in the love and gratitude of the republicans, than in the Pharisaical homage of the federal monarchists [doting admiration of Hamilton's party, the Federalists]. For he was no monarchist from preference of his judgment. The soundness of that gave him correct views of the rights of man, and his severe justice devoted him to them. He has often declared to me that he considered our new constitution as an experiment on the practicability of republican government, and with what dose of liberty man could be trusted for his own good; that he was determined the experiment should have a fair trial, and would lose the last drop of his blood in support of it. And these declarations he repeated to me the oftener and more pointedly, because he knew my suspicions of Colonel Hamilton's views, and probably had heard from him the same declarations which I had, to wit, "that the British constitution, with its unequal representation, corruption and other existing abuses, was the most perfect government which had ever been established on earth, and that a reformation of those abuses would make it an impracticable government." I do believe that General Washington had not a firm confidence in the durability of our government. He was naturally distrustful of men, and inclined to gloomy apprehensions; and I was ever persuaded that a belief that we must at length end in something like a British constitution, had some weight in his adoption of the ceremonies of levees, birth-days, pompous meetings with Congress, and other forms of the same character, calculated to prepare us gradually for a change which he believed possible, and to let it come on with as little shock as might be to the public mind.

These are my opinions of General Washington, which I would vouch at the judgment seat of God, having been formed on an acquaintance of thirty years. I served with him in the Virginia legislature from 1769 to the Revolutionary war, and again, a short time in Congress, until he left us to take command of the army. During the war and after it we corresponded occasionally, and in the four years of my continuance in the office of Secretary of State, our intercourse [interaction] was daily, confidential and cordial. After I retired from that office, great and malignant pains were taken by our federal monarchists, and not entirely without effect, to make him view me as a theorist, holding French principles of government, which would lead infallibly to licentiousness and anarchy. And to this he listened the more easily, from my known disapprobation [disapproval] of the British treaty. I never saw him afterwards, or these malignant insinuations should have been dissipated before his just judgment, as mists before the sun. I felt on his death, with my countrymen that "verily a great man hath fallen this day in Israel."

REVIEWING THE READING

1. How do the strengths and weaknesses of Washington's leadership abilities help explain why he often lost battles of movement in the field but almost never lost when the enemy was in a fortified position?

2. According to Jefferson, what did Washington really think about the American Constitution and the government formed by it?

3. **Using Your Historical Imagination.** Historians must always evaluate the accuracy of their sources, because no sources are ever entirely free from personal bias. How accurate do you believe to be this assessment of Washington's character? Justify your answer.

33

From George
Washington's Farewell
Address.

George Washington's Farewell Address (1796)

In 1796 George Washington was 64 years old. He had served his country well during difficult times. As he prepared to retire from the presidency and return to his beloved Mount Vernon home, he worried about the future of the country he had helped to create.

The following selection is excerpted from Washington's farewell address to the nation. As you read this selection, observe Washington's concerns about our country's relations with foreign nations.

September 17, 1796

Friends and Fellow Citizens: . . . . Observe good faith and justice toward all nations. Cultivate peace and harmony with all. . . .

Against the insidious wiles [sly tricks] of foreign influence (I conjure [beg] you to believe me, fellow citizens) the jealousy [suspicion] of a free people ought to be constantly awake, since history and experience prove that foreign influence is one of the most baneful foes of republican government. But that jealousy, to be useful, must be impartial, else it becomes the instrument of the very influence to be avoided, instead of a defense against it. Excessive partiality [favoritism] for one foreign nation and excessive dislike for another cause those whom they actuate [incite] to see danger only on one side, and serve to veil and even second [support] the arts of influence on the other. Real patriots who may resist the intrigues [plots or schemes] of the favorite are liable to become suspected and odious [offensive], while its tools and dupes [fools] usurp [wrongfully seize] the applause and confidence of the people to surrender their interests.

The great rule of conduct for us in regard to foreign nations is in extending our commercial relations to have with them as little political connection as possible. So far as we have already formed engagements let them be fulfilled with perfect good faith. Here let us stop.

Europe has a set of primary interests which to us have none or a very remote relation. Hence she must be engaged in frequent controversies, the causes of which are essentially foreign to our concerns. Hence, therefore, it must be unwise in us to implicate ourselves by artificial ties in the ordinary vicissitudes [changes] of her politics or the ordinary combinations and collisions of her friendships or enmities.

Our detached and distant situation invites and enables us to pursue a different course. If we remain one people, under an efficient government, the period is not far off when we may defy material injury from external annoyance; when we may take such an attitude as will cause the neutrality we may at any time resolve upon to be scrupulously respected; when belligerent nations, under the impossibility of making acquisitions [claims] upon us, will not lightly hazard [risk] . . . giving us provocation; when we may choose peace or war, as our interest, guided by justice, shall counsel.

Why forego the advantages of so peculiar a situation? Why quit our own to stand upon foreign ground? Why, by interweaving our destiny with that of any part of Europe, entangle our peace and prosperity in the toils of European ambition, rivalship, interest, humor, or caprice [change of mind]?

It is our true policy to steer clear of permanent alliances with any portion of the foreign world, so far, I mean, as we are now at liberty to do it; for let me not be understood as capable of patronizing infidelity [supporting faithlessness] to existing

. . . Why quit our own to stand upon foreign ground?

This portrait of Washington was painted in 1795—just a year before he left the presidency.

engagements. I hold the maxim [proverb] no less applicable to public than to private affairs that honesty is always the best policy. I repeat, therefore, let those engagements be observed in their genuine sense. But in my opinion it is unnecessary and would be unwise to extend them.

Taking care always to keep ourselves by suitable establishments on a respectable defensive posture, we may safely trust to temporary alliances for extraordinary emergencies.

Harmony, liberal intercourse [interaction] with all nations are recommended by policy, humanity, and interest. But even our commercial [trade] policy should hold an equal and impartial [objective] hand, neither seeking nor granting exclusive favors or preferences; consulting the natural course of things; diffusing [spreading out] and diversifying [varying] by gentle means the streams of commerce, but forcing nothing; establishing with powers so disposed, in order to give trade a stable course, to define the rights of our merchants, and to enable the government to support them, conventional rules of intercourse, the best that present circumstances and mutual opinion will permit, but temporary and liable to be from time to time abandoned or varied as experience and circumstances shall dictate; constantly keeping in view that it is folly in one nation to look for disinterested favors from another; that it must pay with a portion of its independence for whatever it may accept under that character; that by such acceptance it may place itself in the condition of having given equivalents for nominal [insignificant] favors, and yet of being reproached [criticized] with ingratitude for not giving more. There can be no greater error than to expect or calculate [plan] upon real favors from nation to nation. It is an illusion which experience must cure, which a just pride ought to discard. . . .

Though in reviewing the incidents of my administration I am unconscious of intentional error, I am nevertheless too sensible of my defects not to think it probable that I may have committed many errors. Whatever they may be, I fervently beseech the Almighty to avert [prevent] or mitigate [reduce] the evils to which they may tend. I shall also carry with me the hope that my country will never cease to view them with indulgence [tolerance], and that, after forty-five years of my life dedicated to its service with an upright zeal, the faults of incompetent abilities will be consigned to oblivion [sent to the unknown], as myself must soon be to the mansions of rest.

REVIEWING THE READING

1. What were Washington's recommendations concerning America's foreign policy? What did he advise concerning existing alliances?

2. What advice did Washington offer about the trade policy of the United States?

3. **Using Your Historical Imagination.** Do you think Washington's advice on foreign policy is useful today, or has it become outdated?

From *America in Literature*, Volume 1, edited by David Levin and Theodore L. Gross.

34

Mike Fink *vs* Davy Crockett (early 1800s)

Many tall tales were created about Davy Crockett, one of the most famous frontiersman in American history. He was an expert with a rifle, a colonel in the Tennessee militia, and a member of Congress— he called himself the "Coonskin Congressman." Mike Fink was a flatboatman—often considered the first of that group of river-boat handlers. It was rumored that he could shoot more accurately than anyone else of his time.

The following selection is one of the tall tales about Davy Crockett and Mike Fink, told by Davy Crockett. As you read this selection, think about the importance of legends and tall tales in American history. Notice also the language and spelling of the tale, which have been left as Davy Crockett might have spoken and written them.

I expect, stranger, you think old Davy Crockett war never beat at the long rifle; but he war tho. I expect there's no man so strong, but what he will find some one stronger. If you havent heerd tell of one Mike Fink, I'll tell you something about him, for he war a helliferocious fellow, and made an almighty fine shot. Mike was a boatman on the Mississip, but he had a little cabbin on the head of the Cumberland [River], and a horrid handsome wife, that loved him the wickedest that ever you see. Mike only worked enough to find his wife in rags, and himself in powder, and lead, and whiskey, and the rest of the time he spent in nocking over bar [bear] and turkeys, and bouncing deer, and sometimes drawing a lead on an injun. So one night I

In this portrait Davy Crockett is dressed as a frontiersman, and carries a long rifle.

fell in with him in the woods, where him and his wife shook down a blanket for me in his wigwam. In the morning sez Mike to me, "I've got the hand-somest wife, and the fastest horse, and the sharpest shooting iron in all Kentuck, and if any man dare doubt it, I'll be in his hair quicker than hell could scorch a feather." This put my dander up, and sez I, "I've nothing to say agin your wife, Mike, for it cant be denied she's a shocking handsome woman, and Mrs. Crockett's in Tennessee, and I've got no horses. Mike, I dont exactly like to tell you you lie about what you say about your rifle, but I'm d—d if you speak the truth, and I'll prove it. Do you see that are cat sitting on the top rail of your potato patch, about a hundred and fifty yards off? If she ever hears agin, I'll be shot if it shant be without ears." So I plazed away, and I'll bet you a horse, the ball cut off both the old tom cat's ears close to his head, and shaved the hair off clean across the skull, as slick as if I'd done it with a razor, and the critter never stirred, nor knew he'd lost his ears till he tried to scatch 'em. "Talk about your rifle after that, Mike!" sez I. "Do you see that are sow away off furder than the eend of the world," sez Mike, "with a litter of pigs round her," and he lets fly. The old sow give a grunt, but never stirred in her tracks, and Mike falls to loading and firing for dear life, till he hadn't left one of them are pigs enough tail to make a tooth-pick on. "Now," sez he, "Col.

Crockett, I'll be pretticulary ableedged to you if you'll put them are pig's tails on again," sez he. "That's onpossible, Mike," sez I, "but you've left one of 'em about an inch to steer by, and if it had a-been my work, I wouldn't have done it so wasteful. I'll mend your host," and so I lets fly, and cuts off the apology he'd left the poor cretur for decency. I wish I may drink the whole of Old Mississip, without a drop of the rale [real] stuff in it, if you wouldn't have thort the tail had been drove in with a hammer. That made Mike a kinder sorter wrothy [angry], and he sends a ball after his wife as she was going to the spring after a gourd full of water, and nocked half her koom out of her head, without stirring a hair, and calls out to her to stop for me take a plizzard at what was left on it. The angeliferous critter stood still as a scarecrow in a cornfield, for she'd got used to Mike's tricks by long practiss. "No, no, Mike," sez I, "Davy Crockett's hand would be sure to shake, if his iron war pointed within a hundred mile of a shemale, and I give up beat, Mike, and as we've had our eye-openers a-ready, we'll now take a flem-cutter, by way of an antiformatic [they have had their wake-up drinks and now will take another as "medicine"], and then we'll disperse."

REVIEWING THE READING

1. According to Davy Crockett, when Mike Fink was not working as a boatman, how did he spend his time?

2. Why did Davy Crockett "give up beat" to Mike Fink?

3. **Using Your Historical Imagination.** Do you think there is any truth to this tall tale? What purpose do you think legends and tall tales serve?

Ranch and Mission Days in Spanish California (ca. 1800)

35

From *Sketches of Early California*, compiled by Donald DeNevi.

For 70 years after the arrival of the first Spanish settlers at San Diego in 1769, California remained a remote outpost of Spanish Mexico, isolated by hundreds of miles from other centers of civilization. California society was dominated by the ranch and the mission, both described in the following account by Guadalupe Vallejo. Vallejo was a descendant of a family that settled in San Diego in 1774. Writing several decades later, he sketched this nostalgic word portrait of California's "ranch and mission days." As you read these excerpts, consider the role played by Native Americans in early California society.

Pioneers

It seems to me that there never was a more peaceful or happy people on the face of the earth than the Spanish, Mexican, and Indian population of Alta California [what is now California] before the American conquest. We were the pioneers of the Pacific coast, building towns and Missions while General Washington was carrying on the war of the Revolution, and we often talk together of the days when a few hundred large Spanish ranches and Mission tracts occupied the whole country from the Pacific to the San Joaquin. . . .

The Jesuit Missions established in Lower California [now Baja California, part of Mexico], at Loreto and other places, were followed by Franciscan Missions in Alta California, with presidios [forts] for the soldiers, adjacent pueblos, or towns, and the granting of large tracts of land to settlers. By 1782 there were nine flourishing Missions in Alta California—San Francisco, Santa Clara, San Carlos, San Antonio, San Luis Obispo, San Buenaventura, San Gabriel, San Juan, and San Diego. . . .

No one need suppose that the Spanish pioneers of California suffered many hardships or privations, although it was a new country. They came slowly, and were well prepared to become settlers. All that was necessary for the maintenance and enjoyment of life according to the simple and healthful standards of those days was brought with them. They had seeds, trees, vines, cattle, household goods, and servants, and in a few years their orchards yielded abundantly and their gardens were full of vegetables. . . .

. . . They came slowly, and were well prepared to become settlers.

The houses of the Spanish people were built of adobe [bricks made of mud and straw], and were roofed with red tiles. They were very comfortable, cool in summer and warm in winter. The clay used to make the bricks was dark brown, not white or yellow, as the adobes in the Rio Grande region and in parts of Mexico.

The Indian houses were never more than one story high, also of adobe, but much smaller and with thinner walls. The inmates covered the earthen floors in part with coarse mats woven of tules [plants that grow in wet areas], on which they slept. The Missions, as fast as possible, provided them with blankets, which were woven under the fathers' personal supervision, for home use and for sale. They were also taught to weave a coarse serge for clothing.

It was between 1792 and 1795, as I have heard, that the governor brought a number of artisans from Mexico, and every Mission wanted them, but there were not enough to go around. There were masons, millwrights, tanners, shoemakers, saddlers, potters, a ribbonmaker, and several weavers. The blankets and the coarse cloth I have spoken of were first woven in the southern Missions, San Gabriel, San Juan Capistrano, and others. About 1797 cotton cloth was also made in a few cases, and the cotton plant

was found to grow very well. Hemp was woven at
Monterey. Pottery was made at Mission Dolores,
San Francisco. Soap was made in 1798, and afterwards
at all the Missions and on many large ranches. The
settlers themselves were obliged to learn trades and
teach them to their servants, so that an educated
young gentleman was well skilled in many arts and
handicrafts. He could ride, of course, as well as the
best cow-boy of the Southwest, and with more grace;
and he could throw the lasso so expertly that I never
heard of any American who was able to equal it.
He could also make soap, pottery, and bricks, burn
lime, tan hides, cut out and put together a pair of
shoes, make candles, roll cigars, and do a great number of things that belong to different trades.

Indian alcaldes [officials] were appointed in the
Mission towns to maintain order. Their duty was
that of police officers; they were dressed better than
the others, and wore shoes and stockings, which
newly appointed officers dispensed with as often
as possible, choosing to go barefoot, or with stockings only. When a vacancy in the office occurred
the Indians themselves were asked which one they
preferred of several suggested by the priest. The
Mission San José had about five thousand Indian
converts at the time of its greatest prosperity, and
a number of Indian alcaldes were needed there. The
alcaldes of the Spanish people in the pueblos were
more like local judges, and were appointed by the
governor. . . .

Missions

The Indian vaqueros, who lived much of the time
on the more distant cattle ranges, were a wild set
of men. I remember one of them, named Martin,
who was stationed in Amador Valley and became
a leader of hill vaqueros, who were very different
from the vaqueros of the large valley near the Missions. He and his friends killed and ate three or
four hundred young heifers [cows] belonging to the

Missions like the one depicted in this lithograph from the 1800s were centers of population and activity throughout California.

Mission, but when Easter approached he felt that he must confess his sins, so he went to Father Narciso and told all about it. The father forgave him, but ordered him to come in from the hills to the Mission and attend school until he could read. The rules were very strict; whoever failed twice in a lesson was always whipped. Martin was utterly unable to learn his letters, and he was whipped every day for a month; but he never complained. He was then dismissed, and went back to the hills. I used to question Martin about the affair, and he would tell me with perfect gravity of manner, which was very delightful, how many calves he had consumed and how wisely the good father had punished him. He knew now, he used to say, how very hard it was to live in the town, and he would never steal again lest he might have to go to school until he had learned his letters.

It was the custom at all the Missions, during
the rule of the Franciscan missionaries, to keep the
young unmarried Indians separate. The young girls
and the young widows at the Mission San José occupied a large adobe building, with a yard behind it,
enclosed by high adobe walls. In this yard some
trees were planted, and a *zanja*, or water-ditch, supplied a large bathing-pond. The women were kept
busy at various occupations, in the building, under
the trees, or on the wide porch; they were taught
spinning, knitting, the weaving of Indian baskets
from grasses, willow rods and roots, and more especially plain sewing. The treatment and occupation
of the unmarried women was similar at the other
Missions. When heathen Indian women came in,
or were brought by their friends, or by the soldiers,
they were put in these houses, and under the charge
of older women, who taught them what to do. . . .

The padres [fathers] always had a school for
the Indian boys. My mother has a *novena*, or "nine-
days' devotion book," copied for her by one of the
Indian pupils of the school at the Mission San José,
early in the century. The handwriting is very neat
and plain, and would be a credit to any one. Many
young Indians had good voices, and these were selected with great care to be trained in singing for
the church choir. It was thought such an honor to
sing in church that the Indian families were all very
anxious to be represented. Some were taught to play
on the violin and other stringed instruments. When
Father Narciso Duran, who was the president of
the Franciscans in California, was at the Mission
San José, he had a church choir of about thirty
well-trained boys to sing the mass. He was himself
a cultivated musician, having studied under some
of the best masters in Spain, and so sensitive was
his ear that if one string was out of tune he could
not continue his service, but would at once turn to
the choir, call the name of the player, and the string
that was out of order, and wait until the matter

was corrected. As there were often more than a dozen players on instruments, this showed high musical ability. Every prominent Mission had fathers who paid great attention to training the Indians in music. . . .

The principal sources of revenue which the Missions enjoyed were the sales of hides and tallow [a substance made from cattle or sheep fat], fresh beef, fruits, wheat, and other things to ships, and in occasional sales of horses to trappers or traders. The Russians at Fort Ross, north of San Francisco, on Bodega Bay, bought a good deal from the Missions. Then too the Indians were sent out to trade with other Indians, and so the Missions often secured many valuable furs, such as otter and beaver, together with skins of bears and deer killed by their own hunters.

. . . The missions often secured . . . furs, such as otter and beaver . . .

The *embarcadero*, or "landing," for the Mission San José was at the mouth of a salt-water creek four or five miles away. When a ship sailed into San Francisco Bay, and the captain sent a large boat up this creek and arranged to buy hides, they were usually hauled there on an ox-cart with solid wooden wheels, called a *carreta*. But often in winter, there being no roads across the valley, each separate hide was doubled across the middle and placed on the head of an Indian. Long files of Indians, each carrying a hide in this manner, could be seen trotting over the unfenced level land through the wild mustard to the *embarcadero*, and in a few weeks the whole cargo would thus be delivered. For such work the Indians always received additional gifts for themselves and families.

I have often been asked about the old Mission and ranch gardens. They were, I think, more extensive, and contained a greater variety of trees and plants, than most persons imagine. The Jesuits had gardens in Baja California as early as 1699, and vineyards and orchards a few years later. The Franciscans in Alta California began to cultivate the soil as soon as they landed. The first grapevines were brought from Lower California in 1769, and were soon planted at all the Missions except Dolores, where the climate was not suitable. Before the year 1800 the orchards at the Missions contained apples, pears, peaches, apricots, plums, cherries, figs, olives, oranges, pomegranates. At San Diego and San Buenaventura Missions there were also sugar canes, date palms, plantains, bananas, and citrons. There were orchards and vineyards in California sufficient to supply all the wants of the people.

REVIEWING THE READING

1. What were the duties of the Indian alcaldes in the mission towns?

2. What religious order was the first to establish missions in California?

3. **Using Your Historical Imagination.** What major differences do you notice between Spanish pioneer society in California and American pioneer society far to the east?

36

From *The Journals of Lewis and Clark*, edited by Bernard DeVoto.

Meriwether Lewis Records a Narrow Escape (1805)

Before the lands west of the Mississippi were formally purchased from France, President Jefferson requested Congress to send out an expedition of exploration to the western territories. Its purposes were to seek out a route west, to make scientific observations, and to establish friendly relations with the Indians. By the time the expedition left St. Louis in 1804, the Louisiana Purchase was a reality. Meriwether Lewis, Jefferson's personal secretary, was the expedition's co-commander, along with William Clark. Most of the members of the Lewis and Clark expedition were regular army soldiers. Lewis and Clark left St. Louis by keelboat and flatboat in 1804 and wintered among the Mandan Indians later that year. Soon after they resumed the trip up the Missouri River in 1805, Lewis described the following events in his daily journal. As you read the excerpts, consider what seems to have been the purpose of Lewis' journal.

Tuesday May 14th 1805.

It was after the sun had set before these men come up with us, where we had been halted by an occurence, which I have now to recappitulate [summarize], and which altho' happily passed without ruinous injury, I cannot recollect but with the utmost trepidation [fear] and horror; this is the upseting and narrow escape of the white perogue [a canoe-like boat]. It happened unfortunately for us this evening that Charbono was at the helm of this Perogue, in stead of Drewyer, who had previously steered her; Charbono cannot swim and is perhaps the most timid waterman in the world; perhaps it was equally unluckey that Capt. C. and myself were both on shore at that moment, a circumstance which rarely happened; and tho' we were on the shore opposite to the perogue, were too far distant to be heard or to do more than remain spectators of her fate; in this perogue were embarked [loaded], our papers, Instruments, books, medicine, a great part of our merchandize and in short almost every article indispensibly necessary to further the views, or insure the success of the enterprize in which we are now launched to the distance of 2200 miles. surfice it to say, that the Perogue was under sail when a sudon squawl of wind struck her obliquely [at an angle], and turned her considerably, . . . the steersman allarmed, in stead of puting, her before the wind, lufted [turned] her up into it, . . . the wind was so violent that it drew the brace of the squarsail out of the hand of the man who was attending it, and instantly upset the perogue and would have turned her completely topsaturva, had it not have been from the resistance mad by the oarning [awning] against the water. In this situation Capt. C. and myself both fired our guns to attract the attention if possible of the crew and ordered the halyards [ropes used to raise and lower sails] to be cut and the sail hawled in, but they did not hear us; . . . such was their confusion and consternation at this moment, that they suffered the perogue to lye on her side for half a minute before they took the sail in. The perogue then wrighted but had filled within an inch of the gunwals; . . . Charbono still crying to his god for mercy, had not yet recollected the rudder, nor could the repeated orders of the Bowsman, Cruzat, bring him to his recollection untill he threatend to shoot him instantly if he did not take hold of the rudder and do his duty. the waves by this time were runing very high, but the fortitude resolution and good conduct of Cruzat saved her; he ordered 2 of the men to throw out the water with some kettles that fortunately were convenient,

> . . . **Capt. C and myself both fired our guns . . .**

while himself and two others rowed her as[h]ore, where she arrived scarcely above the water; . . . we now took every article out of her and lay them to drane as well as we could for the evening, baled out the canoe and secured her.

there were two other men beside Charbono on board who could not swim, and who of course must also have perished had the perogue gone to the bottom. while the perogue lay on her side, finding I could not be heard, I for a moment forgot my own situation, and involluntarily droped my gun, threw aside my shot pouch and was in the act of unbuttoning my coat, before I recollected the folly of the attempt I was about to make; which was to throw myself into the river and indevour [try] to swim to the perogue; . . . . the perogue was three hundred yards distant the waves so high that a pe- rogue could scarcely live in any situation, the water excessively could, and the stream rappid; had I under- taken this project therefore, there was a hundred to one but what I should have paid the forfit of my life for the madness of my project, but this had

Several of the men ac- companying Lewis and Clark kept their own journals of the epic expe- dition. In this drawing from the journal of expe- dition member Patrick Gass, a hunting party is firing their flintlock rifles at bears.

the perogue been lost, I should have valued but little. After having all matters arranged for the evening as well as the nature of the circumstances would permit, we thought it a proper occasion to console ourselves and cheer the sperits of our men and accordingly took a drink of grog [liquor weakened with water] and gave each man a gill of sperits [about 4 ounces of full-strength liquor].

REVIEWING THE READING

1. Why was Lewis so concerned with the swamping and near loss of the pirogue?

2. According to Lewis, why was it unfortunate that Charbono was at the helm of the pirogue?

3. **Using Your Historical Imagination.** What do you think were the purposes of Lewis' journal?

From *Narrative of the Life and Adventures of Charles Ball, a Black Man,* by Charles Ball, from *Plantation and Frontier Documents: 1649–1863,* edited by Ulrich B. Phillips.

37   A Slave Is Resold to South Carolina (ca. 1805)

One of the hardships faced by slaves was the possibility of being sold to new owners. Being sold meant leaving behind friends and familiar surroundings. It could even mean being torn away from family. Wives were often separated from husbands and children from parents. Being sold also meant surviving the hardships of being transported from one location to another, often with little consideration to one's comfort or safety. And the future was always uncertain.

The following selection is excerpted from the personal narrative of Charles Ball. Ball was a slave who experienced the hardship of being sold and transported to the home of his new owner in another state. As you read of his journey from Maryland to South Carolina, note the conditions under which Ball was transported.

My new master, whose name I did not hear, took me that same day across the Patuxent [River], where I joined fifty-one other slaves, whom he had bought in Maryland. Thirty two of these were men and nineteen were women. The women were merely tied together with a rope, about the size of a bed cord, which was tied like a halter round the neck of each; but the men, of whom I was the stoutest and strongest, were very differently caparisoned [harnessed]. A strong iron collar was closely fitted by means of a padlock round each of our necks. A chain of iron about a hundred feet in length was passed through the hasp of each padlock, except at the two ends, where the hasps of the padlocks passed through a link of the chain. In addition to this, we were handcuffed in pairs, with iron staples and bolts, with a short chain about a foot long uniting the handcuffs and their wearers in pairs. In this manner we were chained alternately by the right and left hand. . . .

We were soon on the south side of the river, and taking up our line of march, we travelled about five miles that evening, and stopped for the night at one of those miserable public houses, so frequent in the lower parts of Maryland and Virginia, called "ordinaries."

Our master ordered a pot of mush to be made for our supper; after despatching [eating] which, we all lay down on the naked floor to sleep in our handcuffs and chains. The women, my fellow slaves, lay on one side of the room, and the men who were chained with me, occupied the other. Day at length came, and with the dawn, we resumed our journey towards the Potomac. . . .

Before night we crossed the Potomac, at Hoe's Ferry, and bade farewell to Maryland. At night we stopped at the house of a poor gentleman, at least he appeared to wish my master to consider him a gentleman; and he had no difficulty in establishing his claim to poverty. He lived at the side of the road, in a framed house [wooden], that had never been plastered within, the weather-boards being the only wall. . . . The owner was ragged and his wife and children were in a similar plight. . . . Even this miserable family possessed two slaves, half-starved, half-naked wretches, whose appearance bespoke [showed] them familiar with hunger, and victims of the lash; but there was one pang which they had not known; they had not been chained and driven from their parents or children into hopeless exile.

We left this place early in the morning, and directed our course toward the southwest; our master riding beside us, and hastening our march, sometimes by words of encouragement, and sometimes by threats of punishment. The women took their place in the rear of our line. We halted about nine o'clock for breakfast, and received as much corn bread as we could eat, together with a plate of boiled herring, and about three pounds of pork amongst us. Before we left this place, I was removed from near the middle of the chain, and placed at the front end of it; so that I now became the leader of the file, and held this post of honor until our irons were taken from us, near the town of Columbia, in South Carolina. We continued our route, this day, along the high road between the Potomac and Rappahannock; and I several times saw each of those rivers before night. Our master gave us no dinner today, but we halted a short time before sun-down, and got as much corn mush and sour milk as we could eat, for supper. It was now the beginning of the month of May, and the weather, in the fine climate of Virginia, was very mild and pleasant; so that our master was not obliged to provide us with fire at night. . . .

In Virginia, it appeared to me that the slaves were more rigorously [severely] treated than they were in my native place. It is easy to tell a man of color who is poorly fed, from one who is well supplied with food, by his personal appearance. A half starved negro is a miserable looking creature. His skin

This engraving from the nineteenth century shows a column of slaves being marched through the streets of a southern city.

becomes dry, and appears to be sprinkled over with whitish husks, or scales; the glossiness of his face vanishes; his hair loses its color, and when stricken with a rod, the dust flies from it. These signs of bad treatment I perceived to be very common in Virginia; many young girls who would have been beautiful, if they had been allowed enough to eat, had lost all their prettiness through starvation; their fine glossy hair had become of a reddish color, and stood out round their heads, like long brown wool.

Our master at first expressed a determination to pass through the city of Richmond; but for some reason which he did not make known to us, he changed his mind, and drove us up the country, crossing the Matepony, North Anna and South Anna rivers. For several days we traversed [crossed] a region, which had been deserted by the occupants—being no longer worth culture [cultivation]—and immense thickets of young red cedars now occupied the fields, in digging of which, thousands of wretched slaves, had worn out their lives in the service of merciless masters.

In some places these cedar thickets, as they are called, continued for three or four miles together, without a house to enliven the scene, and with scarcely an original forest tree, to give variety to the landscape.

REVIEWING THE READING

1. What hardships did Ball face on his journey from Maryland to South Carolina?

2. Why did Ball think that the slaves in Virginia were poorly fed?

3. **Using Your Historical Imagination.** Why do you think that the slaveowner treated the male and female slaves differently?

From *I Have Spoken: American History Through the Voices of the Indians,* compiled by Virginia Irving Armstrong.

38

Tecumseh Opposes White Settlement (1810)

Tecumseh was a powerful and celebrated war chief of the Shawnee tribe. He strongly opposed all grants and sales of Indian land to whites. His strong beliefs led him to be particularly troubled by the treaty of Greenville. In this treaty, which was signed without Tecumseh's knowledge, a number of Indian chiefs gave up three million acres of land to the whites in exchange for $10,000.

In a speech made at Vincennes to William Henry Harrison, the governor of the Indiana Territory, Tecumseh voiced his objections to the treaty. While reading the following excerpts from Tecumseh's speech, consider his reasons for believing the Indian chiefs were wrong to sell the land.

Houses are built for you to hold councils in; Indians hold theirs in the open air. I am a Shawnee. My forefathers were warriors. Their son is a warrior. From them I take my only existence. From my tribe I take nothing. I have made myself what I am. And I would that I could make the red people as great as the conceptions of my own mind, when I think of the Great Spirit that rules over us all. . . . I would not then come to Governor Harrison to ask him to tear up the treaty. But I would say to him, "Brother, you have the liberty to return to your own country."

You wish to prevent the Indians from doing as we wish them, to unite and let them consider their lands as the common property of the whole. You take the tribes aside and advise them not to come into this measure. . . . You want by your

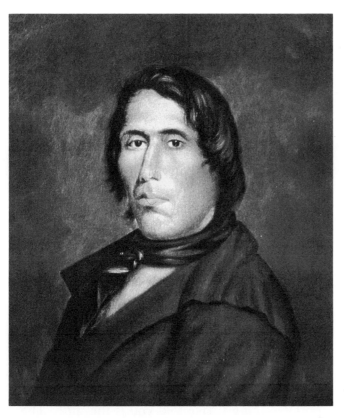

This portrait of Chief Tecumseh was painted from life by an unknown artist.

distinctions of Indian tribes, in allotting to each a particular, to make them war with each other. You never see an Indian endeavor to make the white people do this. You are continually driving the red people, when at last you will drive them onto the great lake, where they can neither stand nor work.

Since my residence at Tippecanoe, we have endeavored to level all distinctions, to destroy village chiefs, by whom all mischiefs are done. It is they who sell the land to the Americans. Brother, this land that was sold, and the goods that was given for it, was only done by a few. . . . In the future we are prepared to punish those who propose to sell land to the Americans. If you continue to purchase them, it will make war among the different tribes, and, at last I do not know what will be the consequences among the white people. Brother, I wish you would take pity on the red people and do as I have requested. If you will not give up the land and do cross the boundary of our present settlements, it will be very hard, and produce great trouble between us.

The way, the only way to stop this evil is for the red men to unite in claiming a common and equal right in the land, as it was at first, and should be now—for it was never divided, but belongs to all. No tribe has the right to sell, even to each other, much less to strangers. . . . *Sell a country! Why not sell the air, the great sea, as well as the earth?* Did not the Great Spirit make them all for the use of his children?

How can we have confidence in the white people?

When Jesus Christ came upon the earth you killed Him and nailed him to the cross. You thought he was dead, and you were mistaken. You have Shakers among you and you laugh and make light of their worship.

Everything I have told you is the truth. The Great Spirit has inspired me.

REVIEWING THE READING

1. Why does Tecumseh believe that the Indian chiefs were wrong to sell the land?

2. According to Tecumseh, why did the white people want to keep the Indians from uniting?

3. **Using Your Historical Imagination.** How do you think Harrison would have answered Tecumseh's claim that the Indians had no right to sell the land?

The British Burn Washington (1814)

39

From *The Campaigns of the British Army at Washington and New Orleans* by George Robert Glieg.

From the start of the War of 1812 until 1814, the British had largely depended on Canadian troops and the Indians to wage war in the United States. In the early part of 1814, however, the British defeated Napoleon in Europe and so were able to send over a large force of British soldiers to battle the Americans on their own soil.

The British plan of attack included the capture of the city of Washington. Toward this end the British troops, led by General Robert Ross, landed at Chesapeake Bay and proceeded to launch an attack on the region. After defeating the American militia in Bladensburg, Maryland, the British troops made their way toward the capital. Once there, the British faced little opposition, for President Madison and other government leaders had escaped the area only a short time before. In retaliation for the earlier burning of Canadian government buildings by American troops, the British soldiers set fire to Washington's government buildings, including the Capitol and the White House. Soon most of Washington was ablaze.

The following excerpts are from the personal account of a young British officer, George R. Glieg, who participated in the attack on Washington. As you read note the action taken by General Ross before he entered the city of Washington.

While the two brigades which had been engaged, remained upon the field to recover their order, the third, which had formed the reserve, and was consequently unbroken, took the lead, and pushed forward at a rapid rate towards Washington.

. . . a flag of truce was sent in with terms.

As it was not the intention of the British government to attempt permanent conquests in this part of America; and as the General was well aware that, with a handful of men, he could not pretend to establish himself, for any length of time, in an enemy's capital, he determined to lay it under contribution, and to return quietly to the shipping. . . .

Such being the intention of General Ross, he did not march the troops immediately into the city, but halted them upon a plain in its immediate vicinity, whilst a flag of truce was sent in with terms. But whatever his proposal might have been, it was not so much as heard; for scarcely had the party bearing the flag entered the street, than they were fired upon from the windows of one of the houses, and the horse of the General himself, who accompanied them, killed. . . . All thoughts of accommodation [truce] were instantly laid aside; the troops advanced forthwith into the town, and having first put to the sword all who were found in the house from which the shots were fired, and reduced it to ashes, they proceeded, without a moment's delay, to burn and destroy every thing in the most distant degree connected with government. In this general devastation were included the Senate-house, the President's palace, an extensive dock-yard and arsenal, barracks for two or three thousand men, several large storehouses filled with naval and military stores, some hundreds of cannon of different descriptions, and nearly twenty thousand stand of small arms. There were also two or three public rope-works which shared the same fate, a fine frigate pierced for sixty guns, and just ready to be launched, several gunbrigs and armed schooners, with a variety of gunboats and small craft. The powder magazines were of course set on fire, and exploded with a tremendous crash, throwing down many houses in their vicinity, partly by pieces of the walls striking them, and partly by the concussion of the air; whilst quantities of shot, shell, and hand grenades, which could not

otherwise be rendered useless, were thrown into the river. . . .

While the third brigade was thus employed, the rest of the army, having recalled its stragglers, and removed the wounded into Bladensburg, began its march towards Washington. Though the battle was ended by four o'clock, the sun had set before the different regiments were in a condition to move, consequently this short journey was performed in the dark. The work of destruction had also begun in the city, before they quitted their ground; and the blazing of houses, ships, and stores, the report of exploding magazines, and the crash of falling roofs, informed them, as they proceeded, of what was going forward. You can conceive nothing finer

This British engraving shows British forces burning Washington, D.C., in 1814.

than the sight which met them as they drew near to the town. The sky was brilliantly illumined by the different conflagrations [fires]; and a dark red light was thrown upon the road, sufficient to permit each man to view distinctly his comrade's face. . . .

I need scarcely observe, that the consternation of the inhabitants was complete . . .

I need scarcely observe, that the consternation [dismay] of the inhabitants was complete, and that to them this was a night of terror. So confident had they been of the success of their troops, that few of them had dreamt of quitting their houses, or abandoning the city; nor was it till the fugitives from the battle began to rush in, filling every place as they came with dismay, that the President himself thought of providing for his safety. That gentleman, as I was credibly [reliably] informed, had gone forth in the morning with the army, and had continued among his troops till the British forces began to make their appearance. Whether the sight of his enemies cooled his courage or not, I cannot say, but, according to my informer, no sooner was the glittering of our arms discernible, than he began to discover that his presence was more wanted in the senate than with the army; and having ridden through the ranks, and exhorted [urged] every man to do his duty, he hurried back to his own house, that he might prepare a feast for the entertainment of his officers, when they should return victorious. . . .

At day-break next morning, the light brigade moved into the city, while the reserve fell back to a height, about half a mile in the rear. Little, however, now remained to be done, because everything marked out for destruction, was already consumed. Of the senate-house, the President's palace, the barracks, the dockyard, &c. nothing could be seen, except heaps of smoking ruins; and even the bridge, a noble structure upwards of a mile in length, was almost wholly demolished. There was, therefore, no farther occasion to scatter the troops, and they were accordingly kept together as much as possible on the Capitol hill.

REVIEWING THE READING

1. According to Glieg, what was the first thing done by General Ross when he halted the troops outside the city of Washington? What was the result of this action?

2. What reason does Glieg give for the fact that so few inhabitants of Washington had left the city before the arrival of the British?

3. **Using Your Historical Imagination**. What evidence can you find in the reading to support the idea that one's point of view can color the reporting of an event?

40

From *I Have Spoken: American History Through the Voices of the Indians*, compiled by Virginia Irving Armstrong.

Red Eagle Surrenders to Jackson (1814)

William Weatherford, known as Red Eagle, was a chief of the Creek Indian tribe. During the War of 1812, Red Eagle led the Creeks in battle against the Americans. On August 30, 1813, the Creek war party attacked Fort Mims in western Alabama. Although Red Eagle urged restraint, his warriors killed between 400 and 500 whites, many of them women and children.

The battles between the American forces and the Creeks came to an end on March 27, 1814, at the Battle of Horseshoe Bend. Led by General Andrew Jackson of Tennessee, the American troops killed 700 of Red Eagle's Creek warriors and completely broke the stronghold of the southern Indians. Following his victory, Jackson issued orders stating that all Creek leaders were to be brought in. Red Eagle, however, had disappeared and could not be found. A few days later he surrendered himself voluntarily to Jackson at Jackson's headquarters. Red Eagle's brave and stirring speech upon his surrender won the admiration of General Jackson, who then pardoned Red Eagle and set him free. As you read the following excerpts from Red Eagle's speech, note the reason he gives for his surrender.

General Jackson, I am not afraid of you. I fear no man, for I am a Creek warrior. I have nothing to request in behalf of myself; you can kill me, if you desire. But I come to beg you to send for the women and children of the war party, who are now starving in the woods. Their fields and cribs [storage bins] have been destroyed by your people, who have driven them to the woods without an ear of corn. I hope that you will send our parties, who will safely conduct them here, in order that they may be fed. I exerted myself in vain to prevent the massacre of the women and children at Fort Mims. I am now done fighting. The Red Sticks [a confederation of Indian tribes formed by Tecumseh] are nearly all killed. . . . I have done the white people all the harm I could; I have fought them, and fought them bravely: if I had an army, I would yet fight, and contend to the last: but I have none; my people are all gone. I can now do no more than weep over the misfortunes of my nation. . . . There was a time when I had a choice, and could have answered you: I have none now—even hope has ended. Once I could animate my warriors to battle; but I cannot animate the dead. My warriors can no longer hear my voice: their bones are at Talladega, Tallushatchee, Emuckfaw, and Tohopeka. . . . If I had been left to contend with the Georgia army, I would have raised corn on one bank of the river, and fought them on the other; but your people have destroyed my nation. . . . I rely upon your generosity.

Chief Red Eagle surrendered to General Jackson after the Creeks' defeat at the Battle of Horseshoe Bend.

REVIEWING THE READING

1. What reason did Red Eagle give to Jackson for coming to him in voluntary surrender?

2. Why did Red Eagle end his fight against the whites?

3. **Using Your Historical Imagination.** Do you think that Red Eagle continued his fight against the whites after he was freed by Jackson? Give reasons for your answer.

41

From "The Legend of
Sleepy Hollow" by
Washington Irving.

Portrait of a Country Schoolteacher, "The Legend of Sleepy Hollow" (1820)

Washington Irving was the first American writer to win a large reputation in Europe, as well as in the United States. The History of New York (1809) and The Sketch-Book of Geoffrey Crayon, Gent. (1820) *firmly established Irving as a major literary figure.*

Irving was also the first American writer to draw upon the rich folklore—tall tales and legends— of his native New York state. "Rip Van Winkle" and "The Legend of Sleepy Hollow" (from The Sketch-Book) *are timeless short stories out of that folkloric tradition. In the following excerpt, Irving describes a country schoolteacher, Ichabod Crane, the ill-fated hero of his tale of Sleepy Hollow. As you read note the role played by the schoolteacher in the rural community.*

In this by-place of nature, there abode, in a remote period of American history, that is to say, some thirty years since, a worthy wight [human being] of the name Ichabod Crane; who sojourned [lived], or, as he expressed it, "tarried," in Sleepy Hollow, for the purpose of instructing the children of the vicinity. He was a native of Connecticut; a state which supplies the Union with pioneers for the mind as well as for the forest, and sends forth yearly its legions of frontier woodsmen and country school-masters. The cognomen [surname] of Crane was not inapplicable to his person. He was tall, but exceedingly lank, with narrow shoulders, long arms and legs, hands that dangled a mile out of his sleeves, feet that might have served for shovels, and his whole frame most loosely hung together. His head was small, and flat at top, with huge ears, large green glassy eyes, and a long snipe nose, so that it looked like a weather-cock, perched upon his spindle neck, to tell which way the wind blew. To see him striding along the profile of a hill on a windy day, with his clothes bagging and fluttering about him, one might have mistaken him for the genius of famine descending upon the earth, or some scarecrow eloped from a cornfield.

His school-house was a low building of one large room, rudely constructed of logs; the windows partly glazed, and partly patched with leaves of old copy-books. It was most ingeniously secured at vacant hours, by a withe [branch or twig] twisted in the handle of the door, and stakes set against the window shutters; so that, though a thief might get in with perfect ease, he would find some embarrassment in getting out; an idea most probably borrowed by the architect, Yost Van Houten, from the mystery of an eel-pot. The school-house stood in a rather lonely but pleasant situation, just at the foot of a woody hill, with a brook running close by, and a formidable birch tree growing at one end of it. From hence the low murmur of his pupils' voices, conning over their lessons, might be heard in a drowsy summer's day, like the hum of a beehive; interrupted now and then by the authoritative voice of the master, in the tone of menace or command; or, peradventure, by the appalling sound of the birch, as he urged some tardy loiterer along the flowery path of knowledge. Truth to say, he was a conscientious man, and ever bore in mind the golden maxim, "Spare the rod and spoil the child."—Ichabod Crane's scholars certainly were not spoiled.

I would not have it imagined, however, that he was one of those cruel potentates [rulers] of the school, who joy in the smart [pain] of their subjects; on the contrary, he administered justice with discrimination rather than severity; taking the burden off the backs of the weak, and laying it on those of the strong. Your mere puny stripling, that winced at the least flourish of the rod, was passed by with indulgence; but the claims of justice were satisfied by inflicting a double portion on some little, tough, wrong-headed, broad-skirted Dutch urchin, who sulked and swelled and grew dogged and sullen beneath the birch. All this he called "doing his duty by their parents"; and he never inflicted a chastisement without following it by the assurance, so consolatory to the smarting urchin, that "he would remember it, and thank him for it the longest day he had to live."

When school hours were over, he was even the companion and playmate of the larger boys; and on holiday afternoons would convoy some of the smaller ones home, who happened to have pretty sisters, or good housewives for mothers, noted for the comforts of the cupboard. Indeed it behooved him to keep on good terms with his pupils. The revenue arising from his school was small, and would have been scarcely sufficient to furnish him with daily bread, for he was a huge feeder, and though lank, had the dilating powers of an anaconda [could swallow a huge meal, as a snake does]; but to help out his maintenance, he was, according to country customs in those parts, boarded and lodged at the houses of the farmers, whose children he instructed. With these he lived successively a week at a time; thus going the rounds of the neighborhood, with all his worldly effects tied up in a cotton handkerchief.

That all this might not be too onerous [a heavy burden] on the purses of his rustic patrons, who are apt to consider the costs of schooling a grievous

> . . . he was a huge feeder, and though lank, had the dilating powers of an anaconda . . .

burden, and school-masters as mere drones, he had various ways of rendering himself both useful and agreeable. He assisted the farmers occasionally in the lighter labors of their farms; helped to make hay; mended the fences; took the horses to water; drove the cows to pasture; and cut wood for the winter fire. He laid aside, too, all the dominant dignity and absolute sway with which he lorded it in his little empire, the school, and became wonderfully gentle and ingratiating [eager to please]. He found favor in the eyes of the mothers, by petting the children, particularly the youngest; and like the lion bold, which whilom [at times] so magnanimously the lamb did hold, he would sit with a child on one knee, and rock a cradle with his foot for whole hours together.

In this illustration from "The Legend of Sleepy Hollow," Ichabod Crane pays an after-school visit to the kitchen of the family with whom he lives.

In addition to his other vocations, he was the singing-master of the neighborhood, and picked up many bright shillings by instructing the young folks in psalmody. It was a matter of no little vanity to him, on Sundays, to take his station in front of the church gallery, with a band of chosen singers; where, in his own mind, he completely carried away the palm [glory] from the parson. Certainly it is, his voice resounded far above the rest of the congregation; and there are peculiar quavers still to be heard in that church, and which may even be heard half a mile off, quite to the opposite side of the mill-pond, on a still Sunday morning, which are said to be legitimately descended from the nose of Ichabod Crane. Thus, by divers little make-shifts in that ingenious way which is commonly denominated "by hook and by crook," the worthy pedagogue [teacher] got on tolerably enough, and was thought, by all who understood nothing of the labor of headwork, to have a wonderfully easy life of it.

The schoolmaster is generally a man of some importance in the female circle of a rural neighborhood; being considered a kind of idle gentlemanlike personage, of vastly superior taste and accomplishments to the rough country swains [young men], and indeed, inferior in learning only to the parson. His appearance, therefore, is apt to occasion some little stir at the tea-table of a farm-house, and the addition of a supernumerary [extra] dish of cakes or sweetmeats, or, peradventure, the parade of a silver tea-pot. Our man of letters, therefore, was peculiarly happy in the smiles of all the country damsels. How he would figure [move around] among them in the church-yard, between services on Sundays! gathering grapes for them from the wild vines that overrun the surrounding trees; reciting for their amusement all the epitaphs on the tombstones; or sauntering, with a whole bevy of them, along the banks of the adjacent mill-pond; while the more bashful country bumpkins hung sheepishly back, envying his superior elegance and address.

> . . . he was a kind of travelling gazette, carrying the whole budget of local gossip from house to house . . .

From his half itinerant life, also, he was a kind of travelling gazette, carrying the whole budget of local gossip from house to house; so that his appearance was always greeted with satisfaction. He was, moreover, esteemed by the women as a man of great erudition [learning], for he had read several books quite through, and was a perfect master of Cotton Mather's history of New England Witchcraft, in which, by the way, he most firmly and potently believed.

He was, in fact, an odd mixture of small shrewdness and simple credulity. His appetite for the marvellous, and his powers of digesting it, were equally extraordinary; and both had been increased by his residence in this spell-bound region. No tale was too gross or monstrous for his capacious swallow. It was often his delight, after his school was dismissed in the afternoon, to stretch himself on the rich bed of clover, bordering the little brook that whimpered by his school-house, and there con over old Mather's direful tales, until the gathering dusk of the evening made the printed page a mere mist before his eyes. Then, as he wended his way, by swamp and stream and awful woodland, to the farmhouse where he happened to be quartered, every sound of nature, at that witching hour, fluttered his excited imagination: the moan of the whip-poor-will [a bird whose cry is heard only at night] from the hill-side; the boding cry of the tree-toad, that harbinger [messenger] of storm; the dreary hooting of the screech-owl, or the sudden rustling in the thicket of birds frightened from their roost. The fire-flies, too, which sparkled most vividly in the darkest places, now and then startled him, as one of uncommon brightness would stream across his path; and if, by chance, a huge blockhead of a beetle came winging his blundering flight against him, the poor varlet was ready to give up the ghost, with the idea that he was struck with a witch's token. His only resource on such occasions, either to drown thought, or drive away evil spirits, was to sing psalm tunes;—and the good people of Sleepy Hollow, as they sat by their doors of an evening, were often filled with awe, at hearing his nasal melody, "in linked sweetness long drawn out," floating with the distant hill, or along the dusky road.

REVIEWING THE READING

1. Why was Crane determined to stay on good terms with the parents of his pupils?

2. What other social functions did the schoolmaster perform for the community?

3. **Using Your Historical Imagination.** In your judgment, how realistic is the description of the life of a country school-teacher?

A Colonial Scrapbook

1

2

3

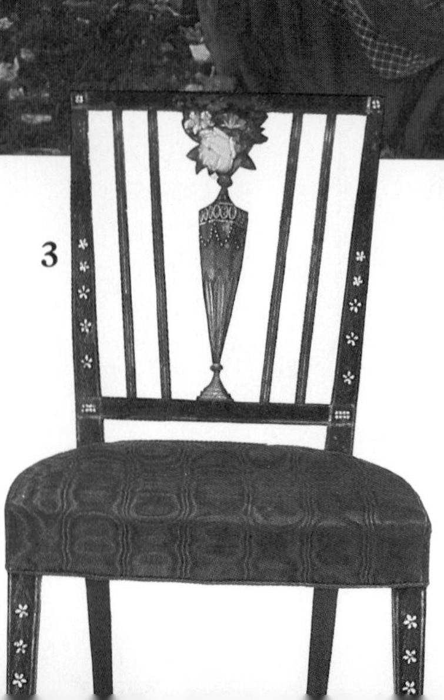

Words of four Syllables.
Ac-com-pa-ny   Accompany
Be-ne-vo·lence   Benevolence
Ce-re·mo-ny   Ceremony
Dif-con-tent-ed   Difcontented
E-ver-laft-ing   Everlafting
Fi-de·li-ty   Fidelity
Glo-ri-fy-ing   Glorifying
Hu-mi-li·ty   Humility
In-fir-mi-ty   Infirmity.
Words of five Syllables.
Ad-mi-ra-ti-on   Admiration
Be-ne-fi-ci al   Beneficial
Con-fo-la-ti-on   Confolation
De-cla-ra-ti-on   Declaration
Ex-hor-ta-ti-on   Exhortation
For-ni-ca-ti-on   Fornication
Ge-ne-ra-ti-on   Generation
Ha-bi-ta-ti-on   Habitation
In-vi-ta-ti-on   Invitation

In Adam's Fall
We Sinned all.

A   Thy Life to Me
B   This Book Atte

C   The Cat doth
     And after fw

D   A Dog wi
     A Thief w

E   An Ea

F

4

1. Spectacles used for reading; 2. woman
demonstrating a method of spinning flax;
3. eighteenth-century chair; 4. pages from *The New
England Primer*; 5. paper currency issued in 1775;
6. man demonstrating use of trough adze to make
a house gutter; 7. reenactment of a colonial dance;
8. silver rattle.

From *Fur Hunters of the Far West* by Alexander Ross.

42

Fur Hunters of the Far West (ca. 1820)

The trade in furs and skins was as old as European settlement in the North America, but in the decades after 1800 it took on new economic importance. The pelt of the beaver was now in great demand in Europe for the manufacture of gentlemen's hats. To exploit the fur resources of the Rocky Mountains and the far northwest, new companies were established, such as the Pacific Fur Company and the North West Fur Company. Alexander Ross, originally from Scotland, joined the North West Fur Company in 1813. Sometime around 1820 he wrote the following account of the daily operations of one of the company's large fur-trapping parties. As you read his description, consider the good and bad features of this sort of life.

A safe and secure spot, near wood and water, is first selected for the camp. Here the chief of the party resides with the property. It is often exposed to danger or sudden attack, in the absence of the trappers, and requires a vigilant eye to guard against the lurking savages. The camp is called headquarters. From hence all the trappers, some on foot, some on horseback, according to the distance they have to go, start every morning in small parties in all directions ranging the distance of some twenty miles around. Six traps is the allowance for each hunter, but to guard against wear and tear, the complement is more frequently ten. These he sets every night and visits again in the morning, sometimes oftener, according to the distance or other circumstances. The beaver taken in the traps are always conveyed [taken] to the camp, skinned, stretched, dried, folded up with the hair in the inside, laid by, and the flesh

used for food. No sooner, therefore, has a hunter visited his traps, set them again, and looked out for some other place, than he returns to the camp to feast and enjoy the pleasures of an idle day.

There is, however, much anxiety and danger in going through the ordinary routine of a trapper's duty. For as the enemy is generally lurking about among the rocks and hiding-places, watching an opportunity, the hunter has to keep a constant look-out, and the gun is often in one hand while the trap is in the other. But when several are together, which is often the case in suspicious places, one-half set the traps and other half keep guard over them. Yet notwithstanding all their precautions some of them fall victims to Indian treachery.

The camp remains stationary [in one place] while two-thirds of the trappers find beaver in the vicinity, but whenever the beaver become scarce the camp is removed to some more favorable spot. In this manner the party keeps moving from place to place during the whole season of hunting. Whenever serious danger is apprehended [forseen], all the

A keelboat of fur traders on the Missouri River is attacked by Indians.

trappers make for the camp. Were we, however, to calculate according to numbers, the prospects from such an expedition would be truly dazzling: say seventy-five men with each six traps, to be successfully employed during five months; that is, two in the spring, and three in the fall, equal to 131 working days, the result would be 58,950 beaver! Practically, however, the case is very different. The apprehension of danger at all times is so great that three-fourths of their time is lost in the necessary steps taken for their own safety. There is also another serious drawback unavoidably accompanying every large party. The beaver is a timid animal. The least noise, therefore, made about its haunt will keep it from coming out for nights together, and noise is unavoidable when the party is large. But when the party is small the hunter has a chance of being more or less successful. Indeed, were the nature of the ground such as to admit of the trappers moving about in safety at all times, and alone, six men with six traps each would in the same space of time and at the same rate kill as many beaver—say 4,716—as the whole seventy-five could be expected to do! And yet the evil is without a remedy, for no small party can exist in these parts. Hence the reason why beaver are so numerous.

REVIEWING THE READING

1. During what part of the year did trapping go on in the Northwest?

2. What major problems did the fur trappers have to face?

3. **Using Your Historical Imagination.** Imagine you are a fur trapper with the North West Fur Company. Describe what you did during one average day in the company's fur camp.

The First American Steam Railroad (1830)

43

From *The Baltimore and Ohio Railroad: Personal Recollections* by John H. B. Latrobe.

The early decades of the nineteenth century were a period of bustling growth and expansion in the United States. Contributing to this growth were new and better means of transporting people and goods from place to place. Perhaps the most significant development in transportation during this time was the steam-driven locomotive, which was first successfully tested in the United States by Peter Cooper in 1830. Cooper hoped to convince officials of the Baltimore and Ohio Railroad to use locomotives rather than horses to pull their trains. To prove the efficiency of machine over animal, Cooper raced his locomotive, the Tom Thumb, *against a horse-drawn coach on September 18, 1830. Although the steam-driven engine was crude by today's standards, it later served to revolutionize transportation in the United States.*

The following selection is excerpted from an account by John H. B. Latrobe. Latrobe was associated with the Baltimore and Ohio Railroad from its beginnings. In the selection Latrobe tells of Cooper's efforts to develop the steam locomotive and of his own eyewitness experiences on the day of the great race. As you read note the circumstances that led to the race's outcome.

In the beginning, no one dreamed of steam upon the road. Horses were to do the work; and even after the line was completed to Frederick, relays of horses trotted the cars from place to place. . . .

To ride in a railroad car in those days was, literally, to go thundering along, the roll of the wheels on the combined rail of stone and iron being almost deafening. . . .

When steam made its appearance on the Liverpool and Manchester Railroad it attracted great attention here. But there was this difficulty about introducing an English engine on an American road. An English road was virtually a straight road. An American road had curves sometimes of as small radius as two hundred feet. . . . For a brief season it was believed that this feature of the early American roads would prevent the use of locomotive engines. The contrary was demonstrated by a gentleman still living in an active and ripe old age, honored and beloved, distinguished for his private worth and for his public benefactions [charitable donations]; one of those to whom wealth seems to have been granted by Providence that men might know how wealth could be used to benefit one's fellow creatures. The speaker refers to Mr. Peter Cooper of New York. Mr. Cooper was satisfied that steam might be adapted to curved roads which he saw would be built in the United States; and he came to Baltimore, which then possessed the only one on which he could experiment, to vindicate [prove] his belief. He had another idea, which was, that the crank could be dispensed with in the change from a reciprocating to a rotary motion [from a back and forth to a circular motion]: and he built an engine to demonstrate both articles of his faith. The machine was not larger than the hand cars used by workmen to transfer themselves from place to place; and as the speaker now recalls its appearance, the only wonder is, that so apparently insignificant a contrivance should ever have been regarded as competent to the smallest results. But Mr. Cooper was wiser than many of the wisest around him. His engine could not have weighed a ton; but he saw in it a principle which the forty-ton engines of to-day have but served to develop and demonstrate.

The boiler of Mr. Cooper's engine was not as large as the kitchen boiler attached to many a range in modern mansions. It was of about the same diameter, but not much more than half as high. It stood upright in the car, and was filled, above the furnace, which occupied the lower section, with vertical tubes. The cylinder was but three-and-a-half inches in diameter, and speed was gotten up by gearing. No natural draught [draft] could have been sufficient to keep up steam in so small a boiler; and Mr. Cooper used therefore a blowing-apparatus, driven by a drum attached to one of the car wheels, over which passed a cord that in its turn worked a pulley on the shaft of the blower. . . .

Mr. Cooper's success was such as to induce him to try a trip to Ellicott's Mills; and an open car, the first used upon the road, already mentioned, having been attached to his engine, and filled with the directors and some friends, the speaker among the rest, the first journey by steam in America was commenced. The trip was most interesting. The curves were passed without difficulty at a speed of fifteen miles an hour; the grades were ascended with comparative ease; the day was fine, the company in the highest spirits, and some excited gentlemen of the party pulled out memorandum books, and when at the highest speed, which was eighteen miles an hour, wrote their names and some connected sentences, to proved that even at that great velocity it was possible to do so. The return trip from the Mills—a distance of thirteen miles—was made in fifty-seven minutes. This was in the summer of 1830.

But the triumph of this Tom Thumb engine was not altogether without a drawback. The great stage [horse-drawn coach] proprietors of the day were Stockton & Stokes; and on this occasion a gallant gray [horse] of great beauty and power was driven by them from town, attached to another car on the second track—for the Company had begun by making two tracks to the Mills—and met the engine at the Relay House on its way back. From this point it was determined to have a race home;

The curves were passed without difficulty at a speed of fifteen miles an hour . . .

On August 28, 1830, a race was held between Cooper's locomotive, the Tom Thumb, and a horse car. Here Cooper's engine is shown just as it passes the horse. The engine, however, eventually lost the race.

and, the start being even, away went horse and engine, the snort of the one and the puff of the other keeping time and tune. At first the gray had the best of it, for his steam would be applied to the greatest advantage on the instant, while the engine had to wait until the rotation of the wheels set the blower to work. The horse was perhaps a quarter of a mile ahead when the safety valve of the engine lifted and the thin blue vapor issuing from it showed an excess of steam. The blower whistled, the steam blew off in vapory clouds, the pace increased, the passengers shouted, the engine gained on the horse, soon it lapped him—the silk was plied—the race was neck and neck, nose and nose—then the engine passed the horse, and a great hurrah hailed the victory. But it was not repeated; for just at this time, when the gray's master was about giving up, the band which drove the pulley, which drove the blower, slipped from the drum, the safety valve ceased to scream, and the engine for want of breath began to wheeze and pant. In vain Mr. Cooper, who was his own engineman and fireman, lacerated [cut] his hands in attempting to replace the band upon the wheel; in vain he tried to urge the fire with light wood; the horse gained on the machine, and passed it; and although the band was presently replaced, and steam again did its best, the horse was too far ahead to be overtaken, and came in the winner of the race. But the real victory was with Mr. Cooper, notwithstanding. He had held fast to the faith that was in him, and had demonstrated its truth beyond peradventure [a doubt]. All honor to his name. . . . In the Musee d'Artillerie at Paris there was preserved old cannon, cotemporary almost with Crecy and Poictiers. In some great museum of internal improvement, and some such will at some future day be gotten up, Mr. Peter Cooper's boiler should hold an equally prominent and far more honored place; for while the old weapons of destruction were ministers of man's wrath, the contrivance we have described was one of the most potential instruments in making available, in America, that vast system which unites remote peoples and promotes that peace on earth and good will to men which angels have proclaimed.

REVIEWING THE READING

1. According to Latrobe, why did people first believe that it would be difficult to use steam engines in the United States?

2. Who was the winner in the race between the locomotive and the horse-drawn coach? What led to this outcome?

3. **Using Your Historical Imagination.** Why do you think Latrobe said "the real victory was with Mr. Cooper," even though it was Cooper who had lost the race?

44

From *The Columbian Orator* by Caleb Bingham.

"On the Starry Heavens," a Reading from *The Columbian Orator* (1830s)

The Columbian Orator *was a widely-used textbook in the academies and other private secondary schools. Its author was educator Caleb Bingham, and the full title he gave his book well described its emphasis:* The Columbian Orator, Containing a Variety of Original and Selected Pieces, Together with Rules Calculated to Improve Youth and Others in the Ornamental Art of Eloquence.

As the title implies, The Columbian Orator *placed great importance on the skills of reading aloud. Many of the readings also taught moral lessons. As you read this anonymous essay on astronomy, consider the moral point of the lesson.*

To us who dwell on its surface, the earth is by far the most extensive orb [globe] that our eyes can any where behold. It is also clothed with verdure [vegetation]; distinguished by trees; and adorned with a variety of beautiful decorations. Whereas, to a spectator placed on one of the planets, it wears a uniform aspect; looks all luminous [light], and no larger than a spot. To beings who dwell at still greater distances, it entirely disappears.

That which we call, alternately, the morning and evening star; as in one part of her orbit, she rides foremost in the procession of night; in the other, ushers in, and anticipates the dawn, is a planetary world; which, with the five others, that so wonderfully vary their mystic dance, are in themselves dark bodies, and shine only by reflection; have fields, and seas, and skies of their own; are furnished with all accommodations for animal subsistence, and are supposed to be abodes of intellectual life. All which, together with this our earthly habitation, are dependant on that grand dispenser of divine munificence [generosity], the sun; receive their light from the distribution of his rays; derive their comfort from his divine agency.

The sun is the great axle of heaven, about which, the globe we inhabit, and other more spacious orbs, wheel their stated courses. The sun, though seemingly smaller than the dial it illuminates, is abundantly larger than this whole earth; on which so many lofty mountains rise, and such vast oceans roll. A line, extending through the centre of that resplendent orb, would measure more than eight hundred thousand miles. A girdle, formed to surround it, would require a length of millions. Were its solid contents to be estimated, the account would overpower our understanding, and be almost beyond the power of language to express.

Are we startled at these reports of astronomy? Are we ready to cry out in a transport of surprise, How mighty is the Being, who kindled such a prodigious [gigantic] fire, and who keeps alive, from age to age, such an enormous mass of flame! Let us attend our philosophic guides, and we shall be brought acquainted with speculations more enlarged, and more amazing.

This sun, with all attendant planets, is but a very little part of the grand machine of the universe. Every star, though in appearance no bigger than the diamond that glitters on a lady's ring, is really a mighty globe; like the sun in size, and in glory; no less spacious, no less luminous than the radiant source of our day. So that every star is not barely a world, but the centre of a magnificent system; has a retinue [following] of worlds, irradiated by its beams, and revolving round its attractive influence. All which are lost to our sight in unmeasurable wilds of ether [uncharted space].

. . . **This sun, with all attendant planets, is but a very little part of the grand machine of the universe.**

That the stars appear like so many diminutive, and scarcely distinguishable points, is owing to their immense and inconceivable distance. Such a distance, that a cannon ball, could it continue its impetuous flight, with unabating rapidity, would not reach the nearest of those twinkling luminaries for more than five hundred thousand years!

Can any thing be more wonderful than these observations? Yes; there are truths far more stupendous; there are scenes far more extensive. As there is no end of the Almighty Maker's greatness, so no imagination can set limits to his creating hand. Could you soar beyond the moon, and pass through all the planetary choir; could you wing your way to the highest apparent star, and take your stand on one of those lofty pinacles of heaven, you would there see other skies expanded; another sun, distributing his inexhaustible beams by day; other stars which gild the horrors of the alternate night; and other, perhaps, nobler systems, established in unknown profusion, through the boundless dimensions of space. Nor do the dominions of the universal Sovereign terminate there. Even at the end of this vast tour, you would find yourself advanced no further than the suburbs of creation; arrived only at the frontiers of the great JEHOVAH's kingdom.

REVIEWING THE READING

1. What does the earth look like from one of the other planets?

2. In writing about the almost inconceivable remoteness of the stars, the author uses an example of the fastest known earthly object. What is this?

3. **Using Your Historical Imagination.** What do you think is the religious lesson implied by the description of "the Starry Sky?"

An Abolitionist Takes a Vow (1831)

45

From *The Liberator*,
edited and published by
William Lloyd Garrison.

*William Lloyd Garrison was an outspoken abolitionist
and one of the organizers of the American Anti-Slavery
Society. Garrison was extremely militant in his cause,
demanding the immediate freedom of all southern slaves.
He held slavery to be the most inhumane of all institutions and blamed even those who tolerated slavery
for its existence.*

*Garrison first began working for abolition as a
writer for Benjamin Lundy's antislavery newspaper,*
The Genius of Universal Emancipation. *But
Lundy's views on abolition proved too tame for the
outspoken Garrison. On January 1, 1831, Garrison
began publishing* The Liberator, *a weekly newspaper dedicated to the immediate abolition of slavery.
The following selection is an article from the first
issue of that newspaper. As you read the selection,
pay special attention to the vow Garrison makes
concerning his involvement with abolition.*

TO THE PUBLIC.

In the month of August, I issued proposals for
publishing "THE LIBERATOR" in Washington
city; but the enterprise, though hailed in different
sections of the country, was palsied [halted] by public
indifference. Since that time, the removal of the
Genius of Universal Emancipation [an antislavery
paper published by Benjamin Lundy] to the Seat
of Government has rendered less imperious [urgent]
the establishment of a similar periodical in that
quarter.

During my recent tour for the purpose of exciting the minds of the people by a series of discourses
on the subject of slavery, every place that I visited
gave fresh evidence of the fact, that a greater revolu-

tion in public sentiment was to be effected in the free states—*and particularly in New England*—than at the south. I found contempt more bitter, opposition more active, detraction [criticism] more relentless, prejudice more stubborn, and apathy more frozen, than among slave owners themselves. Of course, there were individual exceptions to the contrary. This state of things afflicted, but did not dishearten me. I determined, at every hazard, to lift up the standard [banner] of emancipation in the eyes of the nation, *within sight of Bunker Hill and in the birth place of liberty.* That standard is now unfurled; and long may it float, unhurt by the spoliations [plunderings] of time or the missiles of a desperate foe— yea, till every chain be broken, and every bondman set free! Let southern oppressors tremble—let their secret abettors [helpers] tremble—let their northern apologists tremble—let all the enemies of the persecuted blacks tremble.

I deem the publication of my original Prospectus unnecessary, as it has obtained a wide circulation. The principles therein inculcated [expressed] will be steadily pursued in this paper, excepting that I shall not array myself as the political partisan of any man. In defending the great cause of human rights, I wish to derive the assistance of all religions and of all parties.

Assenting to the "self-evident truth" maintained in the American Declaration of Independence, "that all men are created equal, and endowed by their Creator with certain inalienable rights—among which are life, liberty and the pursuit of happiness," I shall strenuously contend [struggle] for the immediate enfranchisement [freedom] of our slave population. In Parkstreet Church, on the Fourth of July, 1829, in an address on slavery, I unreflectingly assented to the popular but pernicious [harmful] doctrine of *gradual* abolition. I seize this opportunity to make a full and unequivocal recantation [withdrawal of the statement], and thus publicly to ask

William Lloyd Garrison, editor of The Liberator, *was a leading northern abolitionist.*

pardon of my God, of my country, and of my brethren the poor slaves, for having uttered a sentiment
so full of timidity, injustice and absurdity. A similar
recantation, from my pen, was published in the Genius of Universal Emancipation at Baltimore, in September, 1829. My conscience is now satisfied.

I am aware, that many object to the severity
of my language; but is there not cause for severity?
I *will be* as harsh as truth, and as uncompromising
as justice. On this subject, I do not wish to think,
or speak, or write, with moderation. No! no! Tell a
man whose house is on fire, to give a moderate
alarm; tell him to moderately rescue his wife from
the hands of the ravisher; tell the mother to gradually
extricate [pull] her babe from the fire into which it
has fallen,—but urge me not to use moderation in
a cause like the present. I am in earnest—I will
not equivocate—I will not excuse—I will not retreat
a single inch—AND I WILL BE HEARD. The apathy of
the people is enough to make every statue leap from
its pedestal, and to hasten the resurrection of the
dead.

It is pretended, that I am retarding the cause
of emancipation by the coarseness of my invective
[language], and the precipitancy [hastiness] of my
measures. *The charge is not true.* On this question my
influence,—humble as it is,—is felt at this moment
to a considerable extent, and shall be felt in coming
years—not perniciously, but beneficially—not as a

The masthead of Garri-son's Liberator, *above, showed readers the senti-ments of the stories inside.*

curse, but as a blessing; and posterity [future genera-
tions] will bear testimony that I was right. I desire
to thank God, that he enables me to disregard "the
fear of man which bringeth a snare," and to speak
his truth in its simplicity and power. And here I
close with this fresh dedication:

'Oppression! I have seen thee, face to face,
And met thy cruel eye and cloudy brow;
But thy soul-withering glance I fear not now—
For dread to prouder feelings doth give place
Of deep abhorrence! Scorning the disgrace
Of slavish knees that at thy footstool bow,
I also Kneel—but with far other vow
Do hail thee and thy herd of hirelings base:—
I swear, while life-blood warms my throbbing
    veins,
Still to oppose and thwart, with heart and
    hand,
Thy brutalising sway—till Afric's chains
Are burst, and Freedom rules the rescued
    land,—
Trampling Oppression and his iron rod:
Such is the vow I take—SO HELP ME GOD!'

WILLIAM LLOYD GARRISON.

REVIEWING THE READING

1. What vow concerning abolition does Garrison make in *The Liberator?*

2. On which American document did Garrison base his views concerning the freeing
   of the slaves? Why was this an appropriate
   document for Garrison to quote?

3. **Using Your Historical Imagination.** What
   do you think Garrison means when he
   states: "I *will be* as harsh as truth, and as
   uncompromising as justice"?

The Confessions of Nat Turner (1831)

46

From *The Confessions of Nat Turner* by Thomas R. Gray.

As the abolitionists continued their fight against the institution of slavery, many southern whites began to fear the possibility of revolt among the slaves. This fear was justified, for a number of uprisings by small groups of slaves indicated the depth of their discontent with bondage.

This discontent expressed itself most sharply on August 21, 1831, in Southampton County, Virginia. On this date Nat Turner, a slave who believed himself divinely chosen to free his people, led a group of followers in a bloody revolt against the whites. They began by killing the family of Turner's owner, and murdered about 60 people before they were finally captured by federal troops and the militia. A number of the slaves involved were executed immediately, and dozens of innocent blacks were killed by groups of angry whites in the weeks that followed. Turner, who had escaped into the woods, was found six weeks later. His conviction at his later trial led to his hanging on November 11.

During his imprisonment Turner dictated an account of his life to a white lawyer, Thomas R. Gray. The following selection is an excerpt from the book that resulted from that account, The Confessions of Nat Turner. *As you read the selection, note Turner's reasons for believing that he was chosen to lead the slaves in revolt.*

All my time, not devoted to my master's service, was spent either in prayer, or in making experiments in casting different things in moulds made of earth, in attempting to make paper, gun-powder, and many other experiments, that although I could

not perfect, yet convinced me of its practicability
if I had the means. I was not addicted to stealing
in my youth, nor have ever been—Yet such was
the confidence of the negroes in the neighborhood,
even at this early period of my life, in my superior
judgment, that they would often carry me with them
when they were going on any roguery [mischief],
to plan for them. Growing up among them, with
this confidence in my superior judgment, and when
this, in their opinions, was perfected by Divine inspiration, from the circumstances already alluded to
[indirectly referred to] in my infancy, and which
belief was ever afterwards zealously inculcated [firmly
fixed in mind] by the austerity [somberness] of my
life and manners, which became the the subject of
remark by white and black.—Having soon [been]
discovered to be great, I must appear so, and therefore
studiously avoided mixing in society, and wrapped
myself in mystery, devoting my time to fasting and
prayer—By this time, having arrived to man's estate,
and hearing the scriptures commented on at meetings, I was struck with that particular passage which
says: "Seek ye the kingdom of Heaven and all things
shall be added unto you." I reflected much on this
passage, and prayed daily for light on this subject—
As I was praying one day at my plough, the spirit
spoke to me, saying "Seek ye the kingdom of Heaven
and all things shall be added unto you." *Question—
what do you mean by the Spirit. Ans.* The Spirit that
spoke to the prophets in former days—and I was
greatly astonished, and for two years prayed continually, whenever my duty would permit—and then
again I had the same revelation, which fully confirmed me in the impression that I was ordained
for some great purpose in the hands of the Almighty.
Several years rolled round, in which many events
occurred to strengthen me in this my belief. At this
time I reverted in my mind to the remarks made
of me in my childhood, and the things that had
been shewn me—and as it had been said of me in

my childhood by those by whom I had been taught to pray, both white and black, and in whom I had the greatest confidence, that I had too much sense to be raised [become proud and feel superior], and if I was, I would never be of any use to anyone as a slave. Now finding I had arrived to man's estate, and was a slave, and these revelations being made known to me, I began to direct my attention to this great object, to fulfil the purpose for which, by this time, I felt assured I was intended. Knowing the influence I had obtained over the minds of my fellow servants, (not by the means of conjuring and such like tricks—for to them I always spoke of such things with contempt) but by the communion of the Spirit whose revelations I often communicated to them, and they believed and said my wisdom came from God. I now began to prepare them for my purpose, by telling them something was about to happen that would terminate in fulfilling the great promise that had been made to me—About this time I was placed under an overseer, from whom I ran away—and after remaining in the woods thirty days, I returned, to the astonishment of the negroes on the plantation, who thought I had made my escape to some other part of the country, as my father had done before. But the reason of my return was, that the Spirit appeared to me and said I had my wishes directed to the things of this world, and not to the kingdom of Heaven, and that I should return to the service of my earthly master—"For he who knoweth his Master's will, and doeth it not, shall be beaten with many stripes, and thus have I chastened [punished] you." And the negroes found fault, and murmured against me, saying that if they had my sense they would not serve any master in the world. And about this time I had a vision—and I saw white spirits and black spirits engaged in battle, and the sun was darkened—the thunder rolled in the Heavens, and blood flowed in streams—and I heard a voice saying, "Such is your luck, such you

. . . I began to direct my attention to this great object, to fulfil the purpose for which . . . I felt assured I was intended.

are called to see, and let it come rough or smooth, you must surely bear it." I now withdrew myself as much as my situation would permit, from the intercourse [interaction] of my fellow servants, for the avowed purpose of serving the Spirit more fully— and it appeared to me, and reminded me of the things it had already shown me, that it would then reveal to me the knowledge of the elements, the revolution of the planets, the operation of tides, and changes of the seasons. After this revelation in the year 1825, and the knowledge of the elements being made known to me, I sought more than ever

In this engraving Nat Turner is depicted at the moment of his capture by local authorities.

to obtain true holiness before the great day of judgment should appear, and then I began to receive the true knowledge of faith. And from the first steps of righteousness until the last, was I made perfect; and the Holy Ghost was with me, and said, "Behold me as I stand in the Heavens"—and I looked and saw the forms of men in different attitudes—and there were lights in the sky to which the children of darkness gave other names than what they really were—for they were the lights of the Saviour's hands, stretched forth from east to west, even as they were extended on the cross on Calvary from the redemption of sinners. And I wondered greatly at these miracles, and prayed to be informed of a certainty of the meaning thereof—and shortly afterwards, while laboring in the field, I discovered drops of blood on the corn as though it were dew from heaven—and I communicated it to many, both white and black, in the neighborhood—and then found on the leaves in the woods hieroglyphic characters [ancient form of writing using pictures to represent sounds or words], and numbers, with the forms of men in different attitudes, portrayed in blood, and representing the figures I had seen before in the heavens. And now the Holy Ghost had revealed itself to me, and made plain the miracles it had shown me—For as the blood of Christ had been shed on this earth, and had ascended to heaven for the salvation of sinners, and was now returning to earth again in the form of dew—and as the leaves on the trees bore the impression of the figures I had seen in the heavens, it was plain to me that the Saviour was about to lay down the yoke he had borne for the sins of men, and the great day of judgment was at hand. About this time I told these things to a white man, (Etheldred T. Brantley) on whom it had a wonderful effect—and he ceased from his wickedness, and was attacked immediately with a cutaneous [skin] eruption, and blood oozed from the pores of his skin, and after praying and fasting nine days, he was healed, and the Spirit appeared to me again, and said, as the Saviour had been baptised so should we be also—and when the white people would not let us be baptized by the church, we went down into the water together, in the sight of many who reviled [made fun of] us, and were baptized by the Spirit—After this I rejoiced greatly, and gave thanks to God. And on the 12th of May, 1828, I heard a loud noise in the heavens, and the Spirit instantly appeared to me and said the Serpent [Satan] was loosened, and Christ had laid down the yoke he had borne for the sins of men, and that I should take it on and fight against the Serpent, for this time was fast approaching when the first should be last and the last should be first. *Ques.* Do you not find yourself mistaken now? *Ans.* Was not Christ crucified? And by signs in the heavens that it would make known to me when I should commence the great work—and until the first sign appeared, I should conceal it from the knowledge of men—And on the appearance of the sign, (the eclipse of the sun last February) I should arise and prepare myself, and slay my enemies with their own weapons.

REVIEWING THE READING

1. When he was a youth, how did Turner spend his spare time? What did his friends and neighbors think of him?

2. What event did Turner take as a sign that it was time to lead the slaves in revolt?

3. **Using Your Historical Imagination.** What actions do you think were taken by southern whites following Nat Turner's revolt to prevent future uprisings?

Frances Kemble Travels by Boat, Stage, Railroad, and Canal (1832–1833)

47

From *Journal* by Frances Anne [Kemble] Butler.

English actress Frances Anne Kemble first visited the United States in 1832. During the next two years she toured various cities and was well received by American audiences. While she traveled, she kept a lively journal of her impressions of American life, which was later published in England. In the following excerpts from her journal, Frances Kemble describes a trip across New York state that involved several different kinds of land and water transport. Consider which of these various forms of travel Kemble found most disagreeable.

The steamboat was very large and commodious [roomy] as all these conveyances are. . . . These steamboats have three stories; the upper one is, as it were, a roofing or terrace on the leads of the second, a very desirable station when the weather is neither too foul, nor too fair; a burning sun being, I should think, as little desirable there, as a shower of rain. The second floor or deck, has the advantage of the ceiling above, and yet, the sides being completely open, it is airy, and allows free sight of the shores on either hand. Chairs, stools, and benches, are the furniture of these two decks. The one below, or third floor, downwards, in fact, the *ground floor*, being the one near the water, is a spacious room completely roofed and walled in, where the passengers take their meals, and resort if the weather is unfavourable. At the end of this room, is a smaller cabin for the use of the ladies, with beds and sofa,

. . . The breakfast was good, and served, and eaten, with decency enough.

and all the conveniences necessary, if they should like to be sick; whither I came and slept till breakfast time. Vigne's account of the pushing, thrusting, rushing, and devouring on board a western steamboat at meal times, had prepared me for rather an awful spectacle; but this, I find, is by no means the case in these more civilized parts, and everything was conducted with perfect order, propriety, and civility. The breakfast was good, and served, and eaten, with decency enough. . . . At about half past ten, we reached the place where we leave the river, to proceed across a part of the State of New Jersey, to the Delaware [River]. . . . Oh, these coaches! English eye hath not seen, English ear hath not heard, nor hath it entered into the heart of Englishman to conceive the surpassing clumsiness and wretchedness of these leathern inconveniences. They are shaped something like boats, the sides being merely leathern pieces, removable at pleasure, but which, in bad weather, are buttoned down to protect the inmates from the wet. There are three seats in this machine; the middle one, having a moveable leathern strap, by way of adossier, runs between the carriage doors, and lifts away, to permit the egress and ingress [leaving and entering] of the occupants of the other seats. . . . For the first few minutes, I thought I must have fainted from the intolerable sensation of smothering which I experienced. However, the leathers having been removed, and a little more air obtained, I took heart of grace, and resigned myself to my fate. Away wallopped the four horses, trotting with their front, and galloping with their hind legs: and away went we after them, bumping, thumping, jumping, jolting, shaking, tossing and tumbling, over the wickedest road, I do think, the cruellest, hard-heartedest road, that ever wheel rumbled upon. Through bog and marsh, and ruts, wider and deeper than any christian ruts I ever saw, with the roots of trees protruding across our path, their boughs every now and then giving us an affectionate scratch through the windows; and, more than once, a half-demolished trunk or stump lying in the middle of the road lifting us up, and letting us down again, with most awful variations of our poor coach body from its natural position. Bones of me! what a road! Even my father's solid proportions could not keep their level, but were jerked up to the roof and down again every three minutes. Our companions seemed nothing dismayed by these wondrous performances of a coach and four, but laughed and talked incessantly, the young ladies, at the very top of their voices, and with the national nasal twang. . . . The few cottages and farm-houses which we passed, reminded me of similar dwellings in France and Ireland; yet the peasantry [farmers] here have not the same excuse for disorder and dilapidation [ruin], as either the Irish or French. The farms had the same desolate, untidy, untended look; the gates broken, the fences carelessly put up, or ill repaired; the farming utensils sluttishly scattered about a littered yard, where the pigs seemed to preside by undisputed right; house-windows broken, and stuffed with paper or clothes; dishevelled women, and barefooted, anomalous [strange] looking human young things. None of the stirring life and activity which such places present in England and Scotland; above all, none of the enchanting mixture of neatness, order, and rustic elegance and comfort, which render so picturesque the surroundings of a farm, and the various belongings of agricultural labour in my own dear country. The fences struck me as peculiar; I never saw any such in England. They are made of rails of wood placed horizontally, and meeting at obtuse angles, so forming a zig-zag wall of wood, which runs over the country like the herringbone seams of a flannel petticoat. At each of the angles, two slanting stakes, considerably higher than the rest of the fence, were driven into the ground, crossing each other at the top, so as to secure the horizontal rails in their position. . . . At the end of fourteen miles we turned into a swampy field, the whole fourteen coachfuls of us, and by the help of heaven, bag and baggage were packed into the coaches which stood on the rail-way ready to receive us. The carriages were not drawn by steam, like those on the Liverpool rail-way, but by horses, with the mere advantage in speed afforded by the iron ledges, which, to be sure, compared with our previous progress through the ruts, was considerable. Our coachful got into the first carriage of the train, escaping, by way of especial grace, the dust which one's predecessors occasion. This vehicle had but two seats, in the usual fashion; each of which held four of us. The whole inside was lined with blazing scarlet leather, and the windows shaded with stuff [wool] curtains of the same refreshing colour; which with full complement of passengers, on a fine, sunny, American summer's day, must make as pretty a little miniature hell as may be, I should think. . . . This railroad is an infinite blessing; 'tis not yet finished, but shortly will be so, and then the whole of that horrible fourteen miles will be performed in comfort and decency, in less than half the time. In about an hour and a half, we reached the end of our rail-road part of the journey, and found another steamboat waiting us, when we all embarked on the Delaware. . . . At about four o'clock, we reached Philadelphia, having performed the journey between that and New York (a distance of a hundred miles,) in less than ten hours, in spite of bogs, ruts, and all other impediments. . . .

We proceeded by canal to Utica, which distance we performed in a day and a night, starting at two from Schenectady, and reaching Utica the next day at about noon. I like travelling by the canal boats very much. Our's was not crowded, and the country through which we passed being delightful, the placid moderate gliding through it, at about four miles and a half an hour, seemed to me infinitely preferable to the noise of wheels, the rumble of a coach, and

the jerking of bad roads, for the gain of a mile an hour. The only nuisances are the bridges over the canal, which are so very low, that one is obliged to prostrate oneself [lie face down] on the deck of the boat, to avoid being scraped off it; and this humiliation occurs, upon average, once every quarter of an hour. . . .

The valley of the Mohawk [River], through which we crept the whole sunshining day, is beautiful from beginning to end; fertile, soft, rich, and occasionally approaching sublimity and grandeur, in its rocks, and hanging woods. We had a lovely day, and a soft blessed sunset, which, just as we came to a point where the canal crosses the river, and where the curved and wooded shores on either side

Kemble preferred the smooth, peaceful trip on a canal boat over the rough ride in a coach.

recede, leaving a broad smooth basin, threw one of the most exquisite effects of light and color, I ever remember to have seen, over the water, and through the sky. . . . We sat in the men's cabin until they began making preparations for bed, and then withdrew into a room about twelve feet square, where a whole tribe of women were getting to their beds. Some half undressed, some brushing, some curling, some washing, some already asleep in their narrow cribs, but all within a quarter of an inch of each other: it made one shudder. . . .

At Utica we dined; and after dinner I slept profoundly. The gentlemen, I believe, went out to view the town, which, twenty years ago, *was not,* and now is a flourishing place, with fine-looking shops, two or three hotels, good broad streets, and a body of lawyers, who had a supper at the house where we were staying, and kept the night awake with champagne, shouting, toasts, and clapping of hands: so much for the strides of civilization through the savage lands of this new world.

REVIEWING THE READING

1. What forms of transport did Kemble use during her trip?

2. Which of these did she find the most uncomfortable?

3. **Using Your Historical Imagination.** Criticizing the disorderly American farms she passed on her trip, Kemble compares them to similar farms she has previously observed in Ireland and France. What do you think she may have meant by the following statement " . . . yet the peasants here have not the same excuse for disorder and dilapidation, as either the Irish or French"?

Frederick Douglass Is Sent to the Slave-Breaker (1833)

48

From *Narrative of the Life of Frederick Douglass* by Frederick Douglass.

Frederick Douglass was one of the most outstanding black abolitionist leaders. An escaped slave, he became a powerful and effective writer and speaker in the antislavery movement. His stories about the horrors of slavery were drawn from personal experience. The following selection, from Douglass' account of being sent to the "slave-breaker" as a young man, is taken from his autobiography. As you read the excerpt, decide what made Edward Covey so effective as a breaker of slaves.

Master Thomas at length said he would stand it no longer. I had lived with him nine months, during which time he had given me a number of severe whippings, all to no good purpose. He resolved to put me out, as he said, to be broken; and, for this purpose, he let [loaned] me for one year to a man named Edward Covey. Mr. Covey was a poor man, farm-renter. He rented the place upon which he lived, as also the hands [workers] with which he tilled it. Mr. Covey had acquired a very high reputation for breaking young slaves, and this reputation was of immense value to him. It enabled him to get his farm tilled with much less expense to himself than he could have had it done without such a reputation. Some slaveholders thought it not much loss to allow Mr. Covey to have their slaves one year, for the sake of the training to which they were subjected, without any other compensation. He could hire young help with great ease, in consequence of this reputation. Added to the natural good qualities of Mr. Covey, he was a professor of religion—a pious soul—a member and a class-leader in the Methodist church. All of this added weight to his reputation as a "nigger-breaker." I was aware of all the facts, having been made acquainted with them by a young man who had lived there. I nevertheless made the change gladly; for I was sure of getting enough to eat, which is not the smallest consideration to a hungry man.

. . . I was now, for the first time in my life, a field hand.

I left Master Thomas's house, and went to live with Mr. Covey, on the 1st of January, 1833. I was now, for the first time in my life, a field hand. In my new employment, I found myself even more awkward than a country boy appeared to be in a large city. I had been at my new home but one week before Mr. Covey gave me a very severe whipping, cutting my back, causing the blood to run, and raising ridges on my flesh as large as my little finger. The details of this affair are as follows: Mr. Covey sent me, very early in the morning of one of our coldest days in the month of January, to the woods, to get a load of wood. He gave me a team of unbroken oxen. He told me which was the in-hand ox, and which the off-hand one. He then tied the end of a large rope around the horns of the in-hand ox, and gave me the other end of it, and told me, if the oxen started to run, that I must hold on upon the rope. I had never driven oxen before, and of course I was very awkward. I, however, succeeded in getting to the edge of the woods with little difficulty; but I had got a very few rods [a rod equals 16.5 feet] into the woods, when the oxen took fright, and started full tilt, carrying the cart against trees, and over stumps, in the most frightful manner. I expected every moment that my brains would be dashed out against the trees. After running thus for a considerable distance, they finally upset the cart, dashing it with great force against a tree, and threw themselves into a dense thicket. How I escaped death, I do not know. There I was, entirely alone, in a thick wood, in a place new to me. My cart was upset and shattered, my oxen were entangled among the young trees, and there was none to help me. After a long spell [time] of effort, I succeeded in getting my cart righted, my oxen disentangled, and again yoked [attached] to the cart. I now proceeded with my team to the place where I had, the day before, been chopping wood, and loaded my cart pretty heavily, thinking in this way to tame my oxen. I then proceeded on my way home. I had now consumed [used] one half of the day. I got out of the woods safely, and now felt out of danger. I stopped my oxen to open the woods gate; and just as I did so, before I could get hold of my ox-rope, the oxen again started, rushed through the gate, catching it between the wheel and the body of the cart, tearing it to pieces, and coming within a few inches of crushing me against the gate-post. Thus twice, in one short day, I escaped death by the merest chance. On my return, I told Mr. Covey what had happened, and how it happened. He ordered me to return to the woods again immediately. I did so, and he followed on after me. Just as I got into the woods, he came up and told me to stop my cart, and that he would teach me how to trifle [fool] away my time, and break gates. He then went to a large gum-tree, and with his axe cut three large switches, and, after trimming them up neatly with his pocket-knife, he ordered me to take off my clothes. He repeated his order. I still made him no answer, nor did I move to strip myself. Upon this he rushed at me with the fierceness of a tiger, tore off my clothes, and lashed me till he had worn out his switches, cutting me so savagely as to leave the marks visible for a long time after. This whipping was the first of a number just like it, and for similar offences.

I lived with Mr. Covey one year. During the first six months, of that year, scarce a week passed without his whipping me. I was seldom free from a sore back. My awkwardness was almost always his

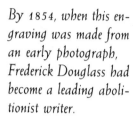

By 1854, when this engraving was made from an early photograph, Frederick Douglass had become a leading abolitionist writer.

excuse for whipping me. We were worked fully up to the point of endurance. Long before day we were up, our horses fed, and by the first approach of day we were off to the field with our hoes and ploughing teams. Mr. Covey gave us enough to eat, but scarce time to eat it. We were often less than five minutes taking our meals. We were often in the field from the first approach of day till its last lingering ray had left us; and at saving-fodder time, midnight often caught us in the field binding blades [tieing together leaves or stalks of grasses].

Covey would be out with us. The way he used to stand it, was this. He would spend the most of his afternoons in bed. He would then come out fresh in the evening, ready to urge us on with his words, example, and frequently with the whip. Mr. Covey was one of the few slaveholders who could and did work with his hands. He was a hardworking man. He knew by himself just what a man or a boy could do. There was no deceiving him. His work went on in his absence almost as well as in his presence; and he had the faculty [ability] of making us feel that he was ever present with us. This he did by surprising us. He seldom approached the spot where we were at work openly, if he could do it secretly. He always aimed at taking us by surprise. Such was his cunning, that we used to call him, among ourselves, "the snake." When we were at work in the cornfield, he would sometimes crawl on his hands and knees to avoid detection, and all at once he would rise nearly in our midst, and scream out, "Ha, ha! Come, come! Dash on, dash on!" This being his mode of attack, it was never safe to stop a single minute. His comings were like a thief in the night. He appeared to us as being ever at hand. He was under every tree, behind every stump, in every bush, and at every window, on the plantation. He would sometimes mount his horse, as if bound to St. Michael's, a distance of seven miles, and in half an hour afterwards you would see him coiled up in the corner of the wood-fence, watching every motion of the slaves. He would, for this purpose, leave his horse tied up in the woods. Again, he would sometimes walk up to us, and give us orders as though he was upon the point of starting on a long journey, turn his back upon us, and make as though he was going to the house to get ready; and, before he would get half way thither [there], he would turn short and crawl into a fence-corner, or behind some tree, and there watch us till the going down of the sun.

Mr. Covey's *forte* [specialty] consisted in his power to deceive. His life was devoted to planning and perpetrating [committing] the grossest deceptions. Every thing he possessed in the shape of learning or religion, he made conform to this disposition to deceive. He seemed to think himself equal to deceiving the Almighty. He would make a short prayer in the morning, and a long prayer at night; and, strange as it may seem, few men would at times appear more devotional than he. The exercises of his family devotions were always commenced with singing; and, as he was a very poor singer himself, the duty of raising the hymn generally came upon me. He would read his hymn, and nod at me to commence. I would at times do so; at others, I would not. My non-compliance [refusal to act] would almost always produce much confusion. To show himself independent of me, he would start and stagger through with his hymn in the most discordant manner. In this state of mind, he prayed with more than ordinary spirit. Poor man! such was his disposition, and success at deceiving, I do verily [truly] believe that he sometimes deceived himself into the solemn belief, that he was a sincere worshipper of the most high God. . . .

If at any one time of my life more than another, I was made to drink the bitterest dregs of slavery, that time was during the first six months of my stay with Mr. Covey. We were worked in all weathers. It was never too hot or too cold; it could never rain, blow, hail, or snow, too hard for us to work in the field. Work, work, work, was scarcely more the order of the day than of the night. The longest days were too short for him, and the shortest nights too long for him. I was somewhat unmanageable when I first went there, but a few months of this discipline tamed me. Mr. Covey succeeded in breaking me. I was broken in body, soul, and spirit. My natural elasticity [adaptability] was crushed, my intellect languished, the disposition to read departed, the cheerful spark that lingered about my eye died; the dark night of slavery closed in upon me; and behold a man transformed into a brute!

REVIEWING THE READING

1. Douglass describes Covey as an effective slave-breaker. He says "His [Covey's] work went on in his absence almost as well as in his presence." Why was this?

2. In what way did Covey's reputation as a slave-breaker benefit him economically?

3. **Using Your Historical Imagination.** What evidence can you find in the reading to show that Douglass was a very untypical slave? Explain.

Old Time Religion at the Camp Meeting (1835)

49

From *Forty Years of American Life, 1821–1861*, by Thomas Low Nichols.

As the line of the frontier moved westward beyond the Mississippi, rude settlements were carved out of the great woods and new social and religious activities were developed. One of these was that special religious gathering called by contemporaries the "camp meeting." At these temporary gathering places, persons from many different religious backgrounds would gather for days of preaching, singing, and religious inspiration. Of all the accounts of the camp meetings that have come down to us in letters, diaries, and personal memoirs, few are as accurate and penetrating as that of Thomas Low Nichols. As you read the following excerpt, note Nichols' reason for saying that camp meetings were absolutely essential for the new "Evangelical denominations" of the frontier.

In the European Churches, Greek, Lutheran, Roman [Catholic], or English, children, baptized in infancy, are afterwards confirmed, considered members of the church, and receive its sacraments. In America, among what are called the Evangelical denominations, there must be, at some period, what is called conversion, getting religion, a change of heart, followed by a public relation of religious experience, a profession of faith, and formal reception into the church. The non-professor [one who does not publicly proclaim his or her faith] becomes a professor, and a church member. But his change is commonly the result of periodical and epidemic [contagious] religious excitements, termed revivals. These sometimes appear to come spontaneously, or, as supposed, by the special outpouring of the Divine Spirit, but they are more often induced by peculiarly earnest and excited preaching, camp meetings, protracted [long] meetings, and systematic efforts to excite the community to religious feeling. Certain energetic and magnetic preachers are called revival preachers, and are hired to preach day and night in one place until there is a revival, and then go to another. Some of these receive considerable sums for their services, and cause revivals wherever they appear.

The camp meetings are mostly held by the Methodists. They gather from a wide district, with tents, provisions, and cooking utensils; form a regular camp in some picturesque forest, by some lake or running stream; a preacher's stand is erected, seats are made of plank, straw laid in a space railed off in front of the preachers for those who are struck with conviction or who wish to be prayed for to kneel upon, and then operations commence.

Ten or twelve preachers have collected, under the leadership of some old presiding elder bishop, who directs the proceedings. Early in the morning, the blowing of a horn wakes the camp to prayers, singing, and a bountiful breakfast: then the day's work begins. People flock in from the surrounding country. Sonorous [loud] hymns, often set to popular song-tunes, are sung by the whole congregation, pealing [echoing] through the forest aisles. Sermon follows sermon, preached with the lungs of Stentors [a reference to a Greek messenger with a powerful voice] and the fervour of an earnest zeal. Prayer follows prayer. The people shout, "Amen!" "Bless the Lord!" "Glory to God!" "Glory! Hallelujah!" They clap their hands, and shout with the excitement. Nervous and hysterical women are struck down senseless, and roll upon the ground. "Mourners" [those who are sorry for their sins] crowd to the anxious seats [special section for prospective converts], to be prayed for. There is groaning, weeping, shouting, praying, singing. Some are suddenly converted, and make the woods ring with joyful shouts of "Glory!" and these exhort others to come and

get religion. After three or four hours of this exciting and exhausting work, a benediction [blessing] is given, and all hands go to work to get dinner. Fires are burning behind each tent, great pots are smoking with savoury food, and, while spiritual affairs are the main business, the physical interests are not neglected. After dinner comes a brief session of gossip and repose. Then there are prayer meetings in the different tents, and the scenes of the morning are repeated at the same time in a dozen or twenty places, and the visitor who takes a place in the center of the camp may hear exhortations, prayers, and singing going on all together and on every side, while at times half a dozen will be praying and exhorting at once in a single group, making "confusion worse confounded."

The early camp meetings often were held in sites known locally for their natural beauty.

. . . Then the horn blows again, and all gather before the preacher's stand, where the scenes of the morning are repeated with increased fervour and effect. A dozen persons may be taken with "the power"—of the Holy Ghost as believed—falling into a state resembling catalepsy [motionlessness]. More and more are brought into the sphere of the excitement. It is very difficult for the calmest and most reasonable person to avoid its influence.

At night, after an interval for supper, the camp is lighted up by lanterns upon the trees and blazing fires of pine-knots. The scene is now wild and beautiful. The lights shine in the tents and gleam in the forest; the rude but melodious Methodist hymns ring through the woods; the ground is glittering with the phosphoric gleam of certain roots which trampling feet have denuded of their bark; the moon shines in the blue vault above the tree tops, and the melancholy scream of the loon, a large waterfowl, comes across the lake on the sighing breeze of night. In this wild and solemn night-scene, the voice of the preacher has double power, and the harvest of converts is increased. A procession is formed of men and women, who march round the camp singing an invitation to the unconverted. They march and sing—

> "Sinners, will you scorn the Saviour?
>   Will you drive Him from your arms?
> Once He died for your behaviour,
>   Now He calls you to His charms."

Or they fill the dim primeval forest with that tumultuous chorus—

> "I am bound for the Kingdom!
> Will you go to Glory with me?
>   O Hallelujah! O Halle hallelujah!
> I am bound for the Kingdom!
> Will you go to Glory with me?
>   O Hallelujah! O praise ye the Lord!"

. . . the moon shines in the blue vault above the tree tops . . .

The recruits fall in—the procession increases. When all are gathered up who can be induced [persuaded] to come, they bring them to the anxious-seats, where they are exhorted and prayed for, with tears, groans, and shouting, and cries of "Glory!"

Then there are prayer meetings in the tents again, with the accumulated excitement of the whole day and evening. At ten o'clock the long, wild note of the horn is heard from the preacher's stand: the night watch is set. Each tent is divided into two compartments, one for men, the other for women; straw is littered down, and all lie down in close rows upon the ground to sleep, and silence reigns in the camp, broken only by the mournful note of the waterfowl and the neighing of horses, fastened, with their forage [food], under the trees. These meetings last a week or longer.

REVIEWING THE READING

1. What were the central characteristics of the new evangelical denominations of the frontier, according to the author?

2. Why was the camp meeting so important to these denominations?

3. **Using Your Historical Imagination.** What factors at the camp meetings helped to promote an emotional religious response in the persons attending them?

50

From *My Eighty Years in Texas* by William Physick Zuber, edited by Janis Boyle Mayfield.

A Mexican Account of San Jacinto (1836)

"Remember the Alamo!" was the stirring cry of the Texans as they engaged in battle with the Mexican army at San Jacinto. The Battle of San Jacinto led to the capture of Mexican General Antonio Lopez de Santa Anna, the "Napoleon of the West." After being given his freedom by Sam Houston, Santa Anna removed his army from Texas, and the Republic of Texas was formed with Houston as its first president.

The following selection is excerpted from an account of the Battle of San Jacinto from the point of view of a Mexican soldier named Delgado, who fought in the battle. Delgado's account forms part of a manuscript of reminiscences written by Texan William Physick Zuber. As you read the selection, note the actions taken by the Mexican troops when they were attacked by the Texans.

April 21, 1836, was the day of Santa Anna's great defeat.

Delgado describes what is known as "the Mexican breastwork": "At daybreak on the twenty-first, His Excellency ordered a breastwork [defensive wall] to be erected for the cannon. It was constructed with packsaddles, sacks of hard bread, baggage, etc. A trifling barrier of branches ran along the front part and right."

The Mexicans had nothing that we call packsaddles. What Delgado or the translator of his statement calls packsaddles were cushions, made of pliant [flexible] leather and filled with hay. The Mexicans called them *terrejos*, and they were used as we use packsaddles. Most of them were so large as to cover a mule's

back from withers to cropper; they were so soft as
to enable the animal to carry a great weight of baggage without being bruised by it. Of about two
hundred captured packmules, I did not observe one
with a sore back.

After the battle I saw what was left of the "breastwork." The "packsaddles, sacks of hard bread, baggage, etc.," had been removed. Two parallel rows
of brush heap, about thirty feet apart, extended about
seventy feet up a rising ground and were about six
or eight feet high. I saw no opening through which
to discharge either cannons or small arms. The brush
would of course have deflected [altered] the course
of rifle balls and weakened their force, but could
be no defense against cannon shot. Its only practical
use for defense would be to arrest [stop] a charge,
as an enemy could not have leaped or climbed over
it. The removed articles might have arrested rifle
balls, but not cannon shot.

A long table, improvised of undressed scantlings
[unseasoned pieces of wood] and planks, extended
nearly the full length of the brush heaps and midway
between them. When I saw this table, it was perfectly
nude, but men who saw it immediately after the
battle said that it was covered with tablespreads
and bore many cakes, bottles of wine, and goblets.
As a defense, this structure was also worthless.

Delgado continues:

"We had the enemy on our right, within a wood,
at long musket range. Our front, though level, was
exposed to the fire of the enemy, who could keep
it up with impunity [freedom from harm] from his
sheltered position. Retreat was easy for him on his
rear and right, while our troops had no room for
maneuvering. We had, in our rear, a small grove
extending to the bay shore, and to New Washington. . . .

"A few hours before the engagement, I submitted
to General Castrillon a few remarks on the situation,
suggested by my limited knowledge. But he answered, 'What can I do, my friend? I know it well,

Mexican general Santa Anna was captured at San Jacinto in the war for Texas independence. But he was released by Sam Houston, who is shown receiving treatment for battle wounds.

but cannot help it. You know that nothing avails here against the caprice, arbitrary will, and ignorance of that man.' This was said in an impassioned [emotional] voice, in close proximity to His Excellency's tent.

"At nine o'clock A.M. General Cos came in with a reinforcement of about five hundred men. His arrival was greeted with a roll of drums and with joyful shouts. As it was reported to His Excellency that these men had not slept the night before, he instructed them to stack their arms, to remove their accoutrements [equipment], and go to sleep in the adjoining grove.

"No important incident took place until 4:30 P.M. At this fatal moment, the bugler on our right sounded the advance of the enemy upon that wing. His Excellency and staff were asleep; the greater part of the men were also sleeping; of the rest, some were eating, others were scattered in the woods in search of boughs to prepare shelter. Our line was composed of musket stacks. Our cavalry were riding bareback, to and from water.

"I stepped upon an ammunition box, the better to observe the movements of the enemy. I saw that

their formation was a mere line in one rank and
very extended. In the center was the Texas flag;
on both wings they had two cannons, well manned.
Their cavalry was opposite to our front, overlapping
our left.

"In this disposition, yelling furiously, with brisk
fire of grape, musketry, and rifles, they advanced
resolutely [boldly] upon our camp. There the utmost
confusion prevailed. General Castrillon shouted on
one side. On the other, Colonel Almonte was giving
orders. Some cried out to commence firing. Others,
to lie down to avoid grapeshot. Among the latter
was His Excellency.

"Then, already some of our men were flying
in groups, terrified, sheltering themselves behind
large trees. I endeavored to force some of them to
fight; but all efforts were vain—the evil was beyond
remedy. They were a bewildered and panic-stricken
herd.

"The enemy kept up a brisk crossfire upon the
woods. Presently, we heard, in close proximity, the
unpleasant noise of their clamor. Meeting no resistance, they dashed upon our deserted camp.

"Then I saw his Excellency running about in
the utmost excitement, wringing his hands, and unable to give an order. General Castrillon was
stretched on the ground, wounded in the leg. Colonel
Trevino was killed, and Col. Marcial Aguirre was
seriously injured. . . .

"Everything being lost, I went, leading my horse,
which I could not mount because the firing had
rendered him restless and fractious [irritable], to join
our men, still hoping that we might be able to defend
ourselves, or to retire under shadow of the night.
This, however, could not be done. It is a known
fact that Mexican soldiers, once demoralized, cannot
be controlled unless they are thoroughly trained
to war.

"On our left, and about a musket shot from
our camp, was a small grove on the bay shore. Our
disbanded herd rushed for it, to obtain shelter from

The men . . . would helplessly crowd together, and were shot down by the enemy . . .

the horrid slaughter carried on all over the prairie by those bloodthirsty usurpers [invaders]. Unfortunately, we met on our way an obstacle difficult to overcome. It was a bayou [creek], not very wide, but rather deep. The men, on reaching it, would helplessly crowd together, and were shot down by the enemy, who was close enough not to miss his aim. It was here that the greatest carnage [destruction] took place.

"Upon reaching that spot, I saw Colonel Almonte swimming across the bayou with his left hand, and holding up the right, in which he grasped his sword.

"I stated before that I was leading my horse; but, in that critical situation, I vaulted upon him, and, with two leaps, he landed me on the opposite side of the bayou. To my sorrow, I had to leave that noble animal mired in that place, . . . As I dismounted, I sank in the mud waist deep, and had great trouble to get out by taking hold of the grass. Both my shoes remained in the bayou. I made an effort to recover them, but soon came to the conclusion that, did I tarry [linger] there, a rifle ball would certainly make an outlet for my soul, as had happened to many a poor fellow around me. Thus I made for the grove, barefooted.

"There I met a number of other officers, with whom I wandered at random, buried in gloomy thoughts upon our tragic disaster. We still had a hope of rallying some of our men, but it was impossible. The enemy's cavalry surrounded the grove, while his infantry penetrated it, pursuing us with fierce and bloodthirsty feelings.

"There they killed Colonel Batres, and it would have been all over with us had not providence placed us in the hands of that noble and generous captain of cavalry Allen, who, by great exertion, saved us repeatedly from being slaughtered by the drunken and infuriated volunteers.

"Then they marched us to their camp. I was barefooted. The prairie had been burned up, and the blades of grass, hardened by fire, penetrated like needles the soles of my feet, so that I could scarcely walk. That did not prevent them from striking me with the butt ends of their guns because I did not walk as fast as they wanted. . . .

"At last, we reached the camp. We were seated on the ground by twos, as we had marched. On the bay shore, our thirst had been quenched with an abundance of water which Allen and others had allowed to pass from hand until all were satisfied. . . .

"After having kept us sitting about an hour and a half, they marched us to the woods, where we saw an immense fire, made up of a huge pile of wood, even whole trees being used. I and some of my comrades were silly enough to believe that we were to be burned alive, in retaliation for those who had been burned in the Alamo. . . . We were considerably relieved when they placed us around the fire to warm ourselves, and dry our clothes."

REVIEWING THE READING

1. According to Delgado, what did he first try to do when the Texas troops advanced into the Mexican camp? How did the Mexican troops respond to Delgado's actions?

2. Why did Delgado and his comrades believe that they were going to be burned alive by the Texans? What was the real reason for the fire?

3. **Using Your Historical Imagination.** Do you think a Texas soldier writing an account of the battle would describe the Texans in the same way they were described by Delgado? Give reasons for your answer.

51

From *Illinois in 1837: A Sketch Descriptive . . . of the State of Illinois,* compiled by S. Augustus Mitchell.

A Settler's Guide to the Illinois Wilderness (1837)

Much of our information about frontier conditions comes from guidebooks written during the early days of settlement. The purpose of these guidebooks was to inform potential settlers about the conditions they faced in particular areas and to attract people interested in buying land. The following excerpts come from a guidebook compiled by S. Augustus Mitchell, who was looking for people to buy land in the state of Illinois. As you read the selection, pay special attention to Mitchell's descriptions of the settlers already living in Illinois.

Upon emigrating to this country, it would be well for an eastern farmer to throw off and forget many of his former habits and practices, and be prepared to accommodate himself to the nature of the soil, and the circumstances of the country; else he will throw away much labour uselessly, and expend money unprofitably. The first object is to find a suitable situation; or, in the language of the country, to *locate* himself. An entire stranger can hardly be expected to judge correctly in relation to soil, and the advantages and disadvantages of location. If he arrives in the dry season of autumn, he will be likely to select a level spot of prairie, with a deep black soil, determined to have rich land at any rate, and perhaps in the spring find himself ploughing in mud and water. If he looks at the appearance of the timber, he will probably be deceived, and overlook some of the best tracts. Advice from those who have long been residents in the country, would save many inconveniences in location.

No emigrant need deceive himself with the notion that he can find a spot which will combine all the advantages, and none of the disadvantages, of the country. On every spot he examines, some indispensable thing will appear to be wanting. Nor is it of any use for a man to travel the country to any great extent, to find as many natural advantages as may satisfy moderate desires. The best policy for an emigrant, after arriving in the Western Country, and fixing upon the district or county in which he intends to reside, is to settle himself on the first spot he finds that he thinks may answer his purpose, and resolve to abide [live] there contentedly. . . .

When an emigrant has fixed his location, he next selects his building spot. Much will depend upon a judicious [wise] choice, in regard to health. An elevated spot of ground, remote from lakes and marshes, and where the air circulates freely from all points of the compass, is desirable. If a river bottom is chosen, the house should be as near the stream, on the highest ground, as is possible, without risk from the washing in of the banks. Settlements directly on the margins of the Mississippi and Missouri are healthy, compared with situations a few hundred yards distant, in the interior of the bottom. Where all other circumstances are equal, the south or south-west side of the timber is the most desirable, as throughout the heat of the summer the winds are usually from the south-west and west, and the timber affords protection from the cold north-winds of winter. But an exposure to the north or north-west is far less disagreeable than would be imagined. In a very few years, by means of orchards and shade trees, sufficient protection can be had.

All confined places should be avoided, such as ravines, and even coves, or points of prairie surrounded by dense timber, unless an opening can be made immediately. The currents in the atmosphere appear to act on the same principles as currents in the water. Where eddies and counter-currents are formed, there impure vapour will con-

All confined places should be avoided . . .

centrate. This is not only true in theory, but holds good in practical observation. . . .

Having fixed on the spot, the next step is to provide cabins or temporary buildings. These, and all other dwellings, should be so arranged as to promote ventilation in the summer. The door and other apertures [openings] should be opposite each other, the chimney at the end; and if a double cabin or one of two rooms is designed, a space of 10 or 12 feet between them should be left and roofed over. Forks may be set in the ground, and porches or sheds may be made on the sides, eight feet in width. The cost is trifling, and they add greatly to the coolness of the dwelling in summer, and its warmth in winter, besides protecting the body of the houses from rains. Hundreds of cabins are made without a nail or particle of iron about them, or a single piece of sawed plank.

The first buildings put up are cabins made of logs, which are constructed after the following manner: Straight trees are felled of a size that a common team can draw, or, as the phrase is, "snake" them to the intended spot. The common form of a large cabin is that called a "double cabin;" that is, two square pens, with an open space between, connected by a roof above and a floor below, so as to form a parallelogram of nearly triple the length of its depth. In the open space the family take their meals, during the pleasant weather; and it serves the threefold purpose of kitchen, lumber-room, and dining-room. The logs of which it is composed are notched on to one another in the form of a square. The roof is covered with thin splits of oak, not unlike staves [shingles]. Sometimes they are made of ash, and in the lower country, of cypress; and they are called clapboards. Instead of being nailed, they are generally confined in their place by heavy timber, laid at right angles across them. This gives the roof of a cabin a unique and shaggy appearance; but if the clapboards have been carefully prepared from good timber, they form a roof sufficiently impervious [resistant] to common rains. The floors are made from short and thick plank, split from the yellow poplar, cottonwood, black walnut, and sometimes oak. They are confined with wooden pins, and are technically called "puncheons." If an emigrant can furnish a few pounds of nails, and a dozen panes of glass, he may add to his comforts; and if a saw-mill is near, and plank or boards cheap, he may save himself the labour of splitting puncheons or slabs for floors and doors. In addition to the cabin, he will need a meat-house, a corn-crib, and stables, all built of logs in the same rough manner. If an emigrant has plenty of money, and sawed lumber can be gotten conveniently, he may put up a frame barn as soon as he pleases. If he has not the advantage of a good spring, he should dig a well immediately, which will cost four or five days' labour, and will stand some time without walling. In making all these improvements, all cash expenses should be avoided as much as possible, unless a man has money to spend freely. The next step is to prepare a farm. If the settler locate himself in barrens, or in timbered land, he has to grub out

A pioneer family begins the hard task of clearing their land and building a home in the wilderness of the American frontier.

the small growth, preparatory to ploughing; that is dig them up by the roots with an instrument called a mattock. It is true, that land covered with bushes can be ploughed, and the stumps left in the ground, as well or better than in the north; but it will require more labour in the end to subdue the sprouts that will strive for the mastery, than to clear the land at once. It usually requires from three to six days' labour to grub an acre. The small growth in timbered lands is taken out in the same manner. If a settler has located himself in a timbered tract, which in this prairie country is wretched policy, he grubs up the small growth, girdles the trees [kills by making a deep cut around the tree], and puts in the plough.

Prairie land requires a strong team, and a large plough kept very sharp, to break it up thoroughly. This must be done well, and every particle of the sward [grassy land] turned over; or it had better be let alone. . . .

> . . . Prairie land requires a strong team, and a large plough kept very sharp, to break it up thoroughly.

The want of adequate supplies of lumber, and of mechanics, renders good buildings more expensive than in the country parts of New-England or New-York.

Merchants' goods, groceries, household-furniture, and almost every necessary and comfort in housekeeping, can be purchased here; and many articles retail at about the same prices as in the Atlantic States.

The following table will exhibit the cost of 320 acres of land, at Congress price, and preparing 160 acres for cultivation or prairie land:

Cost of 320 acres, $1.25 per acre .	$ 400
Breaking up 160 acres prairie, at $2 per acre	320
Fencing into four fields, with a Kentucky fence of eight rails high, with cross stakes	175
Add cost of cabins, corn-cribs, stable &c	250
Making the cost of the farm	$1145

In many instances, a single crop of wheat will pay for the land, for fencing, breaking up, cultivating, harvesting, threshing, and taking to market. All kinds of mechanical labour, especially those in the building line, are in great demand; and workmen, even very coarse and common workmen, get almost any price they ask. Journeymen mechanics get two dollars per day. A carpenter, bricklayer, or mason, wants no other capital to do a first-rate business, and soon become independent, than a set of tools, and habits of industry, sobriety, economy, and enterprize.

Common labourers on the farm obtain from twelve to fifteen dollars per month, including board. Any young man, with industrious habits, can begin here without a dollar, and in a very few years become a substantial farmer. A good cradler [grain cutter] in the harvest-field will earn from one dollar and a half to two dollars per day.

REVIEWING THE READING

1. What advice does Mitchell give about how emigrants should choose land on which to settle?

2. According to Mitchell, what features should a cabin have in order to provide the most comfort?

3. **Using Your Historical Imagination.** If you were a new settler in Illinois in 1837, what information contained in the guidebook would you find most helpful? Refer to specific information from the selection when composing your response and provide reasons for your choices.

52

From *Miscellaneous Writings on Slavery* by William Jay.

Conditions of Free Blacks in the North (1839)

William Jay served as a judge for many years in Westchester County, New York, and was an active and outspoken abolitionist. He helped to organize the New York City Anti-Slavery Society and wrote numerous articles and pamplets on the evils of slavery and the merits of abolishing that institution. In the following excerpts from Jay's collected works, he discusses the situation of free blacks living in those states that do not practice slavery. As you read the selection, note the examples given by Jay that illustrate the continued oppression of blacks living in the free states.

I t appears from the census of 1830, that there were then 319,467 free colored persons in the United States. At the present time the number cannot be less than 360,000. Fifteen States of the Federal Union have each a smaller population than this aggregate [total number]. Hence if the whole mass of human beings inhabiting Connecticut, or New Jersey, or any other of these fifteen States, were subjected to the ignorance and degradation and persecution and terror we are about to describe as the lot of this much-injured people, the amount of suffering would still be numerically less than that inflicted by a professedly [claiming to be] Christian and republican community upon the free negroes. . . .

It is not necessary, for our present purpose, to enter into a particular investigation of the condition of the free negroes in the slave States. We all know that they suffer every form of oppression which the laws can inflict upon persons not actually slaves. That unjust and cruel enactments should proceed from a people who keep two millions of their fellow-men in abject [hopeless] bondage, and who believe such enactments essential to the maintenance of their despotism, certainly affords no cause for surprise.

We turn to the free States, where slavery has not directly steeled our hearts against human suffering, and where no supposed danger of insurrection [revolt] affords a pretext for keeping the free blacks in ignorance and degradation; and we ask, What is the character of the prejudice against color *here?* . . .

With these preliminary remarks we will now . . . consider in order, the various disabilities and oppressions to which they are subjected, either by law or the customs of society.

1. GENERAL EXCLUSION FROM THE ELECTIVE FRANCHISE.

Were this exclusion founded on the want of property, or any other qualification deemed essential to the judicious exercise of the franchise, it would afford no just cause of complaint; but it is founded solely on the color of the skin, and is therefore irrational and unjust. That taxation and representation should be inseparable, was one of the axioms [principles] of the fathers of our Revolution, and one of the reasons they assigned for their revolt from the crown of Britain. But *now*, it is deemed a mark of fanaticism [excessiveness] to complain of the disfranchisement of a whole race, while they remain subject to the burden of taxation. It is worthy of remark, that of the thirteen original States, only *two* were so recreant [unfaithful] to the principles of the Revolution, as to make a *white skin* a qualification for suffrage. But the prejudice has grown with our growth, and strengthened with our strength; and it is believed that in *every* State constitution subsequently formed or revised, (excepting Vermont and Maine, and the revised constitution of Massachusetts,) the crime of a dark complexion has been punished, by debarring [keeping] its possessor from all approach to the ballot-box. The necessary effect of this proscription in aggravating the oppression and degradation of the colored inhabitants, must be obvious to all who call to mind the solicitude [concern] manifested by demagogues, and office-seekers, and law-makers, to propitiate [gain] the good will of all who have votes to bestow. . . .

5. EXCLUSION FROM ALL PARTICIPATION IN THE ADMINIS-
   TRATION OF JUSTICE.

No colored man can be a judge, juror, or constable. . . . In the slave States generally, no black man can enter a court of justice as a witness against a white one. Of course a white man may, with perfect impunity, defraud or abuse a negro to any extent, provided he is careful to avoid the presence of any of his own caste, at the execution of his contract, or the indulgence of his malice. We are not aware that an outrage so flagrant is sanctioned [allowed] by the laws of any *free* State, with one exception. That exception the reader will readily believe can be none other than OHIO. A statute of this State enacts, "that no black or mulatto *person* or *persons* shall hereafter be permitted to be sworn, or give evidence in any court of record or elsewhere, in this State, in any cause depending, or matter of controversy, when either party to the same is a WHITE person; or in any prosecution of the State against any WHITE person." . . .

6. IMPEDIMENTS TO EDUCATION.

No people have ever professed so deep a conviction of the importance of popular education as ourselves, and no people have ever resorted to such cruel expedients [means] to perpetuate abject ignorance. More than one third of the whole population of the slave States are prohibited from learning even to read, and in some of them, free men, if with dark complexions, are subject to stripes [whippings] for teaching their own children. If we turn to the free States, we find that in all of them, without exception, the prejudices and customs of society

HARPER'S WEEKLY.

A JOURNAL OF CIVILIZATION.

Vol. XI.—No. 568.] NEW YORK, SATURDAY, NOVEMBER 16, 1867. [SINGLE COPIES TEN CENTS.
[$4.00 PER YEAR IN ADVANCE.

oppose almost insuperable [insurmountable] obstacles to the acquisition of a liberal education by colored youth. Our academies and colleges are barred against them. We know there are instances of young men with dark skins having been received, under

Although blacks in the north were free, they could not vote until after the Civil War.

peculiar circumstances, into northern colleges; but we neither know nor believe, that there have been a dozen such instances within the last thirty years.

Colored children are very generally excluded from our common schools, in consequence of the prejudices of teachers and parents. In some of our cities there are schools *exclusively* for their use, but in the country the colored population is too sparse to justify such schools; and white and black children are rarely seen studying under the same roof; although such cases do sometimes occur, and then they are confined to elementary schools. Some colored young men, who could bear the expense, have obtained in European seminaries the education denied them in their native land.

It may not be useless to cite an instance of the malignity [spite] with which the education of the blacks is opposed. The efforts made in Connecticut to prevent the establishment of schools of a higher order than usual for colored pupils, are too well known to need a recital here; and her BLACK ACT, prohibiting the instruction of colored children from other States, although now expunged [removed] from her statute book through the influence of abolitionists, will long be remembered to the opprobrium [disgrace] of her citizens. We ask attention to the following illustration of public opinion in another New England State.

In 1834 an academy was built by subscription in CANAAN, New Hampshire, and a charter granted by the Legislature; and at a meeting of the proprietors it was determined to receive all applicants having "suitable moral and intellectual recommendations, without other distinctions;" in other words, without reference to *complexion*. When this determination was made known, a town meeting was forthwith convened, and the following resolutions adopted, [namely]:

"Resolved, that we view with *abhorrence* [horror] the attempt of the abolitionists to

. . . Some colored young men . . . have obtained in European seminaries the education denied them in their native land.

establish in this town a school for the instruction of the sable sons and daughters of Africa,
in common with our sons and daughters.

"Resolved, that we will not associate
with, nor in any way countenance [accept],
any man or woman who shall hereafter persist
in attempting to establish a school in this
town for the *exclusive* education of blacks, *or*
for their education in conjunction with the
whites." . . .

The proprietors of the academy supposing, in
the simplicity of their hearts, that in a free country
they might use their property in any manner not
forbidden by law, proceeded to open their school,
and in the ensuing spring, had twenty-eight white,
and fourteen colored scholars. The crisis had now
arrived when the cause of prejudice demanded the
sacrifice of constitutional liberty and of private property. Another town meeting was convoked [called],
at which, without a shadow of authority, and in
utter contempt of law and decency, it was ordered,
that the academy should be forcibly removed, and
a committee was appointed to execute the abomina-
ble mandate [order]. Due preparations were made
for the occasion, and on the 10th of August, three
hundred men with about two hundred oxen, assembled at the place, and taking the edifice [building]
from off its foundation, dragged it to a distance,
and left it a ruin. No one of the actors in this high-
handed outrage was ever brought before a court of
justice to answer for this criminal and riotous destruction of the property of others.

The transaction we have narrated expresses in
emphatic terms the deep and settled hostility felt
in the free States, to the education of the blacks.
The prejudices of the community render that hostility generally effective without the aid of legal enactments. Indeed, some remaining regard to decency
and the opinion of the world, has restrained the
Legislatures of the free States, with *one exception*, from

consigning [delivering] these unhappy people to ignorance by "decreeing unrighteous decrees," and "framing mischief by a law." Our readers, no doubt, feel that the exception must of course be OHIO.

. . . Ohio legislators . . . enacted a law in 1831, declaring that, "when any appropriation shall be made by the directors of any school district, from the treasury thereof, for the payment of a teacher, the school in such district shall be open"—to whom?—"*to scholars, students, and teachers of every grade, without distinction or preference, whatever,*" as commanded by the constitution? Oh no!—"shall be open to all the WHITE children residing therein!" Such is the impotency [weakness] of written constitutions, where a sense of moral obligation is wanting [lacking] to enforce them. . . .

10. SUBJECTION TO INSULT AND OUTRAGE.

The feeling of the community towards these people, and the contempt with which they are treated, are indicated by the following notice, lately published by the proprietors of a menagerie [zoo], in New York. "The proprietors wish it to be understood, that people of color are not permitted to enter, *except when in attendance upon children and families.*" For two shillings, any white scavenger would be freely admitted, and so would negroes, provided they came in a capacity that marked their dependence; their presence is offensive, *only* when they come as independent spectators, gratifying a laudable [worthy] curiosity.

Even death, the great leveller, is not permitted to obliterate [destroy], among Christians, the distinction of caste, or to rescue the lifeless form of the colored man from the insults of his white brethren. In the porch of a Presbyterian Church, in Philadelphia, in 1837, was suspended a card, containing the form of a deed, to be given to purchasers of lots in a certain burial ground, and to enhance the value of the property, and to entice buyers, the following clause was inserted: "No person of *color*, nor any one who has been the subject of *execution,* shall be interred [buried] in said lot."

Our colored fellow-citizens, like others, are occasionally called to pass from one place to another; and in doing so are compelled to submit to innumerable hardships and indignities. They are frequently denied seats in our stage coaches; and although admitted upon the *decks* of our steamboats, are almost universally excluded from the cabins. Even women have been forced, in cold weather, to pass the night upon deck, and in one instance the wife of a colored clergyman lost her life in consequence of such an exposure.

They are frequently denied seats in our stage coaches . . .

The contempt poured upon these people by our laws, our churches, our seminaries, our professions, naturally invokes upon their heads the fierce wrath of vulgar malignity. In order to exhibit the actual condition of this portion of our population, we will here insert some *samples* of the outrages to which they are subjected, taken from the ordinary public journals.

In an account of the New York riots of 1834, the *Commercial Advertiser* says:

"About twenty poor African (native American) families, have had their all destroyed, and have neither bed, clothing, nor food remaining. Their houses are completely eviscerated [gutted], their furniture a wreck, and the ruined and disconsolate [cheerless] tenants of the devoted houses are reduced to the necessity of applying to the corporation for bread."

The example set in New York was zealously followed in Philadelphia.

"Some arrangement, it appears, existed between the mob and the white inhabitants, as the dwelling-houses of the latter, contiguous to the residences of the blacks, were illuminated and left undisturbed, while the huts of the negroes were singled out with unerring certainty. The furniture found in these houses was generally broken up and destroyed—beds ripped open and their contents scattered in the streets. . . . The number of houses assailed [attacked] was not less than twenty. . . ." *Philadelphia Gazette.*

"No one case is reported of an attack having been *invited* or *provoked* by the residents of the dwellings assailed or destroyed. The extent of the depredations committed on the *three* evenings of riot and outrage can only be judged of by the number of houses damaged or destroyed. So far as ascertained, this amounts to FORTY-FIVE. One of the houses assaulted was occupied by an unfortunate cripple, who, unable to fly from the fury of the mob, was so beaten by some of the ruffians, that he has since died in consequence of the bruises and wounds inflicted. . . ." *National Gazette.*

REVIEWING THE READING

1. Give five examples from the selection of the type of discrimination faced by free blacks living in some of the free states.

2. What happened in Canaan, New Hampshire, when a new school there admitted both black children and white children? What action was taken by the court following this event?

3. **Using Your Historical Imagination.** Why do you think that discrimination against a group of people continues even after laws are passed to forbid such practices?

A Woman's Advice to Women (1840s)

From *A Treatise on Domestic Economy, for the Use of Young Ladies at Home, and at School* by Catherine E. Beecher.

53

Catherine Beecher, the sister of famous novelist Harriet Beecher Stowe, ran a school for young women—a "ladies seminary"—during the 1840s. Like many similar schools of the period, Beecher's school taught much of what today would be called home economics, as well as basic skills of reading, writing, and arithmetic. As you read the excerpts from Beecher's book A Treatise on Domestic Economy, consider whether Beecher seems more concerned with the dictates of fashion or with practical matters in her advice to women.

On Clothing

The clothing ought always to be proportioned to the constitution and habits. A person of strong constitution, who takes much exercise, needs less clothing than one of delicate and sedentary [inactive] habits. According to this rule, women need much thicker and warmer clothing, when they go out, than men. But how different are our customs, from what sound wisdom dictates! Women go out with thin stockings, thin shoes, and open necks, when men are protected by thick woollen hose and boots, and their whole body encased in many folds of flannel and broadcloth. . . .

But the practice, by which females probably suffer most, is, the use of *tight dresses*. Much has been said against the use of corsets by ladies. But these may be worn with perfect safety, and be left off, and still injury, such as they often produce, be equally felt. It is the *constriction* [tightness] of the dress that is to be feared, and not any particular article that produces it. A frock [dress], or a belt, may be so tight, as to be even worse than a corset, which would more equally divide the compression [squeezing together].

So long as it is the fashion to admire, as models of elegance, the wasp-like figures which are presented at the rooms of mantuamakers [dressmakers] and milliners [creators of women's hats], there will be hundreds of foolish women, who will risk their lives and health to secure some resemblance to these deformities of the human frame. But it is believed, that all sensible women, when they fairly understand the evils which result from tight dressing, and learn the *real* model of taste and beauty for a perfect female form, will never risk their own health, or the health of their daughters, in efforts to secure one which is as much at variance with good taste, as it is with good health. . . .

The rule of safety, in regard to the tightness of dress, is this. Every person should be dressed so loosely, that, *when sitting in the posture used in sewing, reading, or study,* THE LUNGS *can be as fully and as easily inflated, as they are without clothing.* . . .

The English ladies set our countrywomen a good example, in accommodating their dress to times and seasons. The richest and noblest among them wear warm cotton hose and thick shoes, when they walk for exercise; and would deem it vulgar to appear, as many of our ladies do, with thin hose and shoes, in damp or cold weather. Any mode [style] of dress, not suited to the employment, the age, the season, or the means [income] of the wearer, is in bad taste.

On Cleanliness

The importance of cleanliness, in person and dress, can never be fully realized, by persons who are ignorant of the construction of the skin, and of the influence which its treatment has on the health of the body. Persons deficient [lacking] in such knowledge, frequently sneer at what they deem the foolish and fidgety particularity of others, whose frequent ablu-

tions [washings] and changes of clothing, exceed [go beyond] their own measure of importance.

The popular maxim, that "dirt is healthy," has probably arisen from the fact, that playing in the open air is very beneficial to the health of children, who thus get dirt on their persons and clothes. But it is the fresh air and exercise, and not the dirt, which promotes the health. . . .

The benefits arising from a proper care of the skin, is the reason why bathing has been so extensively practised by civilized nations. The Greeks and Romans considered bathing as indispensable to daily comfort, as much so, as their meals; and public baths were provided for all classes. In European coun-

This illustration from a women's magazine of the mid-1800s shows how women were expected to look.

tries, this practice is very prevalent [widespread], but there is no civilized nation which pays so little regard to the rules of health, on this subject, as our own. To wash the face, feet, hands, and neck, is the extent of the ablutions practised by perhaps the majority of our people. . . .

(Because many families had servants to help care for their large homes, Beecher also offered advice about the way a woman should train her domestic help. After describing the basic tools needed for washing dishes, she recommends posting the following set of procedures in the kitchen.)

Rules for Washing Dishes

1. Scrape the dishes, putting away any food which may remain on them, and which it may be proper to save for future use. Put grease into the grease-pot, and whatever else may be on the plates, into the slop-pail [garbage pail]. Save tea-leaves for sweeping. Set all the dishes, when scraped, in regular piles; the smallest at the top.

2. Put the nicest articles in the wash-dish, and wash them in hot suds, with the swab [strips of cloth attached to a stick] or nicest dish-cloth. Wipe all metal articles, as soon as they are washed. Put all the rest into the rinsing-dish, which should be filled with hot water. When they are taken out, lay them to drain on the waiter [tray]. Then rinse the dish-cloth, and hang it up, wipe the articles washed, and put them in their places.

3. Pour in more hot water, wash the greasy dishes with the dish-cloth made for them; rinse them, and set them to drain. Wipe them, and set them away. Wash the knives and forks, *being careful that the handles are never put in water;* wipe them, and then lay them in a knife-dish, to be scoured.

4. Take a fresh supply of clean suds, in which, wash the milk-pans, buckets, and tins. Then rinse and hang up this dish-cloth, and take the other; with which, wash the roaster, gridiron [grate on

which food is broiled], pots, and kettles. Then wash
and rinse the dish-cloth, and hang it up. Empty
the slop-bucket and scald it. Dry metal teapots and
tins before the fire. Then put the fireplace in order,
and sweep and dust the kitchen.

REVIEWING THE READING

1. Does Beecher emphasize practicality or
   fashion in her recommendations to
   women?

2. What does she think about the wearing
   of tight dresses?

3. **Using Your Historical Imagination.** In
   what two statements does Catherine
   Beecher sum up her philosophy of proper
   dress? Do you agree or disagree with this?

54

From *Life on the Mississippi* by Mark Twain.

Mark Twain Describes a "Lightning Pilot" (ca. 1840)

The era of the steamboat was an exciting time in American history, and no one paints a more colorful picture of that time than author Mark Twain. Twain, whose real name was Samuel Clemens, took his pen name from his days as a young steamboat pilot on the Mississippi River. In those days, steamboat crew members called "leadsmen" would measure the depth of the water with an instrument divided into segments. One of these segments, the "twain," measured a depth of 2 fathoms, or 12 feet. Thus the leadsman would call out "mark twain" to indicate that the river water was a safe depth of two fathoms.

The following selection is taken from Life on the Mississippi, *Twain's semiautobiographical tale of a young man's experiences aboard a Mississippi steamboat. In the excerpt the narrator has convinced the pilot of the* Paul Jones, *Mr. Bixby, to allow him to travel with the steamboat so that he can better learn the river. As you read the selection, pay special attention to the event that occurs near Hat Island.*

When I returned to the pilothouse St. Louis was gone and I was lost. Here was a piece of river which was all down in my book but I could make neither head nor tail of it: you understand, it was turned around. I had seen it when coming upstream but I had never faced about to see how it looked when it was behind me. My heart broke again, for it was plain that I had got to learn this troublesome river *both ways.*

The pilothouse was full of pilots, going down to "look at the river." What is called the "upper river" (the two hundred miles between St. Louis and Cairo, where the Ohio comes in) was low, and the Mississippi changes its channel so constantly that the pilots used to always find it necessary to run down to Cairo to take a fresh look when their boats were to lie in port a week, that is, when the water was at a low stage. A deal of this "looking at the river" was done by poor fellows who seldom had a berth [job] and whose only hope of getting one lay in their being always freshly posted and therefore ready to drop into the shoes of some reputable pilot for a single trip, on account of such pilot's sudden illness or some other necessity. And a good many of them constantly ran up and down inspecting the river, not because they ever really hoped to get a berth but because (they being guests of the boat) it was cheaper to "look at the river" than stay ashore and pay board. In time these fellows grew dainty in their tastes and only infested boats that had an established reputation for setting good tables. All visiting pilots were useful, for they were always ready and willing, winter or summer, night or day, to go out in the yawl [small boat] and help buoy the channel or assist the boat's pilots in any way they could. They were likewise welcomed because all pilots are tireless talkers when gathered together, and as they talk only about the river they are always understood and are always interesting. Your true pilot cares nothing about anything on earth but the river, and his pride in his occupation surpasses the pride of kings.

. . . all pilots are tireless talkers when gathered together . . .

We had a fine company of these river inspectors along this trip. There were eight or ten, and there was abundance [plenty] of room for them in our great pilothouse. Two or three of them wore polished silk hats, elaborate shirt-fronts, diamond breastpins, kid gloves, and patent-leather boots. They were

choice in their English, and bore themselves with
a dignity proper to men of solid means and prodigious
[extraordinary] reputation as pilots. The others were
more or less loosely clad, and wore upon their heads
tall felt cones that were suggestive of the days of
the Commonwealth [English government under Oli-
ver and Richard Cromwell: 1649–1660].

I was a cipher [an unimportant person] in this
august [grand] company and felt subdued, not to
say torpid [sluggish]. I was not even of sufficient
consequence to assist at the wheel when it was necessary to put the tiller hard down in a hurry; the
guest that stood nearest did that when occasion required—and this was pretty much all the time, because of the crookedness of the channel and the
scant water. I stood in a corner, and the talk I listened
to took the hope all out of me. One visitor said to
another:

"Jim, how did you run Plum Point, coming up?"

"It was in the night there, and I ran it the way
one of the boys on the *Diana* told me; started out
about fifty yards above the woodpile on the false
point and held on the cabin under Plum Point till
I raised the reef—quarter less twain [12 feet]—then
straightened up for the middle bar till I got well
abreast the old one-limbed cottonwood in the bend,
then got my stern on the cottonwood and head
on the low place above the point, and came through
abooming—nine and a half."

"Pretty square crossing, ain't it?"

"Yes, but the upper bar's working down fast."

Another pilot spoke up and said:

"I had better water than that and ran it lower
down; started out from the false point—mark twain
—raised the second reef abreast the big snag in
the bend and had quarter less twain."

One of the gorgeous ones remarked:

"I don't want to find fault with your leadsmen
but that's a good deal of water for Plum Point, it
seems to me."

There was an approving nod all around as this quiet snub dropped on the boaster and "settled" him. And so they went on talk-talk-talking. Meantime, the thing that was running in my mind was, "Now, if my ears hear aright, I have not only to get the names of all the towns and islands and bends, and so on by heart, but I must even get up a warm personal acquaintanceship with every old snag and one-limbed cottonwood and obscure woodpile that ornaments the banks of this river for twelve hundred miles; and more than that, I must actually know where these things are in the dark, unless these guests are gifted with eyes that can pierce through two miles of solid blackness. I wish the piloting business was in Jericho and I had never thought of it."

At dusk Mr. Bixby tapped the big bell three times (the signal to land) and the captain emerged from his drawing room in the forward end of the "texas," [officers' quarters] and looked up inquiringly. Mr. Bixby said:

"We will lay up here all night, captain."

"Very well, sir."

That was all. The boat came to shore and was tied up for the night. It seemed to me a fine thing that the pilot could do as he pleased, without asking so grand a captain's permission. I took my supper and went immediately to bed, discouraged by my day's observations and experiences. My late voyage's notebooking was but a confusion of meaningless names. It had tangled me all up in a knot every time I had looked at it in the daytime. I now hoped for respite [relief] in sleep, but no, it reveled all through my head till sunrise again, a frantic and tireless nightmare.

Next morning I felt pretty rusty and low-spirited. We went booming along, taking a good many chances, for we were anxious to "get out of the river" (as getting out to Cairo was called) before night should overtake us. But Mr. Bixby's partner, the other pilot, presently grounded the boat and

> . . . I must even get up a warm personal acquaintance-ship with every old snag and one-limbed cottonwood and obscure woodpile that ornaments the banks of this river for twelve hundred miles . . .

we lost so much time getting her off that it was plain the darkness would overtake us a good long way above the mouth. This was a great misfortune, especially to certain of our visiting pilots, whose boats would have to wait for their return, no matter how long that might be. It sobered the pilothouse talk a good deal. Coming upstream, pilots did not mind low water or any kind of darkness; nothing stopped them but fog. But downstream work was different; a boat was too nearly helpless with a stiff current pushing behind her, so it was not customary to run downstream at night in low water.

The pilot house of a typical river steamer provided passengers and crew with a clear view of river traffic.

There seemed to be one small hope, however: if we could get through the intricate and dangerous Hat Island crossing before night, we could venture the rest, for we would have plainer sailing and better water. But it would be insanity to attempt Hat Island at night. So there was a deal of looking at watches all the rest of the day and a constant ciphering [calculating] upon the speed we were making; Hat Island was the eternal subject; sometimes hope was high and sometimes we were delayed in a bad crossing and down it went again. For hours all hands lay under the burden of this suppressed excitement; it was even communicated to me and I got to feeling so solicitous [low] about Hat Island, and under such an awful pressure of responsibility, that I wished I might have five minutes on shore to draw a good, full, relieving breath and start over again. We were standing no regular watches. Each of our pilots ran such portions of the river as he had run when coming upstream, because of his greater familiarity with it, but both remained in the pilothouse constantly.

An hour before sunset Mr. Bixby took the wheel and Mr. W—— stepped aside. For the next thirty minutes every man held his watch in his hand and was restless, silent, and uneasy. At last somebody said, with, a doomful sigh:

"Well, yonder's Hat Island—and we can't make it."

All the watches closed with a snap, everybody sighed and muttered something about its being "too bad, too bad—ah, if we could *only* have got here half an hour sooner!" and the place was thick with the atmosphere of disappointment. Some started to go out but loitered, hearing no bell tap to land. The sun dipped behind the horizon, the boat went on. Inquiring looks passed from one guest to another, and one who had his hand on the doorknob and had turned it, waited, then presently took away his hand and let the knob turn back again. We bore steadily down the bend. More looks were exchanged

. . . **The dead silence and sense of waiting became oppressive.**

and nods of surprised admiration—but no words. Insensibly the men drew together behind Mr. Bixby, as the sky darkened and one or two dim stars came out. The dead silence and sense of waiting became oppressive. Mr. Bixby pulled the cord and two deep, mellow notes from the big bell floated off on the night. Then a pause, and one more note was struck. The watchman's voice followed from the hurricane deck:

"Labboard [larboard—left side of ship] lead, there! Stabboard [starboard—right side of ship] lead!"

The cries of the leadsmen began to rise out of the distance and were gruffly repeated by the word-passers on the hurricane deck.

"M-a-r-k three! M-a-r-k three! Quarter-less-three! Half twain! Quarter twain! M-a-r-k twain! Quarter-less—"

Mr. Bixby pulled two bell ropes and was answered by faint jinglings far below in the engine room, and our speed slackened. The steam began to whistle through the gauge cocks. The cries of the leadsmen went on—and it is a weird sound, always, in the night. Every pilot in the lot was watching now, with fixed eyes, and talking under his breath. Nobody was calm and easy but Mr. Bixby. He would put his wheel down and stand on a spoke, and as the steamer swung into her (to me) utterly invisible marks—for we seemed to be in the midst of a wide and gloomy sea—he would meet and fasten her there. Out of the murmur of half-audible talk one caught a coherent [clear] sentence now and then—such as:

"There; she's over the first reef all right!"

After a pause, another subdued voice:

"Her stern's coming down just *exactly* right, by *George!* Now she's in the marks; over she goes!"

Somebody else muttered:

"Oh, it was done beautiful—*beautiful!*"

Now the engines were stopped altogether and we drifted with the current. Not that I could see the boat drift, for I could not, the stars being all gone by this time. This drifting was the dismalest work; it held one's heart still.

Presently I discovered a blacker gloom than that which surrounded us. It was the head of the island. We were closing right down upon it. We entered its deeper shadow, and so imminent [immediate] seemed the peril that I was likely to suffocate, and I had the strongest impulse to do something, anything, to save the vessel. But still Mr. Bixby stood by his wheel, silent, intent as a cat, and all the pilots stood shoulder to shoulder at his back.

"She'll not make it!" somebody whispered.

The water grew shoaler [shallower] and shoaler by the leadsman's cries, till it was down to:

"Eight-and-a-half! E-i-g-h-t feet! E-i-g-h-t feet! Seven-and—"

Mr. Bixby said warningly through his speaking tube to the engineer:

"Stand by, now!"

"Aye, aye, sir!"

"Seven-and-a-half! Seven feet! Six-and—"

We touched bottom! Instantly Mr. Bixby set a lot of bells ringing, shouted through the tube, "Now, let her have it—every ounce you've got!" then to his partner, "Put her hard down! snatch her! snatch her!" The boat rasped and ground her way through the sand, hung upon the apex [tip] of disaster a single tremendous instant, and then over she went! And such a shout as went up at Mr. Bixby's back never loosened the roof of a pilothouse before!

There was no more trouble after that. Mr. Bixby was a hero that night, and it was some little time, too, before his exploit ceased to be talked about by river men.

Fully to realize the marvelous precision required in laying the great steamer in her marks in that murky waste of water, one should know that not only must she pick her intricate way through snags and blind reefs, and then shave the head of the island so closely as to brush the overhanging foliage [vegetation] with her stern, but at one place she must pass almost within arm's reach of a sunken and invisible wreck that would snatch the hull timbers from under her if she should strike it—and destroy a quarter of a million dollars' worth of steamboat and cargo in five minutes, and maybe a hundred and fifty human lives into the bargain.

The last remark I heard that night was a compliment to Mr. Bixby, uttered in soliloquy and with unction [to himself with emotion] by one of our guests. He said:

"By the Shadow of Death, but he's a lightning pilot!"

REVIEWING THE READING

1. What two reasons are given by the narrator for the fact that pilots often went to "look at the river"?

2. What did Mr. Bixby do at Hat Island? Why did someone call him a "lightning pilot"?

3. **Using Your Historical Imagination.** What details does Twain use in the story to create an atmosphere of suspense?

Tocqueville Describes American Attitudes About Work (1840)

55

From *Democracy in America* by Alexis de Tocqueville.

In 1831 the French government sent young Alexis de Tocqueville to the United States to study the American prison system. While in America Tocqueville found that his interest was captured by far more than just the prisons. He was especially impressed by the American spirit of democracy, with its twin promises of equality and freedom. Tocqueville noted that one of the ways in which the Americans demonstrated this democratic spirit was in their attitudes about work. In the following excerpts from his book Democracy in America, *Tocqueville discusses his observations on this topic. As you read the selection, note the way in which the Americans and the Europeans differ in their attitudes toward work.*

Amongst a democratic people, where there is no hereditary wealth, every man works to earn a living, or has worked, or is born of parents who have worked. The notion of labour is therefore presented to the mind on every side as the necessary, natural, and honest condition of human existence. Not only is labour not dishonourable amongst such a people, but it is held in honour: the prejudice is not against it, but in its favour. In the United States a wealthy man thinks that he owes it to public opinion to devote his leisure to some kind of industrial or commercial pursuit, or to public business. He would think himself in bad repute if he employed his life solely in living. It is for the purpose of escaping this obligation to work, that so many rich Americans come to Europe, where they find some scattered remains of aristocratic society, amongst which idleness is still held in honour.

Equality of conditions not only ennobles the notion of labour in men's estimation, but it raises the notion of labour as a source of profit. . . .

No profession exists in which men do not work for money; and the remuneration [pay] which is common to them all gives them all an air of resemblance. This serves to explain the opinions which the Americans entertain with respect to different callings. In America no one is degraded because he works, for everyone about him works also; nor is anyone humiliated by the notion of receiving pay, for the President of the United States also works for pay. He is paid for commanding, other men for obeying orders. In the United States professions are more or less laborious, more or less profitable; but they are never either high or low: every honest calling is honourable. . . .

The United States of America have only been emancipated for half a century from the state of colonial dependence in which they stood to Great Britain: the number of large fortunes there is small, and capital is still scarce. Yet no people in the world has made such rapid progress in trade and manufactures as the Americans: they constitute at the present day the second maritime nation in the world; and although their manufactures have to struggle with almost insurmountable natural impediments [obstacles], they are not prevented from making great and daily advances. In the United States the greatest undertakings and speculations are executed without difficulty, because the whole population is engaged in productive industry, and because the poorest as well as the most opulent [wealthy] members of the commonwealth are ready to combine their efforts for these purposes. The consequence is, that a stranger is constantly amazed by the immense public works executed by a nation which contains, so to speak, no rich men. The Americans arrived but as yesterday on the territory which they inhabit, and they have already changed the whole order of nature for their own advantage. They have joined the Hudson [River] to the Mississippi, and made the Atlantic Ocean communicate with the Gulf of Mexico, across a continent of more than five hundred leagues [about 2,000 miles] in extent which separates the two seas. The longest railroads which have been constructed up to the present times are in America. But what most astonishes me in the United States, is not so much the marvellous grandeur of some undertakings, as the innumerable multitude of small ones. Almost all the farmers of the United States combine some trade with agriculture; most of them make agriculture itself a trade. It seldom happens that an American farmer settles for good upon the land which he occupies: especially in the districts of the far West he brings land into tillage in order to sell it again, and not to farm it: he builds a farmhouse on the speculation that, as the state of the country will soon be changed by the increase of population, a good price will be gotten for it. Every year a swarm of the inhabitants of the North arrive in the Southern States, and settle in the parts where the cotton-plant and the sugar-cane grow. These men cultivate the soil in order to make it produce in a few years enough to enrich them; and they already look forward to

Alexis de Tocqueville was a French statesman who observed American democracy at work during a visit to the United States and wrote favorably about it when he returned home.

the time when they may return home to enjoy the competency [money] thus acquired. Thus the Americans carry their business-like qualities into agriculture; and their trading passions are displayed in that as in their other pursuits.

The Americans make immense progress in productive industry, because they all devote themselves to it at once; and for this same reason they are exposed to very unexpected and formidable embarrassments. As they are all engaged in commerce, their commercial affairs are affected by such various and complex causes that it is impossible to foresee what difficulties may arise. As they are all more or less engaged in productive industry, at the least shock given to business [such as a recession] all private fortunes are put in jeopardy at the same time, and the State is shaken. I believe that the return of these commercial panics is an endemic [native] disease of the democratic nations of our age. It may be rendered less dangerous, but it cannot be cured; because it does not originate in accidental circumstances, but in the temperament of these nations.

REVIEWING THE READING

1. According to Tocqueville, how do wealthy Americans view work? How does this view differ from the view of wealthy Europeans?

2. Give two examples from the selection that illustrate Tocqueville's observation that the Americans had changed the order of nature for their own advantage.

3. **Using Your Historical Imagination.** What do you think Tocqueville meant by his statement that commercial panics originate "in the temperament" of democratic nations?

A Native American Trickster Tale (1840s)

56

From "The Upper World," in *Nine Tales of Coyote* by Fran Martin.

Similar to tall tales, Native American trickster tales focus on the qualities that a society values, such as creativity, intelligence, and shrewdness. In trickster tales, however, the heros are animals. These animals usually use their ingenuity to solve problems or to get out of scrapes. The following selection is an excerpt from a trickster tale told by the Nez Perce Indians of Idaho and eastern Oregon and Washington. As you read the selection, note how Coyote's trick backfires on him.

O f all the creatures the old men speak of, the cleverest was Coyote. He was a small animal, yellowish-gray, like a bright-eyed little dog with a brush for a tail. But for all his small size, he was a medicine man, which means that he knew and practiced the arts of magic. Powerful and shrewd as he was, however, he could never resist a joke. So he was known far and wide as a rascal and a trickster, but not until his visit to the Upper World did he get the respect he deserved. This is how it happened:

One day as Coyote was loping along about his business, he heard the noise of a big powwow in the valley. Being a sociable creature, he had to go and see what the discussion was about. He found all the animals at the foot of the tallest pine tree, arguing about which of their number was the greatest medicine man.

"Poor idiots!" Coyote muttered. "They've forgotten me!"

But he was smart enough to say it to himself.

"I am the most powerful!" one of them would shout.

"You? No, I am! I am!" And they began to squabble. They roared, cawed, yowled, whistled, bellowed, bawled, and screeched, until they fell on their sides, panting, with their tongues lolling out, and the Thunder Bird woke on the mountain and stirred his scales. Then Coyote opened his mouth and spoke for the first time.

"We must set ourselves a test," he suggested. "Who is brave enough to climb the tallest pine to the Eagle's nest?"

The tallest pine was so high that its top was lost among the clouds, but all the animals wanted to have a try. Red Squirrel scooted easily up the long straight trunk, but he was so scatterbrained he forgot what he was doing, and ran chattering down the other side. Grizzly Bear had to give up when the tree began to sway beneath his weight.

After a while came the turn of little Black Bear. Up, up he went; but just as he was about to reach his goal, Coyote winked at the Eagle's nest and it shot up fifty feet higher. Black Bear was astonished at that, but he took a long breath and bravely went on climbing. When his head was almost on a level with the nest, Coyote slyly winked again, and up it shot another fifty feet. Then for good measure he winked again, several times in a row. By this time Black Bear was so confused that it was all he could do to scramble back to safety. Only Coyote was left to try.

Using his strongest medicine-magic, he charmed himself into his man form. He cautioned the others not to watch him climb, for if they did they would go against his medicine, and he would never be able to come back down the tree.

Coyote grasped the dry, scaly trunk with his man-arms, and set his man-moccasins on whatever small bumps and bolls he could find to support them. At first he climbed quickly, but before long he felt

Chief Joseph was a leader of the Nez Perce Indians.

the medicine-magic begin to drain away. When he came to the first big branch of the tree, he threw one leg across it and braced himself, panting for breath. Cool air from the snowfields washed across his face, and the drops of sweat dried from his eyelashes. When his sight was cleared, he saw the meadow lying small and green below him. And there were all the animals, in a ring around the tree, with their mouths wide open and their heads tipped back, watching him climb in spite of all his warnings. So that was why he was losing his magic power.

"Look down! Look down! Don't watch me!" he cried, and the foolish animals remembered and hung their heads.

Again the medicine-magic made it easy for Coyote, and up, up he went, into the thin clear air among the snow peaks. But once more he felt the strength draining fast out of his arms and legs. Bitterly he regretted those extra times he had winked at the Eagle's nest. He looked down, and there! They were watching him again.

"Look down, look down!" called Coyote in despair.

But the medicine-magic had left him for good . . .

But the medicine-magic had left him for good, and he knew he could never get back to earth again by way of the pine tree. There was nothing left to do but keep on climbing. . . . Soon the towering peaks looked as tiny as ant-heaps, and at last through drifting clouds he caught a dizzy glimpse of the whole round world at once, with the four outer worlds that lie at the points of the compass. His brain reeled at the sight and he thought he must fall, but just at that moment he came to a hole in the sky. With trembling hands he pulled himself through, and fell headlong on the grass. . . .

Then he walked across the blowing fields toward a little gray tepee in the distance. Outside sat two gray-bearded spiders, spinning their silvery thread. Never had Coyote seen two creatures so old and skinny and gray. . . .

"Greetings, Ancients," he said, bowing. "What is the name of your country?"

One of the spiders answered, in a cracked old voice, "This is Ah-cum-kinny-coo. The Upper World."

"Then you must be my grandfathers!" cried Coyote. "My grandfathers are said to live in the Upper World!"

He began to dance and spin about for joy, but the first of the spiders stopped him.

"Never," he croaked.

And the other said, "Our grandson is Coyote."

And the first said, "Yes, Coyote; and he lives on earth."

"Watch!" said Coyote gleefully, and as they watched he charmed himself, and changed back to his animal form.

Then the two ancients rose from their spinning, and greeted Coyote as their grandson. . . . From far below they heard a sorrowful wailing. It was the animals lamenting [mourning] Coyote, their mightiest medicine man.

"I would go back if I could," said Coyote, "but they watched me climb and drained away my magic."

"That's soon mended," said the most ancient of the spiders. He gave Coyote one end of the silver thread and told him to let himself down through the hole in the sky. . . . Fast as he shot down, the silver thread unreeled above him, slowing his fall, and swung him slow and slower, like a giant swing, until he landed soft as a feather among his friends. One whole long year they had passed there, bewailing their loss, for a day in the Upper World is a year in the land below. They were full of joy when Coyote appeared, and ready to listen to his words.

"Soon the human race is coming," Coyote told them. "But never again will anyone go to the Upper World and return."

Then Coyote bound golden tobacco leaves with the end of the silver thread, and quickly the spiders pulled it up through the sky and closed the hole behind it.

REVIEWING THE READING

1. What trick did Coyote play on the other animals? How did Coyote's trick backfire on him?

2. Who does Coyote meet in the Upper World? How does he get back to the earth?

3. **Using Your Historical Imagination.** It was not until Coyote visited the Upper World that he earned the respect of the other animals. What aspects of Coyote's personality and actions do you think earned him this respect?

From *The Slave Narratives of Texas*, edited by Ronnie C. Tyler and Lawrence R. Murphy.

57 | Six Texas Slave Narratives (1840–1859)

Oral history is a valuable information-gathering tool used by historians to add to our store of knowledge about particular events or particular time periods. Collecting oral histories involves interviewing people who experienced the event or lived through the time period and recording their oral responses. Oral history has been particularly valuable in adding to our knowledge about the institution of slavery and the conditions under which the slaves lived. The following selection contains six oral histories collected from people who lived as slaves in Texas. As you read the selection, note the often brutal conditions under which some of the former slaves lived.

Wes Brady

Some white folks might want to put me back in slavery if I told you how we were used in slavery time, but you asked me for the truth. The overseer straddled his big horse at three o'clock in the morning, rousting the hands off to the field. He got them all lined up, and then came back to the house for breakfast. The rows were a mile long, and no matter how much grass was in them, if you left one sprig on your row, they beat you nearly to death. Lots of times they weighed cotton by candlelight. All the hands took dinner to the field in buckets, and the overseer gave them fifteen minutes to get dinner. He'd start cuffing some of them over the head when it was time to stop eating and go back to work. He'd go to the house and eat his dinner, and then he'd come back and look in all the buckets, and if a piece of anything that was there when he left

was eaten, he'd say you were losing time and had
to be whipped. . . .

The little chaps would pick up egg shells and
play with them, and if the overseer saw them he'd
say they were stealing eggs and give them a beating.
I saw long lines of slaves chained together driven
by a white man on a horse down the Jefferson road.

The first work I did was dropping corn, and
then I worked in the cow pen and was a sheep
herder. All us house chaps had to shell a half bushel
of corn every night to feed the sheep. Many times
I have walked through the quarters when I was a
little chap crying for my mother. We mostly only
saw her on Sunday. Us children were in bed when
the folks went to the field and came back. I remember
waking up at night lots of times and seeing her
make a little mush on the coals in the fireplace,
but she always made sure that overseer was asleep
before she did that.

Mary Kincheon Edwards

We picked about 100 pounds of cotton in one basket.
I didn't mind picking cotton, because I never did
have a backache. I picked two and three hundred
pounds a day, and one day I picked 400. Sometimes
the prize was given by massa to the slave who picked
the most. The prize was a big cake or some clothes.
Picking cotton was not so bad, because we were
used to it and had a fine time of it. I got a dress
one day and a pair of shoes another day for picking
most. I was so fast I took two rows at a time.

The women brought oil cloths to the field, so
they could make a shady place for the children to
sleep, but those who were big enough had to pick.
Sometimes they sang:

O–ho, I's going home,
And cuss the old overseer.

We had an ash hopper and used drip lye for
making barrels of soap and hominy. The way we

Cotton plantations in the American South depended on slave labor to harvest the cotton crop.

tested the lye was to drop an egg in it, and if the egg floated the lye was ready to put in the grease for making the soap. We threw greasy bones in the lye, and that made the best soap. The lye ate the bones.

Sarah Ashley

I used to have to pick cotton, and sometimes I picked 300 pounds and toted it a mile to the cotton house. Some picked 300 to 800 pounds of cotton and had

to tote the bag a whole mile to the gin. If they
didn't get the work done, they got whipped till they
had blisters on them. Then if they didn't do it, the
man on a horse went down the rows and whipped
them with a paddle made with holes in it and burst
the blisters. I never got whipped, because I always
got my 300 pounds. We had to go early to do
that, when the horn goes early, before daylight.
We had to take the victuals [food] in the bucket
to the house.

Preely Coleman

I grew big enough to hoe and then to plow. We
had to be ready for the field by daylight and the
conch was blown, and massa called out, "All hands
ready for the field." At 11:30 he blew the conch,
which was the mussel shell, you know, again, and
we ate dinner, and at 12:30 we had to be back at
work. But massa wouldn't allow no kind of work
on Sunday.

Massa Tom made us wear shoes, because there
were so many snags and stumps our feet got sore,
and they were red russet shoes. I'll never forget them;
they were so stiff at first we could hardly stand
'em.

Phoebe Henderson

After they brought us to Texas in 1859, I worked
in the field many a day, plowing and hoeing, but
the children didn't do much except carry water.
When they got tired, they'd say they were sick,
and the overseer let them lie down in the shade.
He was a good and kindly man and when we did
wrong, and we told him he forgave us, and he didn't
whip the boys because he was afraid they'd run away.

I worked in the house, too. I spun seven curts
[sic] a day, and every night we ran two looms, making
large curts for plow lines. We made all our clothes.
We didn't wear shoes in Georgia, but in this place
the land was rough and strong, so we couldn't go

barefooted. A black man that worked in the shop measured our feet and made us two pairs a year.

Sarah Ford

The overseer was Uncle Big Jake, who was black like the rest of us, but he was so mean I suspect the devil made him overseer down below a long time ago. That was the bad part of Massa Charles, because he let Uncle Jake whip the slaves so much that some like my papa who had spirit was all the time running away. And even if your stomach is full and you have plenty of clothes, that bullwhip on your bare hide made you forget the good part, and that's the truth.

Uncle Big Jake sure worked the slaves from early morning till night. When you are in the field, you'd better not lag none. When it's falling weather the hands were put to work fixing this and that. The women who had little children didn't have to work so hard. They worked around the sugar house and come 11 o'clock they quit and cared for the babies till 1 o'clock and then worked till 3 o'clock and quit.

REVIEWING THE READING

1. According to Wes Brady, why were the slave children beaten for playing with egg shells? Who beat these children?

2. According to Sarah Ford, why did slaves like her father try to run away? What was her impression of the overseer?

3. **Using Your Historical Imagination.** Why do you think the use of oral history is of particular value in teaching us about the conditions under which slaves lived?

Charles Dickens Tells of the Delights of Travel in America (1842)

58

From *American Notes for General Circulation* by Charles Dickens.

English novelist Charles Dickens first visited America in 1842, and—like many British travelers before and after him—published a book about his experiences. Dickens was a humorist and his American Notes *doubtless contains some exaggerations, but he does manage to convey a sense of the hardships of travel in early nineteenth-century America. On this particular journey from Washington to Richmond, Dickens set out by steamboat, then transferred to horse coach. Coach travel was common in Europe at this time; note in the excerpt how Dickens compares American coach travel with European.*

We were to proceed in the first instance by steamboat: and as it is usual to sleep on board, in consequence of the starting-hour being four o'clock in the morning, we went down to where she lay, at that very uncomfortable time for such expeditions when slippers are most valuable, and a familiar bed, in the perspective of an hour or two, looks uncommonly pleasant. . . .

I go on board . . . open the door of the gentlemen's cabin; and walk in. Somehow or other—from its being so quiet I suppose—I have taken it into my head that there is nobody there. To my horror and amazement it is full of sleepers in every stage, shape, attitude, and variety of slumber: in the berths, on the chairs, on the floors, on the tables, and particularly round the stove, my detested enemy. I take another step forward, and slip upon the shining face of a black steward, who lies rolled in a blanket on the floor. He jumps up, grins, half in pain and half in hospitality; whispers my own name in my ear; and groping among the sleepers, leads me to my berth. Standing beside it, I count these slumbering passengers, and get past forty. There is no use in going further, so I begin to undress. As the chairs are all occupied, and there is nothing else to put my clothes on, I deposit them upon the ground: not without soiling my hands, for it is in the same condition as the carpets in the Capitol, and from the same cause. Having but partially undressed, I clamber on my shelf, and hold the curtain open for a few minutes while I look round on all my fellow travellers again. That done, I let it fall on them, and on the world: turn round: and go to sleep.

I wake, of course, when we get under weigh [way], for there is good deal of noise. The day is then just breaking. Everybody wakes at the same time. Some are self-possessed directly, and some are much perplexed to make out where they are until they have rubbed their eyes, and leaning on one elbow, looked about them. Some yawn, some groan, nearly all spit, and a few get up. I am among the risers: for it is easy to feel, without going into the fresh air, that the atmosphere of the cabin, is vile in the last degree. I huddle on my clothes, go down into the fore-cabin, get shaved by the barber, and wash myself. The washing and dressing apparatus for the passengers generally, consists of two jack towels, three small wooden basins, a keg of water and a ladle to serve it out with, six square inches of looking-glass, two ditto ditto of yellow soap, a comb and brush for the head, and nothing for the teeth. Everybody uses the comb and brush, except myself. Everybody stares to see me using my own; and two or three gentlemen are strongly disposed to banter me on my prejudices, but don't. When I have made my toilet [finished grooming], I go upon the hurricane-deck [top deck], and set in for two hours of hard walking up and down. The sun is rising brilliantly; we are passing Mount Vernon, where Washington lies buried; the river is wide and rapid; and its banks are beautiful. All the glory and splendour of the day are coming on, and growing brighter every minute.

At eight o'clock, we breakfast in the cabin where I passed the night, but the windows and doors are all thrown open, and now it is fresh enough. There is no hurry or greediness apparent in the despatch of the meal. It is longer than a travelling breakfast with us [the English]; more orderly; and more polite.

Soon after nine o'clock we come to Potomac Creek, where we are to land: and then comes the oddest part of the journey. Seven stagecoaches are preparing to carry us on. . . . The coaches are something like the French coaches, but not nearly so good. In lieu of springs, they are hung on bands of the strongest leather. There is very little choice or difference between them; and they may be likened to the car portion of the swings at an English fair, roofed, put upon axle-trees and wheels, and curtained with painted canvas. They are covered with mud from the roof to the wheel-tire, and have never been cleaned since they were first built.

The tickets we have received on board the steamboat are marked No. I, so we belong to coach No. I. . . . There is only one outside passenger, and he sits upon the box. As I am that one, I climb up; and while they are strapping the luggage on the roof, and heaping it into a kind of tray behind, have a good opportunity of looking at the driver.

He is a negro—very black indeed. . . . But somebody in authority cries "Go ahead!" as I am making these observations. The mail [coach] takes the lead in a four-horse wagon, and all the coaches follow in procession: headed by No. I.

By the way, whenever an Englishman would cry "All right!" an American cries "Go ahead!" which

During his visit to America in 1842, English novelist Charles Dickens found traveling conditions to be somewhat different from those in his own country.

is somewhat expressive of the national character of the two countries.

The first half mile of the road is over bridges made of loose planks laid across two parallel poles, which tilt up as the wheels roll over them; and IN the river. The river has a clayey bottom and is full of holes, so that half a horse is constantly disappearing unexpectedly, and can't be found again for some time.

But we get past even this, and come to the road itself, which is a series of alternate swamps and gravel-pits. A tremendous place is close before us, the black driver rolls his eyes, screws his mouth up very round, and looks straight between the two leaders, as if he were saying to himself, "we have done this often before, but *now* I think we shall have a crash." He takes a rein in each hand; jerks and pulls at both; and dances on the splashboard with both feet (keeping his seat, of course) like the late lamented Ducrow on two of his fiery coursers [horses]. We come to the spot, sink down in the mire nearly to the coach windows, tilt on one side at an angle of forty-five degrees, and stick there. The insides scream dismally; the coach stops; the horses flounder; all the other six coaches stop; and their four-and-twenty horses flounder likewise: but merely for company, and in sympathy with ours. Then the following circumstances occur.

BLACK DRIVER (to the horses). "Hi!"

Nothing happens. Insides scream again.

BLACK DRIVER (to the horses). "Ho!"

Horses plunge, and splash the black driver.

GENTLEMAN INSIDE (looking out). "Why, what on airth——"

Gentleman receives a variety of splashes and draws his head in again, without finishing his question or waiting for an answer.

BLACK DRIVER (still to the horses). "Jiddy! Jiddy!"

Horses pull violently, drag the coach out of the hole, and draw it up a bank; so steep, that the

. . . **We come to the spot, sink down in the mire nearly to the coach windows** . . .

black driver's legs fly up into the air, and he goes back among the luggage on the roof. But he immediately recovers himself and cries (still to the horses),

"Pill!"

No effect. On the contrary, the coach begins to roll back upon No. 2, which rolls back upon No. 3, which rolls back upon No. 4, and so on, until No. 7 is heard to curse and swear, nearly a quarter of a mile behind.

BLACK DRIVER (louder than before). "Pill!"

Horses make another struggle to get up the bank, and again the coach rolls backward.

BLACK DRIVER (louder than before). "Pe-e-e-ill!"

Horses make a desperate struggle.

BLACK DRIVER (recovering spirits). "Hi, Jiddy, Jiddy, Pill!"

Horses make another effort.

BLACK DRIVER (with great vigour). "Ally Loo! Hi. Jiddy, Jiddy. Pill. Ally Loo!"

Horses almost do it.

BLACK DRIVER (with his eyes starting out of his head). "Lee den. Lee, dere. Hi. Jiddy, Jiddy. Pill. Ally Loo. Lee-e-e-e-e!"

They run up the bank, and go down again on the other side at a fearful pace. It is impossible to stop them, and at the bottom there is a deep hollow, full of water. The coach rolls frightfully. The insides scream. The mud and water fly about us. The black driver dances like a madman. Suddenly we are all right by some extraordinary means, and stop to breathe.

A black friend of the black driver is sitting on a fence. The black driver recognises him by twirling his head round and round like a harlequin [clown], rolling his eyes, shrugging his shoulders, and grinning from ear to ear. He stops short, turns to me, and says:

"We shall get you through sa, like a fiddle, and hope a please you when we get you through sa. Old 'ooman at home sir:" chuckling very much.

"Outside gentleman sa, he often remember old 'oo-man at home sa," grinning again.

"Aye, aye, we'll take care of the old woman. Don't be afraid."

The black driver grins again, but there is another hole, and beyond that, another bank, close before us. So he stops short: cries (to the horses again) "Easy. Easy den. Ease. Steady. Hi. Jiddy. Pill. Ally. Loo," but never "Lee!" until we are reduced to the very last extremity, and are in the midst of difficulties, extrication [escape] from which appears to be all but impossible.

And so we do the ten miles or thereabouts in two hours and a half; breaking no bones, though bruising a great many; and in short getting through the distance, "like a fiddle."

This singular kind of coaching terminates at Fredericksburgh, whence there is a railway to Richmond.

REVIEWING THE READING

1. What was to Dickens the chief hardship of the steamboat?

2. How did Dickens compare American coach travel to that with which he was familiar in Europe?

3. **Using Your Historical Imagination.** What do you think the novelist may have meant by observing that "whenever an English-man would cry 'All right!' an American cries 'Go ahead!' which is somewhat expressive of the national character of the two countries."

Dorothea Dix Pleads for Reform of Insane Asylums (1843)

59

From *Memorial to the Legislature of Massachusetts* by Dorothea Dix.

Dorothea Dix was an early crusader against the inhumane treatment of the retarded and the insane in Massachusetts prisons. Dix did not content herself with criticism at a distance but visited many state prisons herself and collected hard information with which to shock the legislature into action. The selection below is taken from her Memorial to the Legislature of Massachusetts, *presented in 1843. As you read the excerpt, consider what reform Dix is suggesting to the legislature.*

About two years since leisure afforded opportunity and duty prompted me to visit several prisons and almshouses [homes for the poor] in the vicinity of this metropolis, I found, near Boston, in the jails and asylums for the poor, a numerous class brought into unsuitable connection with criminals and the general mass of paupers [people who rely on public money for help]. I refer to idiots and insane persons, dwelling in circumstances not only adverse [unfavorable] to their own physical and moral improvement, but productive of extreme disadvantages to all other persons brought into association with them. I applied myself diligently to trace the causes of these evils, and sought to supply remedies. As one obstacle was surmounted [overcome], fresh difficulties appeared. Every new investigation has given depth to the conviction that it is only by decided, prompt, and vigorous legislation the evils to which I refer, and which I shall proceed more fully to illustrate, can be remedied. I shall be obliged to speak with great plainness, and to reveal many things revolting to the taste,

Dorthea Dix's plea to the legislature for better treatment of mental patients was the beginning of reform in Massachusetts. She went on to work for the building of state hospitals for the mentally ill throughout the United States.

and from which my woman's nature shrinks with peculiar sensitiveness. But truth is the highest consideration. I tell *what I have seen*—painful and shocking as the details often are—that from them you may feel more deeply the imperative [important] obligation which lies upon you to prevent the possibility of a repetition or continuance of such outrages upon humanity. If I inflict pain upon you, and move you to horror, it is to acquaint you with sufferings which you have the power to alleviate [lessen], and make you hasten to the relief of the victims of legalized barbarity.

I come to present the strong claims of suffering humanity. I come to place before the Legislature of Massachusetts the condition of the miserable, the desolate, the outcast. I come as the advocate of the helpless, forgotten, insane, and idiotic men and women; of beings sunk to a condition from which the most unconcerned would start with real horror; of beings wretched in our prisons, and more wretched in our almshouses. And I cannot suppose it needful to employ earnest persuasion, or stubborn argument, in order to arrest and fix attention upon a subject only the more strongly pressing in its claims because it is revolting and disgusting in its details.

I must confine myself to few examples, but am ready to furnish other and more complete details, if required. If my pictures are displeasing, coarse, and severe, my subjects, it must be recollected, offer no tranquil, refined, or composing features. The condition of human beings, reduced to the extremest states of degradation and misery, cannot be exhibited in softened language, or adorn a polished page.

I proceed, gentlemen, briefly to call your attention to the present state of insane persons confined within this Commonwealth, in *cages, closets, cellars, stalls, pens! Chained, naked, beaten with rods, and lashed into obedience*. . . .

REVIEWING THE READING

1. What is Dix's basic criticism of the way insane and retarded persons are treated in Massachusetts?

2. What are "paupers"?

3. **Using Your Historical Imagination.** However discreetly, who does Dix blame for these abuses? What is likely to have been the response of the legislature?

60

From *Down the Santa Fe Trail and into Mexico: The Diary of Susan Shelby Magoffin, 1846–1847,* edited by Stella M. Drumm.

A Teenage Bride on the Santa Fe Trail (1846)

In the spring of 1846, 19-year-old Susan Shelby Magoffin became one of the first women to travel the Santa Fe Trail from Missouri to New Mexico. A recent bride, Magoffin accompanied her trader husband and his wagon train of goods on the long and dangerous trip across plains and deserts to Santa Fe. She kept a daily journal—lively and personal—of her experiences. It survived in manuscript, known only to a few historians, until it was published in 1926. As you read the following excerpts from her journal, consider Magoffin's impressions of the hardships faced on the Santa Fe Trail.

*C*amp No. 18 On the wide Prairie. Sunday June 28th, 1846. This is my third Sabbath on the Plains. And how does conscience tell me it has been spent? Oh, may my heavenly father grant me pardon for my wickedness! Did I not in the very beginning of it forget—yes, and how can I be pardoned for the great sin—that it was the Holy Sabbath, appointed by my heavenly father for a day of rest—and classed it so much with the days of the week, that I regularly took out my week's work, knitting. Oh, how could I ever have been so thoughtless, so unmindful of my duty and my eternal salvation!

Passed the whole day with little wood, and no water for the cattle, but some little about in puddles. Had some difficulty in crossing a swampy place, this evening; the teamsters [people driving the wagons] had to mow grass and put in it, before they could pass their teams.

Noon. No. 20. Little Arkansas River. June 30th, 1846.
Come my feeble pen, put on thy specks and assist
this full head to unburthen itself! Thou hast a longer
story than is usual to tell. How we left *Camp No.
19* yesterday (Monday) morning after a sleepless
night, our tent was pitched in the musquito region
and when will the God Somnus [sleep] make his
appearance in such quarters? It was slap, slap, all
the time, from one party of the combatants, while
the others came with a buz and a bite.

We traveled till 11 o'clock with the hope of
finding water for the weary cattle. The sun was excessively oppressive. Col. Owens' mule teams left us
entirely, but his oxen like ours were unable to stand
the heat. They were before us and stoped—we followed their example, as much from necessity as any
thing else. The oxen, some of them staggered under
their yokes, and when we turned out for want of
water—there was none within five miles of us that
we knew of—some of the most fatigued absolutely
crept under the wagons for shade, and did not move
till they were driven up in the evening. One poor
thing fell in the road and we almost gave him up
for lost. His driver though, rather a tender hearted
lad I presume, went with a bucket to a *mud hole*
and brought the *wet mud* which was a little cool,
and *plastered his body over with it.* He then got all the
water from the water kegs after the men had drank,
which was not more than two or three tin cups
full; he took this and opening the ox's mouth poured
it down his throat. He then made a covering over
him with ox yokes standing up and blankets spread
over. In the course of an hour or two the poor
thing could get up, and walk. But his great thirst
for water led him to searching the deep grass, and
when the wagons started at 5 o'clock, he could not
be found. Roman, the old Mexican who attended
the loose stock, hunted some time for him, but to
no purpose. Other sick ones needed his attention
and it was probable this one had gone back to last

> . . . We
> traveled till 11
> o'clock with the
> hope of finding
> water for the
> weary cattle.

night's camp ground, and as it was too far to send on an uncertainty and pressing times, we gave up the search.

It blew up a little cooler towards sunset and we travelled pretty well, to make water was our object; both man and beast were craving it. The former could occasionally find a little to quench his parched thirst, by searching ravines that were grown up with tall weeds, this tho' muddy, and as warm as a scorching sun beaming into it all day could make it, was a luxurious draught [drink]. Now, about dark, we came into the musquito regions, and I found to my great *horror* that I have been complaining all this time for nothing, yes absolutely for *nothing;* for some two or hundred or even thousands are nothing compared with what we now encountered. The carriage mules became so restless that they passed all the wagons and switching their tails from side to side, as fast as they could, and slaping their ears, required some strength of our Mexican driver to hold them in. He would jerk the reins and exclaim *"bola los animal[es] cómo estande bravos!"* [Ho, animals! how wild you are!] The moon was not very bright and we could not see far before us. Suddenly one of the mules sprang to one side, reared, and pitched till I really believed we should turn over. Magoffin discouvered something lying in the road, and springing from the carriage pulled me out. It was a dead ox lying immediately in our way, and it is no wonder the mule was frightened.

In my own hurry to get out I had entirely forgotten the musquitoes, and on returning to the carriage I found my feet covered with stings, and my dress full, where they had gotten on me in the grass. About 10 o'clock we came upon a dark ravine, over which *las caras* [*los carros*—the wagons] would probably experience some difficulty in passing, so we stoped to see them over. The mules became perfectly frantic, and nothing could make them stand. They were turned out to shift for themselves, and Magoffin

seeing no other alternative than to remain there all night, tied his head and neck up with pocket handkerchiefs and set about having the tent stretched. I drew my feet up under me, wraped my shawl over my head, till I almost smothered with heat, and listened to the din without. And such a noise as it was, I shall pray ever to be preserved. Millions upon millions were swarming around me, and their knocking against the carriage *reminded me of a hard rain.* It was equal to any of the plagues of Egypt [the torments sent by God to convince the Egyptians to release the Israelites]. I lay almost in a perfect stupor, the heat and stings made me perfectly sick, till Magoffin came to the carriage and told me to *run if I could,* with my shawl, bonnet and shoes on (and without opening my mouth, Jane said, for they would *choke* me) straight to the bed. When I got there they pushed me straight in under the musquito bar, which had been tied up in some kind of a fashion, and oh, dear, what a relief it was to breathe again. There I sat in my cage, like an imprisoned creature frightened half to death.

　　Magoffin now rolled himself up some how with all his cloths on, and lay down at my side, he dare not raise the bar to get in. I tried to sleep and

In the 1840s teenage bride Susan Magoffin traveled in a wagon train like this one heading west on the Santa Fe Trail.

. . . On awakening this morning I found my forehead, arms and feet covered with knots.

towards daylight succeeded. On awaking this morning I found my forehead, arms and feet covered with knots. They were not little red places as musquitos generally make, but they were knots, some of them quite as large as a pea. We knocked up [took down] the tent as quick as possible and without thinking of breakfast came off to this place, passing on our way our own wagons and those of Col. Owens encamped at Mud Creek.

On our arrival here the buffalo [robe] and pillow were spread out and I layed down to sleep and I can say it took no rocking to accomplish the end. The tent was stretched with the intention of remaining here all night. The crossing is quite difficult, the sun extremely warm and it was supposed the oxen could not go on. About 11 o'clock *mi alma* [literally "my heart," referring to her husband] came and raised me by my hand entirely up onto my feet without waking me. The whole scene had entirely changed. The sky was perfectly dark, wind blowing high, the atmosphere cool and pleasant and *no musquitoes*, with every appearance of a hard storm.

At 12 o'clock breakfast was ready, and after drinking a cup of tea I fell on the bed completely worn out. After two or three hours sound sleep I got up washed, combed my head, put on clean cloths—a luxury on the plains by the way—and sallied forth in the cool air somewhat refreshed. I brought out my writing implements and here I am.

. . . *July 4th 1846. Pawnee Fork. Saturday.* What a disasterous *celebration* I have today. It is certainly the greatest miracle that I have my head on my shoulders. I think I can never forget it if I live to be as old as my grandmother.

The wagons left Pawnee Rock some time before us.—For I was anxious to see this wonderful curiosity. We went up and while *mi alma* with his gun and pistols kept watch, for the wily Indian may always be apprehended here, it is a good lurking place and they are ever ready to fall upon any unfortunate trader behind his company—and it is necessary to be careful, so while *mi alma* watched on the rock above and Jane stood by to watch if any should come up on the front side of me, I cut my name, among the many hundreds inscribed on the rock and many of whom I knew. It was not done well, for fear of Indians made me tremble all over and I hurried it over in any way. This I remarked would be quite an adventure to celebrate the 4th! but woe betide I have yet another to relate.

The wagons being some distance ahead we rode on quite briskly to overtake them. In an hour's time we had driven some six miles, and at *Ash creek* we came up with them. No water in the creek and the crossing pretty good only a tolerably steep bank on the first side of it, all but two had passed over, and as these were not up we drove on ahead of them to cross first. The bank though a little steep was smooth and there could be no difficulty in riding down it.—However, we had made up our minds always to walk down such places in case of accident, and before we got to it *mi alma* hallowed "woe" as he always does when he wishes to stop, but as there was no motion made by the driver to that effect, he repeated it several times and with much vehemence [force]. We had now reached the very verge [edge] of the cliff and seeing it a good way and apparently less dangerous than jumping out as we were, he said "go on." The word was scarcely from his lips, ere we were whirled completely over with a perfect crash. One to see the wreck of that carriage now with the top and sides entirely broken to pieces, could never believe that people had come out of it alive. But strange, wonderful to say, we are almost entirely unhurt! I was considerably stunned at first and could not stand on my feet. *Mi alma* forgetting himself and entirely enlisted for my safety carried me in his arms to a shade tree, almost entirely without my knowledge, and rubing my face and hands with whiskey soon brought me entire to myself.—My back and side are a little hurt, but is very small compared with what it might have been. *Mi alma* has his left hip and arm on which he fell both bruised and strained, but not seriously. Dear creature 'twas for me he received this, for had he not caught me in his arms as we fell he could have saved himself entirely. And then I should perhaps have been killed or much crushed for the top fell over me, and it was only his hands that kept it off of me. It is better as it is, for we can sympathise more fully with each other.

It was a perfect mess that; of people, books, bottles—one of which broke, and on my head too I believe—guns, pistols, baskets, bags, boxes and the dear knows what else. I was insensible to it all except when something gave me a hard knock and brought me to myself. We now sought refuge in Jane's carriage for our own could only acknowledge its incapability.

REVIEWING THE READING

1. What hardships of the trail are described in this part of Susan Magoffin's account?

2. How would you describe Magoffin's attitude toward this dangerous and difficult journey?

3. **Using Your Historical Imagination.** As a young woman of the mid-nineteenth century, Susan Magoffin wrote of the hardships and dangers of life on the trail that she regarded as extraordinary—not part of ordinary existence. From a modern perspective, what other aspects of life on the trail, which she simply took for granted, would we probably regard as hardships?

Emily Dickinson Describes Mount Holyoke Seminary (1847)

61

From *A Hundred Years of Mount Holyoke College* by Arthur C. Cole.

Of all the changes taking place in the United States in the early to mid-nineteenth century, none was more dramatic than those taking place in the field of education. As new colleges sprang up across the country, the demand for equal education for women grew stronger. Among the fortunate young women of the time to be given an opportunity to attend college was 16-year-old Emily Dickinson, who would later be recognized as one of America's finest poets.

In 1847 Dickinson left her home in Amherst, Massachusetts, to attend the Mount Holyoke Female Seminary (now Mount Holyoke College), a women's school founded by Mary Lyon. Dickinson would remain there for just one year. The following selection is an excerpt from a letter she wrote just six weeks after arriving at the school. As you read try to determine why Dickinson left the seminary after only one year there.

Mt. Holyoke Seminary. Nov. 6, 1847

My Dear Abiah,

I am really at Mt. Holyoke Seminary and this is to be my home for a long year. Your affectionate letter was joyfully received and I wish that this might make you as happy as your's did me. It has been nearly six weeks since I left home and that is a longer time, than I was ever away from home before now. I was very homesick for a few days and it seemed to me I could not live here. But I am now contented and quite happy, if I can be happy when absent from my dear home and friends.

This is a drawing from a daguerreotype, an early kind of photography of Emily Dickinson. She once described herself as "small, like a wren" and was painfully shy. Still, she wrote over 1,000 "letters" to the world through intense poems of great insight.

You may laugh at the idea, that I cannot be happy when away from home, but you must remember that I have a very dear home and that this is my first trial in the way of absence for any length of time in my life.

As you desire it, I will give you a full account of myself since I first left the paternal roof. I came to S. Hadley six weeks ago next Thursday. I was much fatigued with the ride and had a severe cold besides, which prevented me from commencing my examinations until the next day, when I began. I finished them in three days and found them about what I had anticipated, though the old scholars say, they are more strict than they have ever been before. As you can easily imagine, I was much delighted to finish without failures and I came to the conclusion then, that I should not be at all homesick, but the reaction left me as homesick a girl as it is not usual to see. I am now quite contented and am very much occupied now in reviewing the Junior studies, as I wish to enter the middle class. The school is very large, and though quite a number have left, on account of finding the examinations more difficult than they anticipated, yet there are nearly 300 now. Perhaps you know that Miss Lyon is raising her standard of scholarship a good deal, on account of the number of applicants this year and on account of that she makes the examinations more severe than usual. You cannot imagine how trying they are, because if we cannot go through them all in a specified time, we are sent home. I cannot be too thankful that I got through as soon as I did and I am sure that I never would endure the suspense which I endured during those three days again for all the treasures of the world.

I room with my Cousin Emily, who is a Senior. She is an excellent room-mate and does all in her power to make me happy. You can imagine how pleasant a good room-mate is for you have been away to school so much. Everything is pleasant and happy here and I think I could be no happier at any other school away from home. Things seem much more like home than I anticipated and the teachers are all very kind and affectionate to us. They call on us frequently and urge us to return their calls and when we do, we always receive a cordial [warm] welcome from them.

I will tell you my order of time for the day, as you were so kind as to give me your's. At 6 o'clock, we all rise. We breakfast at 7. Our study hours begin at 8. At 9 we all meet in the Seminary Hall for devotions [religious exercises]. At 10 1/4 I recite a review of Ancient History in connection with which we read Goldsmith and Grimshaw. At 11 I recite a lesson in "Pope's Essay on Man" which is merely transposition. At 12 I practise Calisthenics [exercises] and at 12 1/4 read until dinner which is at 12 1/2. After dinner from 1 1/2 until 2 I sing in Seminary Hall. From 2 3/4 until 3 3/4 I practise upon the Piano. At 3 3/4 I go to Section, where we give in all our accounts for the day including

Although she attended college at Mount Holyoke Seminary for a year, Emily Dickinson lived most of her life at home. She wrote more than 1,700 poems, which were not found and published until after her death in 1886.

Absence—Tardiness—Communications—Breaking Silent Study hours—Receiving Company in our rooms and ten thousand other things which I will not take time or place to mention. At 4 1/2 we go into Seminary Hall and receive advice from Miss Lyon in the form of a lecture. We have supper at 6 and silent study hours from then until the retiring bell, which rings at 8 3/4 but the tardy bell does not ring until 9 3/4, so that we don't often obey the first warning to retire.

Unless we have a good and reasonable excuse for failure upon any of the items that I mentioned above, they are recorded and a *black mark* stands against our names. As you can easily imagine, we do not like very well to get "exceptions" as they are called scientifically here. My domestic work is not difficult and consists in carrying the knives from the 1st tier of tables at morning and noon, and at night washing and wiping the same quantity of knives. I am quite well and hope to be able to spend the year here free from sickness. You have probably heard many reports of the food here and if so I can tell you, that I have yet seen nothing corresponding to my ideas on that point, from what I have heard. Everything is wholesome and abundant and much nicer than I should imagine could be provided for almost 300 girls. We have also a great variety upon our tables and frequent changes. One thing is certain and that is, that Miss Lyon and all the teachers, seem to consult our comfort and happiness in everything they do and you know that is pleasant. When I left home I did not think I should find a companion or a dear friend in all the multitude. I expected to find rough and uncultivated manners, and to be sure I have found some of that stamp, but on the whole, there is an ease and grace and a desire to make one another happy, which delights and at the same time surprises me very much. I find no Abby or Abiah or Mary but I love many of the girls. Austin [Emily's brother] came to see me

One thing is certain and that is, that Miss Lyon and all the teachers, seem to consult our comfort and happiness in everything they do . . .

when I had been here about two weeks and brought Viny and Abby. I need not tell you how delighted I was to see them all nor how happy it made me to hear them say that "they were *so lonely.*" It is a sweet feeling to know that you are missed and that your memory is precious at home. . . .

Abiah, you must write me often and I shall write you as often as I have time. But you know I have many letters to write now I am away from home. Cousin Emily says "give my love to Abiah."

From your aff. EMILY, E. D.

REVIEWING THE READING

1. Why do you think Dickinson left the seminary after only one year?

2. There were some things Dickinson liked about the school and other things she did not. What did she like, and what did she dislike?

3. **Using Your Historical Imagination.** Considering the times, what kind of career do you think the Mount Holyoke Seminary expected its students to pursue? Do the classes Dickinson mentions reflect this?

From "Civil Disobedience" by Henry David Thoreau, in *The Portable Thoreau,* edited by Carl Bode.

62

Henry Thoreau Goes to Jail (1848)

America's war with Mexico from 1846 to 1847 was viewed by many Americans as simply a way of adding southern territory, which would eventually be opened to slavery. Among the antislavery protesters of the war was author/naturalist Henry David Thoreau of Massachusetts. In 1848 Thoreau chose to go to jail rather than pay a toll tax to the state government. In his famous essay "Civil Disobedience," Thoreau explains his reasons for choosing jail as one way of protesting the government's support of the war.

Thoreau's essay was first delivered as a lecture in 1847 in a public hall in Concord, Massachusetts, and was published a year later in Aesthetic Papers. *Later, famous civil rights leaders, such as Mohandas Gandhi of India and Martin Luther King, Jr., of the United States, would look to the words of Thoreau for inspiration. As you read the following excerpts from Thoreau's essay, try to determine what he believed to be the best way to fight civil wrongs.*

I heartily accept the motto, "That government is best which governs least"; and I should like to see it acted up to more rapidly and systematically. Carried out, it finally amounts to this, which also I believe, "That government is best which governs not at all"; and when men are prepared for it, that will be the kind of government which they will have. Government is at best but an expedient [means to an end]; but most governments are usually, and all governments are sometimes, inexpedient. The objections which have been brought against a standing army, and they are many and weighty, and deserve to prevail, may also at last be brought against a standing government. The standing army is only an arm of the standing government. The government itself, which is only the mode which the people have chosen to execute their will, is equally liable to be abused and perverted before the people can act through it. Witness the present Mexican war, the work of comparatively a few individuals using the standing government as their tool; for, in the outset, the people would not have consented to this measure.

This American government—what is it but a tradition, though a recent one, endeavoring to transmit itself unimpaired to posterity, but each instant losing some of its integrity? It has not the vitality and force of a single living man; for a single man can bend it to his will. . . .

Unjust laws exist: shall we be content to obey them, or shall we endeavor to amend them, and obey them until we have succeeded, or shall we transgress [break] them at once? Men generally, under such a government as this, think that they ought to wait until they have persuaded the majority to alter them. They think that, if they should resist, the remedy would be worse than the evil. But it is the fault of the government itself that the remedy *is* worse than the evil. *It* makes it worse. Why is it not more apt to anticipate and provide for reform? Why does it not cherish its wise minority? Why does it cry and resist before it is hurt? Why does it not encourage its citizens to be on the alert to point out its faults, and *do* better than it would have them? Why does it always crucify Christ, and excommunicate [cut off from the church] Copernicus and Luther, and pronounce Washington and Franklin rebels?

One would think, that a deliberate and practical denial of its authority was the only offence never contemplated by government; else, why has it not assigned its definite, its suitable and proportionate,

Henry David Thoreau went to jail to demonstrate his belief that government should not control individuals' lives.

penalty? If a man who has no property refuses but once to earn nine shillings for the State, he is put in prison for a period unlimited by any law that I know, and determined only by the discretion of those who placed him there; but if he should steal ninety times nine shillings from the State, he is soon permitted to go at large again.

If the injustice is part of the necessary friction of the machine of government, let it go, let it go: perchance it will wear smooth—certainly the machine will wear out. If the injustice has a spring, or a pulley, or a rope, or a crank, exclusively for itself, then perhaps you may consider whether the remedy will not be worse than the evil; but if it is of such a nature that it requires you to be the agent of injustice to another, then, I say, break the law. Let your life be a counter-friction to stop the machine. What I have to do is to see, at any rate, that I do not lend myself to the wrong which I condemn. . . .

I do not hesitate to say, that those who call themselves Abolitionists [those against slavery] should at once effectually withdraw their support, both in person and property, from the government of Massachusetts, and not wait till they constitute a majority of one, before they suffer the right to prevail through them. I think that it is enough if they have God on their side, without waiting for that other one. Moreover, any man more right than his neighbors constitutes a majority of one already.

I meet this American government, or its representative, the State government, directly, and face to face, once a year—no more—in the person of its tax-gatherer; this is the only mode in which a man situated as I am necessarily meets it; and it then says distinctly, Recognize me; and the simplest, the most effectual, and, in the present posture of affairs, the indispensablest mode of treating with it on this head, of expressing your little satisfaction with and love for it, is to deny it then. My civil neighbor, the tax-gatherer, is the very man I have to deal with—for it is, after all, with men and not with parchment that I quarrel—and he has voluntarily chosen to be an agent of the government. . . .

I know this well, that if one thousand, if one hundred, if ten men whom I could name—if ten *honest* men only—ay, if *one* HONEST man, in this State of Massachusetts, *ceasing to hold slaves*, were actually to withdraw from this copartnership, and be locked up in the county jail therefor, it would be the abolition of slavery in America. For it matters not how small the beginning may seem to be: what is once well done is done forever. . . .

Under a government which imprisons any unjustly, the true place for a just man is also a prison. The proper place today, the only place which Massachusetts has provided for her freer and less desponding [discouraged] spirits, is in her prisons, to be put out and locked out of the State by her own act, as they have already put themselves out by their principles. It is there that the fugitive slave, and the Mexican prisoner on parole, and the Indian come to plead the wrongs of his race should find them; on that separate, but more free and honorable, ground, where the State places those who are not *with* her, but *against* her—the only house in a slave State in which a free man can abide with honor. . . .

I have paid no poll-tax for six years. I was put into a jail once on this account, for one night; and, as I stood considering the walls of solid stone, two or three feet thick, the door of wood and iron, a foot thick, and the iron grating which strained the light, I could not help being struck with the foolishness of that institution which treated me as if I were mere flesh and blood and bones, to be locked up. I wondered that it should have concluded at length that this was the best use it could put me to, and had never thought to avail itself of my services in some way. I saw that, if there was a wall of stone between me and my townsmen, there was a still more difficult one to climb or break through before they could get to be as free as I was. I did not for a moment feel confined, and the walls seemed a great waste of stone and mortar. I felt as if I alone of all my townsmen had paid my tax. They plainly did not know how to treat me, but behaved like persons who are underbred. In every threat and in every compliment there was a blunder; for they thought that my chief desire was to stand the other side of that stone wall. I could not but smile to see how industriously they locked the door on my meditations, which followed them out again without let or hindrance, and *they* were really all that was dangerous. As they could not reach me, they had resolved to punish my body; just as boys, if they cannot come at some person against whom they have a spite, will abuse his dog. I saw that the State was half-witted, that it was timid as a lone woman with her silver spoons, and that it did not know its friends from its foes, and I lost all my remaining respect for it, and pitied it. . . .

The night in prison was novel [unusual] and interesting enough. The prisoners in their shirtsleeves were enjoying a chat and the evening air in the doorway, when I entered. But the jailer said, "Come, boys, it is time to lock up"; and so they dispersed, and I heard the sound of their steps returning into the hollow apartments [cells]. . . .

It was like traveling into a far country, such as I had never expected to behold, to lie there for one night. It seemed to me that I never had heard the town clock strike before, nor the evening sounds of the village; for we slept with the windows open, which were inside the grating. It was to see my native village in the light of the Middle Ages, and our Concord was turned into a Rhine stream, and visions of knights and castles passed before me. There were the voices of old burghers [citizens] that I heard in the streets. I was an involuntary spectator and auditor of whatever was done and said in the kitchen of the adjacent [adjoining] village inn—a wholly new and rare experience to me. It was a closer view of my native town. I was fairly inside of it. I never had seen its institutions before. This is one of its peculiar institutions; for it is a shire town [a New England town where a court with a jury meets]. I began to comprehend what its inhabitants were about.

In the morning, our breakfasts were put through the hole in the door, in small oblong-square tin pans, made to fit, and holding a pint of chocolate, with brown bread, and an iron spoon. When they called for the vessels again, I was green enough to return what bread I had left; but my comrade seized it, and said that I should lay that up for lunch or dinner. Soon after he was let out to work at haying in a neighboring field, whither he went every day, and would not be back till noon; so he bade me good-day, saying that he doubted if he should see me again.

When I came out of prison—for some one interfered, and paid that tax—I did not perceive that great changes had taken place on the common [village square], such as he observed who went in a youth and emerged a tottering and gray-headed man; and yet a change had to my eyes come over the scene—the town, and State, and country—greater than any that mere time could effect. I saw yet more distinctly the State in which I lived. I saw to what extent the people among whom I lived could be trusted as good neighbors and friends; that their friendship was for summer weather only; that they did not greatly propose to do right; that they were a distinct race from me by their prejudices and superstitions, as the Chinamen and Malays are; that in their sacrifices to humanity they ran no risks, not even to their property; that after all they were not so noble but they treated the thief as he had treated them, and hoped, by a certain outward observance and a few prayers, and by walking in a particular straight though useless path from time to time, to save their souls. This may be to judge my neighbors harshly; for I believe that many of them are not aware that they have such an institution as the jail in their village.

It was formerly the custom in our village, when a poor debtor came out of jail, for his acquaintances to salute him, looking through their fingers, which were crossed to represent the grating of a jail window, "How do ye do?" My neighbors did not thus salute me, but first looked at me, and then at one another, as if I had returned from a long journey. I was put into jail as I was going to the shoemaker's to get a shoe which was mended. When I was let out the next morning, I proceeded to finish my errand, and, having put on my mended shoe, joined a huckleberry party, who were impatient to put themselves under my conduct; and in half an hour—for the horse was soon tackled—was in the midst of a huckleberry field, on one of our highest hills, two miles off, and then the State was nowhere to be seen.

This is the whole history of "My Prisons."

REVIEWING THE READING

1. According to Thoreau, what is the most effective way a person can fight civil wrongs?

2. What did Thoreau believe a person should do if he or she believed a law to be unjust?

3. **Using Your Historical Imagination.** On two occasions mentioned in the reading, someone else paid Thoreau's taxes to either keep him out of jail or get him released. Each time, Thoreau considered the act "unfortunate" or "interfering." Why do you think he felt this way?

Horace Mann on Education and Poverty (1848)

63

From *Twelfth Annual Report, Massachusetts Board of Education.*

Between the 1820s and the 1850s in the United States, people became more and more aware of the need for public education. The state of Massachusetts, under the direction of Secretary of Education Horace Mann, instituted many changes in public education that later became models for public schools all over the country. Mann saw to it that more money was provided for the school system, that teachers were properly trained and better paid, that better schools were built, and that laws were passed requiring students to attend school.

Horace Mann believed that only through public education could the country progress. As you read the following excerpts from his twelfth annual report to the Massachusetts Board of Education, try to determine why Mann also believed that education was the key to ending poverty.

A State should . . . seek the solution of such problems as these: To what extent can competence [knowledge] displace pauperism [poverty]? How nearly can we free ourselves from the low-minded and the vicious, not by their expatriation [removal], but by their elevation? To what extent can the resources and powers of Nature be converted into human welfare, the peaceful arts of life be advanced, and the vast treasures of human talent and genius be developed? How much of suffering, in all its forms, can be relieved? or, what is better than relief, how much can be prevented? Cannot the classes of crimes be lessened, and the number of criminals in each class be diminished?

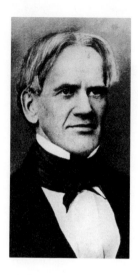

Horace Mann's work for education during the 1800s was instrumental in the development of the public school system in the United States.

. . . The distance between the two extremes of society is lengthening, instead of being abridged. With every generation, fortunes increase on the one hand, and some new privation is added to poverty on the other. We are verging towards those extremes of opulence [wealth] and of penury [poverty], each of which unhumanizes the human mind. . . .

I suppose it to be the universal sentiment of all those who mingle any ingredient of benevolence [caring] with their notions on political economy, that vast and overshadowing private fortunes are among the greatest dangers to which the happiness of the people in a republic can be subjected. Such fortunes would create a feudalism of a new kind. . . .

Now, surely nothing but universal education can counterwork this tendency to the domination of capital and servility of labor. . . . If education be equably diffused [equally spread out], it will draw property after it by the strongest of all attractions; for such a thing never did happen, and never can happen, as that an intelligent and practical body of men should be permanently poor. Property and labor in different classes are essentially antagonistic; but property and labor in the same class are essentially fraternal. . . .

Education, then, beyond all other devices of human origin, is the great equalizer of the conditions of men,—the balance-wheel of the social machinery. I do not here mean that it so elevates the moral nature as to make men disdain and abhor and oppression of their fellow-men. This idea pertains to another of its attributes. But I mean that it gives each man the independence and the means by which he can resist the selfishness of other men. It does better than to disarm the poor of their hostility towards the rich: it prevents being poor. Agrarianism [a movement for equal distribution of land] is the revenge of poverty against wealth. The wanton destruction of the property of others—the burning of hay-ricks [haystacks] and corn-ricks, the demolition of machinery because it supersedes [replaces] hand-labor, the sprinkling of vitriol [acid] on rich dresses—is only agrarianism run mad. Education prevents both the revenge and the madness. On the other hand, a fellow-feeling for one's class or caste is the common instinct of hearts not wholly sunk in selfish regards for person or for family. The spread of education, by enlarging the cultivated class or caste, will open a wider area over which the social feelings will expand; and, if this education should be universal and complete, it would do more than all things else to obliterate [erase] distinctions in society. . . .

But the beneficent [helpful] power of education would not be exhausted, even though it should peaceably abolish all the miseries that spring from co-existence, side by side, of enormous wealth and squalid want. It has a higher function. Beyond the power of diffusing old wealth, it has the prerogative [power] of creating new. It is a thousand times more lucrative [profitable] than fraud, and adds a thousand-fold more to a nation's resources than the most successful conquests. Knaves and robbers can obtain only what was before possessed by others. But education creates or develops new treasures,—treasures not before possessed or dreamed of by any one.

REVIEWING THE READING

1. Why did Mann believe that education was the key to ending poverty?

2. According to Mann, who was responsible for seeing that young people were properly educated?

3. **Using Your Historical Imagination.** What do you think Mann meant when he called education "the balance-wheel of the social machinery"? Do you agree or disagree with this statement? Explain your answer.

64

From *History of Woman Suffrage*, edited by Susan B. Anthony, Elizabeth Cady Stanton, and Matilda Joslyn Gage.

The Seneca Falls Declaration of Woman's Rights (1848)

As the cry for an end to slavery in the United States grew stronger during the 1830s and 1840s, women began adding their voices to the cause. Many men, however, resented women speaking out in public. They thought it was unfeminine and that women should not be concerned about social issues. The women were often forbidden to speak at public gatherings. Many of these women resented being treated as second-class citizens. They soon realized that they were being discriminated against in many of the same ways that the slaves were. They were not allowed to vote, did not have the same rights as men to an education, and were not allowed to own property.

In 1848 Elizabeth Cady Stanton and Lucretia Coffin Mott organized a Woman's Rights Convention at Seneca Falls, New York. During the convention, the nearly 300 male and female delegates drew up The Seneca Falls Declaration of Woman's Rights. *As you read the following excerpt from the declaration, notice its similarity to the Declaration of Independence, and think about why the delegates would choose this particular format.*

THE SENECA FALLS DECLARATION OF 1848

When, in the course of human events, it becomes necessary for one portion of the family of man to assume among the people of the earth a position different from that which they have hitherto occupied, but one to which the laws of nature and of nature's God entitle them, a decent respect to the opinions of mankind requires that they should declare the causes that impel them to such a course.

We hold these truths to be self-evident: that all men and women are created equal; . . .

The history of mankind is a history of repeated injuries and usurpations [taking control of] on the part of man toward woman, having in direct object the establishment of an absolute tyranny over her. To prove this, let facts be submitted to a candid world.

He has never permitted her to exercise her inalienable right to the elective franchise [to vote].

He has compelled her to submit to laws, in the formation of which she had no voice.

He has withheld from her rights which are given to the most ignorant and degraded men—both natives and foreigners.

Having deprived her of this first right of a citizen, the elective franchise, thereby leaving her without representation in the halls of legislation, he has opposed her on all sides.

He has made her, if married, in the eye of the law, civilly dead.

He has taken from her all right in property, even to the wages she earns.

> . . . He has taken from her all right in property, even to the wages she earns.

He has made her, morally, an irresponsible being, as she can commit many crimes with impunity [without fear of punishment], provided they be done in the presence of her husband. In the covenant of marriage, she is compelled to promise obedience to her husband, he becoming, to all intents and purposes, her master—the law giving him power to deprive her of her liberty, and to administer chastisement [punishment].

He has so framed the laws of divorce, as to what shall be the proper causes, and in case of separation, to whom the guardianship of the children shall be given, as to be wholly regardless of the happiness of women—the law, in all cases, going upon a false

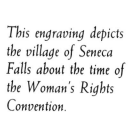

This engraving depicts the village of Seneca Falls about the time of the Woman's Rights Convention.

supposition of the supremacy of man, and giving all power into his hands.

After depriving her of all rights as a married women, if single, and the owner of property, he has taxed her to support a government which recognizes her only when her property can be made profitable to it.

He has monopolized nearly all the profitable employments, and from those she is permitted to follow, she receives but a scanty remuneration [payment]. He closes against her all the avenues to wealth and distinction which he considers most honorable to himself. As a teacher of theology, medicine, or law, she is not known.

He has denied her the facilities for obtaining a thorough education, all colleges being closed against her.

He allows her in Church, as well as State, but a subordinate position, claiming Apostolic authority for her exclusion from the ministry, and with some exceptions, from any public participation in the affairs of the Church.

He has created a false public sentiment by giving to the world a different code of morals for men and women, by which moral delinquencies which exclude women from society, are not only tolerated, but deemed of little account in man.

He has usurped the prerogative of Jehovah himself, claiming it as his right to assign for her a sphere of action, when that belongs to her conscience and to her God.

He has endeavored, in every way that he could, to destroy her confidence in her own powers, to lessen her self-respect, and to make her willing to lead a dependent and abject [hopeless] life.

Now, in view of this entire disfranchisement of one-half the people of this country, their social and religious degradation—in view of the unjust laws above mentioned, and because women do not feel themselves aggrieved, oppressed, and fraudulently deprived of their most sacred rights, we insist that they have immediate admission to all the rights and privileges which belong to them as citizens of the United States.

In entering upon the great work before us, we anticipate no small amount of misconception, misrepresentation, and ridicule; but we shall use every instrumentality within our power to effect our object. We shall employ agents, circulate tracts, petition the State and National legislatures, and endeavor to enlist the pulpit and the press in our behalf. We hope this Convention will be followed by a series of Conventions embracing every part of the Country.

RESOLUTIONS

WHEREAS, The great precept of nature is conceded to be, that "man shall pursue his own true and substantial happiness." Blackstone [a famous English judge] in his Commentaries remarks, that this law of Nature being coequal with mankind, and dictated by God himself, is of course superior in obligation to any other. It is binding over all the globe, in all countries and at all times, no human laws are of any validity if contrary to this, and such of them as are valid, derive all their force, and all their validity, and all their authority, mediately and immediately, from this original; therefore,

Resolved, That such laws as conflict, in any way, with the true and substantial happiness of woman, are contrary to the great precept of nature and of

. . . woman is man's equal— was intended to be so by the Creator . . .

no validity, for this is "superior in obligation to any other."

Resolved, That all laws which prevent woman from occupying such a station in society as her conscience shall dictate, or which place her in a position inferior to that of man, are contrary to the great precept of nature, and therefore of no force or authority.

Resolved, That woman is man's equal—was intended to be so by the Creator, and the highest good of the race demands that she should be recognized as such.

Resolved, That the women of this country ought to be enlightened in regard to the laws under which they live, that they may no longer publish their degradation [low state] by declaring themselves satisfied with their present position, nor their ignorance, by asserting that they have all the rights they want.

Resolved, That inasmuch as man, while claiming for himself intellectual superiority, does accord [give] to woman moral superiority, it is pre-eminently his duty to encourage her to speak and teach, as she has an opportunity, in all religious assemblies.

Resolved, That the same amount of virtue, delicacy, and refinement of behavior that is required of woman in the social state, should also be required of man, and the same transgressions should be visited [imposed] with equal severity on both man and woman.

Resolved, That the objection of indelicacy and impropriety, which is so often brought against woman when she addresses a public audience, comes with a very ill-grace from those who encourage, by their attendance, her appearance on the stage, in the concert, or in feats of the circus.

Resolved, That woman has too long rested satisfied in the circumscribed limits which corrupt customs and a perverted application of the Scriptures have marked out for her, and that it is time she should move in the enlarged sphere which her great Creator has assigned her.

Resolved, That it is the duty of women of this country to secure to themselves their sacred right to the elective franchise.

Resolved, That the equality of human rights results necessarily from the fact of the identity of the race in capabilities and responsibilities.

Resolved, therefore, That, being invested by the Creator with the same capabilities, and the same consciousness of responsibility for their exercise, it is demonstrably the right and duty of woman, equally with man, to promote their righteous cause by every righteous means; and especially in regard to the great subjects of morals and religion, it is self-evidently her right to participate with her brother in teaching them, both in private and in public, by writing and by speaking, by any instrumentalities proper to be used, and in any assemblies proper to be held; and this being a self-evident truth growing out of the divinely implanted principles of human nature, any custom or authority adverse to it, whether modern or wearing the hoary [stale] sanction of antiquity, is to be regarded as a self-evident falsehood, and at war with mankind.

REVIEWING THE READING

1. Why do you think the delegates chose to write their Declaration in a format similar to the Declaration of Independence?

2. What rights and privileges were the delegates asking for?

3. **Using Your Historical Imagination.** Many of the rights the women demanded required major changes in the laws of the United States. What other things do you think they were asking for that could be granted to them immediately?

65

From *Life on the Plains and among the Diggings* by Alonzo Delano.

Notes from a Forty-Niner's Diary (1849)

On January 24, 1848, a carpenter named James W. Marshall, who worked at Sutter's mill near San Francisco, California, found flakes of gold in the American River. The word spread, other finds soon followed, and before long, the whole country knew about the gold to be found in California.

At the time there were about 15,000 people living in California. By the end of 1849 the population had increased to more than 100,000. Among the thousands of forty-niners, as the California gold prospectors came to be known, was a man named Alonzo Delano who later wrote about his experience. As you read the following excerpts describing Delano's trek across the country, try to imagine the extreme hardships faced by many of the forty-niners.

Ascending to the top of an inclined plain, the long-sought, the long-wished-for and welcome valley of Sacramento, lay before me, five or six miles distant. . . .

In May, 1850, a report reached the settlements that a wonderful lake had been discovered, an hundred miles back among the mountains, towards the head of the Middle Fork of Feather River, the shores of which abounded with gold, and to such an extent that it lay like pebbles on the beach. An extraordinary ferment [activity] among the people ensued, and a grand rush was made from the towns, in search of this splendid El Dorado [legendary city of gold]. Stores were left to take care of themselves, business of all kinds was dropped, mules were suddenly bought up at exorbitant prices, and crowds started off to search for the golden lake.

Days passed away, when at length adventurers began to return, with disappointed looks, and their worn out and dilapidated garments showed that they had "seen some service," and it proved that, though several lakes had been discovered, the Gold Lake *par excellence* was not found. The mountains swarmed with men, exhausted and worn out with toil and hunger; mules were starved, or killed by falling from precipices [steep cliffs]. Still the search was continued over snow forty or fifty feet deep, till the highest ridge of the Siérra was passed, when the disappointed crowds began to return, without getting a glimpse of the grand *desideratum* [what they hoped to find], having had their labor for their pains. Yet this sally [trip] was not without some practical and beneficial results. The country was more perfectly explored, some rich diggings were found, and, as usual, a few among the many were benefitted. A new field for enterprize was opened, and within a month, roads were made and traversed by wagons, trading posts were established, and a new mining country was opened, which really proved in the main [reality] to be rich, and had it not been for the gold-lake fever, it might have remained many months undiscovered and unoccupied. . . .

From the mouth of Nelson's Creek to its source, men were at work in digging. Sometimes the stream was turned from its bed, and the channel worked; in other places, wing dams were thrown out, and the bed partially worked; while in some, the banks only were dug. Some of these, as is the case everywhere in the mines, paid well, some, fair wages, while many were failures. One evening, while waiting for my second supply of goods, I strolled by a deserted camp. I was attracted to the ruins of a shanty [hut], by observing the effigy [dummy] of a man standing upright in an old torn shirt, a pair of ragged pantaloons, and boots which looked as if they had

Miners in the California goldfields in the late 1800s washed away thousands of pounds of rock and soil hoping to uncover hidden grains or nuggets of gold.

been clambering over rocks since they were made—in short, the image represented a lean, meagre, worn-out and woe-begone miner, such as might daily be seen at almost every point in the upper mines. On the shirt was inscribed, in a good business hand, "My claim failed—will you pay the taxes?" (an allusion to the tax on foreigners.) Appended [attached] to the figure was a paper, bearing the following words: "Californians—Oh, Californians, look at me! once fat and saucy as a privateersman, but now—look ye—a miserable skeleton. In a word, I am a used up man. . . ."

Ludicrous as it may appear, it was a truthful commentary on the efforts of hundreds of poor fellows in the "golden land." This company had penetrated the mountain snows with infinite labor, in the early part of the season, enduring hardships of no ordinary character—had patiently toiled for weeks, living on the coarsest fare; had spent time and money in building a dam and digging a race [channel] through rocks to drain off the water; endured wet and cold, in the chilling atmosphere of the country, and when the last stone was turned, at the very close of all this labor, they did not find a single cent to reward them for their toil and privations, and what was still more aggravating, a small, wing dam, on the very claim below them, yielded several thousand dollars. Having paid out their money, and lost their labor, they were compelled to abandon the claim, and search for other diggings, where the result might be precisely the same. . . .

The population of Independence represented almost every State in the Union, while France, England, Ireland, Germany, and even Bohemia [Czechoslovakia], had their delegates. As soon as breakfast was dispatched, all hands were engaged in digging and washing gold in the banks, or in the bed of the stream. When evening came, large fires were built, around which the miners congregated, some engrossed with thoughts of home and friends, some to talk of new discoveries, and richer diggings somewhere else; or, sometimes a subject of debate was started, and the evening was whiled away in pleasant, and often instructive, discussion, while many, for whom this kind of recreation had not excitement enough, resorted to dealing monte [a card game], on a small scale, thus either exciting or keeping up a passion for play. Some weeks were passed in this way under the clear blue sky of the mountains, and many had made respectable piles. I highly enjoyed the wild scenery, and, quite as well, the wild life we were leading, for there were many accomplished and intelligent men; and a subject for amusement or debate was rarely wanting. As for ceremony or dress, it gave us no trouble: we were all alike. . . . At length a monte dealer arrived, with a respectable bank.

A change had been gradually coming over many of our people, and for three or four days several industrious men had commenced drinking, and after the monte bank was set up, it seemed as if the long smothered fire burst forth into a flame. Labor, with few exceptions, seemed suspended, and a great many miners spent their time in riot and debauchery. . . . The monte dealer, who, in his way was a gentleman, and honorable according to the notions of that class of men, won in two nights three thousand dollars! When he had collected his taxes on our bar, he went to Onion Valley, six miles distant, and lost in one night four thousand, exemplifying [illustrating] the fact, that a gambler may be rich to-day, and a beggar to-morrow.

REVIEWING THE READING

1. What types of hardships did the forty-niners face in the gold camps?

2. Why do you think the California Gold Rush could be considered an international affair? Where did the forty-niners come from?

3. **Using Your Historical Imagination.** The author talks about the card dealer who won a lot of money at one camp only to lose it and more at another camp. Why do you think Delano may have been talking about the forty-niners as well as the card dealer when he said "a gambler may be rich today, and a beggar tomorrow"?

Mexicans in "the Diggings" (1849)

66

From *The Decline of the Californios: A Social History of the Spanish-speaking Californians, 1846–1890* by Leonard Pitt.

Why did the native Spanish population of California, the Californios, fail to take full advantage of the great gold strikes right on their doorstep? Historian Leonard Pitt gives reasons in the following excerpt from his book The Decline of the Californios. *Some Hispanic Californians had good luck from the outset. Don Antonio Coronel took 45 ounces of gold in a day. But soon he found himself competing with Chileans, Mexicans, Germans, French, and all the Yankee rogues who flocked to California. Consider what happened to Californios in the gold fields.*

As news of the discovery spread in 1848, Californios [Hispanic Californians] speedily converged on the Sierra from all directions and, in a sense, made up for lost time. The experience of Angeleños was typical. With Don Antonio Coronel taking on the function of patron, the thirty Californios, Sonorans, and Indian servants had good luck from the outset. They immediately enticed some mountain tribesmen to accept baubles in exchange for gold nuggets and, after spying out the Indians' trove and plying them with more trinkets, they obtained their digging labor into the bargain. In one day Antonio himself ended up with 45 ounces of gold; Dolores Sepúlveda found a 12-ounce nugget; and Señor Valdez discovered a boulder buried only 3 feet down which had once blocked the flow of an ancient alluvial stream and produced a towelful of nuggets in a short time. He sold his claim to Lorenzo Soto, who took out a whopping 52 pounds of gold in eight days and then sold it to Señor Machado, who also became rich. Even a Sonoran servant became fabulously wealthy overnight.

In this illustration, Mexican miners use a method called "winnowing" to separate gold from soil. As they shake the cloth, the grains of dirt are blown away, but the heavier gold remains.

In all, about 1,300 native Californians mined gold in 1848, the year of the bonanzas. If they had missed the opportunity to discover Sierra gold in the past, they did not do so now; nearness to the placers [mineral-bearing soil deposits] gave them the head start on the thousands of prospectors still getting their wits together for the voyage halfway around the world. The Californios had additional advantages in knowing precisely where and how to find gold and in gladly pooling their resources and dividing their labor. As a result, the organized Californios, though less numerous than the 4,000 individualistic Yankees in the mines that year, probably extracted as much gold as they. Coronel, a struggling Mexican schoolteacher, had pocketed enough gold to become a prominent landowner, viticulturist [grape grower], and community leader. He and many other Californios resolved to make a second expedition the next year. They dismissed the news that a few Californios had been harried from their claims by fist-swinging Oregon Yankees, who refused to acknowledge that the Treaty of Guadalupe Hidalgo granted some Mexicans full citizenship: in 1848 "everything ended peacefully."

In the year that followed, the story changed drastically. Coronel's return trip to the mines began badly, with a near-fatal brawl in a Sonora saloon. One day he and *compadre* Juan Padilla were waiting for the wet January weather to clear, when a former Bear Flagger began to bully Padilla for having served as Bernardo Garcia's henchman in the wartime atrocity against Cowie and Fowler. Padilla insisted that the charge was a lie, and the American replied with an assault. After a severe beating, Padilla lay in an upstairs room, hovering near death for several weeks, while below his accuser continued to threaten his life. Only Coronel's good reputation and the intercession of friendly Americans restrained the former Bear Flagger.

After nursing his friend back to life, Coronel returned to the Sierra. He fell in among Chileans,

Mexicans, and Germans doing well at dry diggings until confronted with posters declaring that foreigners had no right to be there and must leave the mines at once; resistance would be met by force. Although this threat never materialized, excitement mounted. In a nearby camp, a Mexican gambler's tent had been raided, and some Yankees accused five foreigners of stealing 5 pounds of gold. Coronel's associates doubted the accusation against at least one apparently honorable man and raised 5 pounds of gold to offer as ransom. Coronel conferred with a Yankee delegation and gave them the gold. The delegates then retired to consider the offer but never re-emerged from the drunken and agitated crowd, which by then numbered into the hundreds. The money did no good; all five prisoners were convicted and flogged at once, and two of them, a Frenchman and a Chilean, were charged with a previous murder and robbery. Guilty or not, the pair scarcely understood enough of the proceedings to reply to the accusations. When Coronel next saw them they were standing in a cart, lashed together back to back and pinned with a note warning away defenders such as might come from Coronel's camp. A horse then jolted the cart from under the men, and California had witnessed its first lynching. That incident resulted, Coronel thought, from a declining gold supply and the Yankees' increasing jealousy of successful Spanish Americans.

As quickly as possible Don Antonio led his group away from the newly named "Hangtown," and resettled in the remote northern mines. But even there a hundred gringos appeared with the gruff announcement that the entire riverbed belonged exclusively to Americans who would tolerate no foreigners. Furious, some of Coronel's people who had reached the limit of their endurance planned armed resistance, even at the cost of their lives, but Coronel held back and sadly announced, "For me gold mining is finished."

As the only true native-born citizens they did have a legitimate place in the mines . . .

By July many other Californios had cause to echo Coronel's words. As the only true native-born citizens they did have a legitimate place in the mines, yet they knew no way to convince 100,000 hostile strangers of this truth. Fisticuffs or hand combat simply was not the Californians' style. Consequently, one of them carried into the field of combat a safe-conduct pass, signed by the army's secretary of state, which certified him as a bona fide citizen deserving of every right and privilege, of every lawful aid and protection. What good the pass did is not recorded, but the attacks mounted. For most Californios, the best answer was to go home and stay there: "Don't go to the mines on any account," one *paisano* advised another. Out of pride, which prevented them from being converted into aliens by Yankee rogues and upstarts, few Californians ventured back into the maelstrom [fuss] after 1849.

Musing over the gold rush from a safe distance, the Californians once more concluded that outsiders were, by and large, despicable [hateful]. Mariano Vallejo said of the forty-niners without sparing any nationality, "The good ones were few and the wicked many." Hugo Reid ticked off the list of troublemakers:

. . . vagabonds from every quarter of the globe. Scoundrels from nowhere, rascals from Oregon, pickpockets from New York, accomplished gentlemen from Europe, interlopers from Lima and Chile, Mexican thieves, gamblers of no particular spot, and assassins manufactured in Hell for the expressed purpose of converting the highways and biways into theatres of blood; then, last but not least, Judge Lynch with his thousand arms, thousand sightless eyes, and five-hundred lying tongues.

The Californians now simply reverted to their customary circular logic, which held that evil came from outsiders, that outsiders were mostly evil, and that evil mothered evil. In no other way could they

explain the ugly behavior of so many people, especially Americanos.

After a century of slow population growth, during which the arrival of twenty-five cholos [persons
of mixed Mexican and Indian blood] or fifty Americans seemed a momentous occasion, suddenly and
without warning California faced one of the swiftest,
largest, and most varied folk migrations of all time.
More newcomers now arrived each day in California
than had formerly come in a decade. Briefly told,
the story of the Californians in the gold rush is
their encounter with 100,000 newcomers in the single year of 1849—80,000 Yankees, 8,000 Mexicans,
5,000 South Americans, and several thousand miscellaneous Europeans—and with numbers that swelled
to a quarter million by 1852. Even assuming the
goodwill of every last one of these strangers, they
outnumbered the Californians ten and fifteen times
over and reduced them to feelings of insignificance.

REVIEWING THE READING

1. How successful were native Califor-
    nians— Californios—in the bonanza year
    of 1848?

2. How did mining for gold in the Sierras
    turn sour for Californios?

3. **Using Your Historical Imagination.** It is
    said that practically all the gold found
    or mined in the history of time is still
    present in our world—because it is so
    scarce and useful. Gold does not corrode.
    It is durable in any climate. Working with
    your classmates, imagine and discuss the
    history of one nugget of gold from its
    first discovery to its use today.

67

From *Blackfoot Lodge Tales* by George B. Grinnell.

The Blackfoot Genesis (1800s)

The Blackfoot Indians had lived on the Northern Plains for centuries, hunting the buffalo, the antelope, and—in the mountains—the bighorn sheep. They had a reputation as brave and formidable warriors, and American fur trappers and traders soon learned to treat them with great respect. The Blackfoot explained their presence on the Plains with the following legend (written down in the late nineteenth century but probably much older than that). As you read the excerpt, consider the use of this kind of legend in Blackfoot society.

All animals of the Plains at one time heard and knew him, and all birds of the air heard and knew him. All things that he had made understood him when he spoke to them—the birds, the animals, and the people.

Old Man was traveling about, south of here, making the people. He came from the south, traveling north, making animals and birds as he passed along. He made the mountains, prairies, timber, and brush first. So he went along, traveling northward, making things as he went, putting rivers here and there, and falls on them, putting red paints here and there in the ground—fixing up the world as we see it today. He made the Milk River [the Teton] and crossed it, and, being tired, went up on a little hill and lay down to rest. As he lay on his back, stretched out on the ground, with arms extended, he marked himself out with stones—the shape of his body, head, legs, arms, and everything. There you can see those rocks today. After he had rested, he went on northward, and stumbled over a knoll and fell down on his knees. The he said, "You are a bad thing to be stumbling against"; so he raised up two large buttes there, and named them the Knees, and they are called so to this day. He went on farther north, and with some of the rocks he carried with him he built the Sweet Grass Hills.

Old Man covered the plains with grass for the animals to feed on. He marked off a piece of ground, and in it he made to grow all kinds of roots and berries—camas, wild carrots, wild turnips, sweetroot, bitterroot, sarvis berries, bull berries, cherries, plums, and rosebuds. He put trees in the ground. He put all kinds of animals on the ground. When he made the bighorn with its big head and horns, he made it out on the prairie. It did not seem to travel easily on the prairie; it was awkward and could not go fast. So he took it by one of its horns, and led it up into the mountains, and turned it loose; and it skipped about among the rocks and went up fearful places with ease. So he said, "This is the place that suits you; this is what you are fitted for, the rocks, and the mountains." While he was in the mountains, he made the antelope out of dirt, and turned it loose, to see how it would go. It ran so fast that if fell over some rocks and hurt itself. He saw that this would not do, and took the antelope down on the prairie, and turned it loose; and it ran away fast and gracefully, and he said, "This is what you are suited to."

One day Old Man determined that he would make a woman and a child; so he formed them both—the woman and the child, her son—of clay. After he had molded the clay in human shape, he said to the clay, "You must be people," and then he covered it up and left it, and went away. The next morning he went to the place and took the covering off, and saw that the clay shapes had changed a little. The second morning there was still more change, and the third still more. The fourth morning he went to the place, took the covering off, looked at the images, and told them to rise

This engraving from the nineteenth century depicts a Blackfoot Indian chief holding symbols of his rank.

and walk; and they did so. They walked down to the river with their Maker, and then he told them that his name was Na'pi, Old Man.

As they were standing by the river, the woman said to him, "How is it? Will we always live, will there be no end to it? He said: "I have never thought of that. We will have to decide it. I will take this buffalo chip and throw it in the river. If it floats, when people die, in four days they will become alive again; they will die for only four days. But if it sinks, there will be an end to them." He threw the chip into the river, and it floated. The woman turned and picked up a stone, and said: "No, I will throw this stone in the river; if it floats we will always live, if it sinks people must die, that they may always be sorry for each other." The woman threw the stone into the water, and it sank. "There," said Old Man, "you have chosen. There will be an end to them."

It was not many nights after that the woman's child died, and she cried a great deal for it. She said to Old Man: "Let us change this. The law that you first made, let that be a law." He said: "Not so. What is made law must be law. We will undo nothing that we have done. The child is dead, but it cannot be changed. People will have to die."

REVIEWING THE READING

1. Who was Na'pi, Old Man?

2. Why were legends created and passed from generation to generation?

3. **Using Your Historical Imagination.** Judging from this example, what would be the usual topics covered by the origin legend or legends of people? What topics are dealt with here?

On the Underground Railroad (ca.1850)

68

From *Reminiscences* by Levi Coffin.

Levi Coffin, a Quaker who lived in Cincinnati during the 1850s, was one of the most important organizers of the so-called "underground railroad," a widespread organization of abolitionists who helped runaway slaves escape north to freedom. In the following excerpts from his Reminiscences, *published in 1876, Coffin tells how one group of 28 slaves crossed the Ohio River from the slave state of Kentucky and then were helped north on the "railroad." As you read consider what general conclusions you can draw about the underground railroad and how it functioned.*

The fugitives generally arrived in the night, and were secreted among the friendly colored people or hidden in the upper room of our house. They came alone or in companies, and in a few instances had a white guide to direct them.

One company of twenty-eight that crossed the Ohio River at Lawrenceburg, Indiana—twenty miles below Cincinnati—had for conductor a white man whom they had employed to assist them. The character of this man was full of contradictions. He was a Virginian by birth and spent much of his time in the South, yet he hated slavery. He was devoid of [without] moral principle, but was a true friend to the poor slave. . . .

The company of twenty-eight slaves referred to, all lived in the same neighborhood in Kentucky, and had been planning for some time how they could make their escape from slavery. This white man—John Fairfield—had been in the neighborhood for some weeks buying poultry, etc., for market, and though among the whites he assumed to be very pro-slavery, the negroes soon found that he was their friend.

He was engaged by the slaves to help them across the Ohio River and conduct them to Cincinnati. They paid him some money which they had managed to accumulate. The amount was small, considering the risk the conductor assumed, but it was all they had. Several of the men had their wives with them, and one woman a little child with her, a few months old. John Fairfield conducted the party to the Ohio River opposite the mouth of the Big Miami, where he knew there were several skiffs tied to the bank, near a wood-yard. When I asked him afterward if he did not feel compunctions of conscience [have second thoughts] for breaking these skiffs loose and using them, he replied: "No; slaves are stolen property, and it is no harm to steal boats or anything else that will help them gain their liberty." The entire party crowded into three large skiffs or yawls, and made their way slowly across the river. The boats were overloaded and sank so deep that the passage was made in much peril. The boat John Fairfield was in was leaky, and began to sink when a few rods [a rod equals 16.5 feet] from the Ohio bank, and he sprang out on the sand-bar, where the water was two or three feet deep, and tried to drag the boat to the shore. He sank to his waist in mud and quicksands, and had to be pulled out by some of the negroes. The entire party waded out through mud and water and reached the shore safely, though all were wet and several lost their shoes. They hastened along the Bank toward Cincinnati, but it was now late in the night and daylight appeared before they reached the city. Their plight was a most pitiable one. They were cold, hungry and exhausted; those who had lost their shoes in the mud suffered from bruised and lacerated [cut] feet, while to add to their discomfort, a drizzling rain fell during the latter part of the night. They could not enter the city for their appearance would at once proclaim them to be fugitives. When they reached the outskirts of the city, below Mill Creek, John Fairfield hid them as well as he could in ravines that had been washed in the sides of the steep hills, and told them not to move until he returned. He then went directly to John Hatfield, a worthy colored man, a deacon in the Zion Baptist Church, and told his story. He had applied to Hatfield before and knew him to be a great friend to the fugitives—one who had often sheltered them under his roof and aided them in every way he could.

. . . When he arrived, wet and muddy, at John Hatfield's house, he was scarcely recognized. He soon made himself and his errand known, and Hatfield at once sent a messenger to me, requesting me to come to his house without delay, as there were fugitives in danger. I went at once and met several prominent colored men who had also been summoned. While dry clothes and a warm breakfast were furnished to John Fairfield, we anxiously discussed the situation of the twenty-eight fugitives who were lying, hungry and shivering, in the hills in sight of the city.

Several plans were suggested, but none seemed practicable. At last I suggested that some one should go immediately to a certain German livery stable in the city and hire two coaches, and that several colored men should go out in buggies and take the women and children from their hiding-places, then that the coaches and buggies should form a procession as if going to a funeral, and march solemnly along the road leading to Cumminsville, on the west side of Mill Creek. In the western part of Cumminsville was the Methodist Episcopal burying ground, where a certain lot of ground had been set apart for the use of the colored people. They should pass this and continue on the Colerain pike till they reached a right-hand road leading to College Hill. At the latter place they would find a few colored families, living in the outskirts of the village, and

> . . . John Fairfield hid them as well as he could in ravines . . .

could take refuge among them. Jonathan Cable, a Presbyterian minister, who lived near Farmer's College, on the west side of the village, was a prominent abolitionist, and I knew that he would give prompt assistance to the fugitives.

I advised that one of the buggies should leave the procession at Cumminsville, after passing the burying-ground, and hasten to College Hill to apprise [tell] friend Cable of the coming of the fugitives, that he might make arrangements for their reception in suitable places. My suggestions and advice were agreed to, and acted upon as quickly as possible, John Hatfield agreeing to apprise friend Cable of the coming of the fugitives. We knew that we must act quickly and with discretion, for the fugitives were in a very unsafe position, and in great danger of being discovered and captured by the police, who were always on the alert for runaway slaves.

While the carriages and buggies were being procured, John Hatfield's wife and daughter, and other colored women of the neighborhood, busied themselves in preparing provisions to be sent to the fugitives. A large stone jug was filled with hot coffee, and this, together with a supply of bread and other provisions, was placed in a buggy and sent on ahead of the carriages, that the hungry fugitives might receive some nourishment before starting.

The house in this photo was one of the stations of the underground railroad, where escaping slaves were hidden as they made their way to Canada.

The conductor of the party, accompanied by John Hatfield, went in the buggy, in order to apprise the fugitives of the arrangements that had been made, and have them in readiness to approach the road as soon as the carriages arrived. Several blankets were provided to wrap around the women and children, whom we knew must be chilled by their exposure to the rain and cold. The fugitives were very glad to get the supply of food, the hot coffee especially being a great treat to them, and felt much revived. About the time they finished their breakfast the carriages and buggies drove up and halted in the road, and the fugitives were quickly conducted to them and placed inside. The women in the tight carriages wrapped themselves in the blankets, and the woman who had a young babe muffled it closely to keep it warm, and to prevent its cries from being heard. The little thing seemed to be suffering much pain, having been exposed so long to the rain and cold.

All the arrangements were carried out, and the party reached College Hill in safety, and were kindly received and cared for. . . .

When it was known by some of the prominent ladies of the village that a large company of fugitives were in the neighborhood, they met together to prepare some clothing for them. Jonathan Cable ascertained [determined] the number and size of the shoes needed, and the clothes required to fit the fugitives for traveling, and came down in his carriage to my house, knowing that the Anti-Slavery Sewing Society had their depository there. I went with him to purchase the shoes that were needed, and my wife selected all the clothing we had that was suitable for the occasion; the rest was furnished by the noble women of College Hill.

I requested friend Cable to keep the fugitives as secluded as possible until a way could be provided for safely forwarding them on their way to Canada. Friend Cable was a stockholder in the Underground

Railroad, and we consulted together about the best route, finally deciding on the line by way of Hamilton, West Elkton, Eaton, Paris and Newport, Indiana. West Elkton, twenty-five or thirty miles from College Hill, was the first Underground Railroad depot. That line always had plenty of locomotives and cars in readiness. I agreed to send information to that point, accordingly wrote to one of my particular friends at West Elkton, informing him that I had some valuable stock on hand which I wished to forward to Newport, and requested him to send three two-horse wagons—covered—to College Hill, where the stock was resting, in charge of Jonathan Cable. . . .

The three wagons arrived promptly at the time mentioned, and a little after dark took in the party, together with another fugitive, who had arrived the night before, and whom we added to the company. They went through to West Elkton safely that night, and the next night reached Newport, Indiana. With little delay they were forwarded on from station to station through Indiana and Michigan to Detroit, having fresh teams and conductors each night, and resting during the day. I had letters from different stations, as they progressed, giving accounts of the arrival and departure of the train, and I also heard of their safe arrival on the Canada shore.

REVIEWING THE READING

1. What motivated Virginian John Fairfield to help the slaves escape?

2. What is indicated by Coffin's use of the term "stock" (meaning merchandise) in his letter to West Elkton?

3. **Using Your Historical Imagination.** What conclusions can you draw from Coffin's account about the nature of the underground railroad?

A Contemporary Account of Harriet Tubman (1850s)

69

From *Commonwealth*, July 17, 1864, and *Freeman's Record*, March 1865, in *The Underground Railroad* by Charles L. Blockson.

Harriet Tubman was an escaped slave who returned many times to the South to lead other slaves to freedom. She was an individual of great courage and strong personality who impressed all who met her, including the anonymous author of the selection that follows. This account of Tubman was based on actual interviews in the abolitionist journals Commonwealth *and* Freeman's Record. *As you read the excerpts, think about the strategies used by Tubman in her successful raids into Maryland.*

One of the teachers lately commissioned by the New-England Freedmen's Aid Society is probably the most remarkable woman of this age. That is to say, she has performed more wonderful deeds by the native power of her own spirit against adverse circumstances than any other. She is well known to many by the various names which her eventful life has given her, Harriet Garrison, Gen. Tubman, &c.; but among the slaves she is universally known by her well earned title of Moses,—Moses the deliverer. She is a rare instance, in the midst of high civilization and intellectual culture, of a being of great native powers, working powerfully, and to beneficient ends, entirely untaught by schools or books.

Her maiden name was Araminta Ross. She is the granddaughter of a native African, and has not a drop of white blood in her veins. She was born in 1820 or 1821, on the Eastern Shore of Maryland. Her parents were slaves, but married and faithful to each other, and the family affection is very strong. She claims that she was legally freed by a will of her first master, but his wishes were not carried into effect.

She seldom lived with her owner, but was usually "hired out" to different persons. She once "hired her time," and employed it in rudest farming labors, ploughing, carting, driving the oxen, &c., to so good advantage that she was able in one year to buy a pair of steers worth forty dollars.

When quite young she lived with a very pious mistress; but the slaveholder's religion did not prevent her from whipping the young girl for every slight or fancied fault. Araminta found that this was usually a morning exercise; so she prepared for it by putting on all the thick clothes she could procure to protect her skin. She made sufficient outcry, however, to convince her mistress that her blows had full effect; and in the afternoon she would take off her wrappings, and dress as well as she could. When invited into family prayers, she preferred to stay on the landing, and pray for herself; "and I prayed to God," she says "to make me strong and able to fight and that's what I've allers prayed for ever since." It is in vain to try to persuade her that her prayer was a wrong one. She always maintains it to be sincere and right, and it has certainly been fully answered. . . .

Owing to changes in her owner's family, it was determined to sell her and some other slaves; but her health was so much injured, that a purchaser was not easily found. At length she became convinced that she would soon be carried away, and she decided to escape. . . .

Wise judges are we of each other!—She was only quitting home, husband, father, mother, friends, to go out alone, friendless and penniless into the world.

She remained two years in Philadelphia working hard and carefully hoarding her money. Then she hired a room, furnished it as well as she could, bought a nice suit of men's clothes, and went back to Maryland for her husband. But the faithless man had taken

During the 1850s Harriet Tubman made 19 trips from the North to the South and led about 300 slaves to freedom. Always a fighter for freedom, she also joined the movement for woman's rights that started in the late 1850s in New York and New England.

to himself another wife. . . . Thus all personal aims died out of her heart; and with her simple brave motto, "I can't die but once," she began the work which has made her Moses,—the deliverer of her people. Seven or eight times she has returned to the neighborhood of her former home, always at the risk of death in the most terrible forms, and each time has brought away a company of fugitive slaves, and led them safely to the free States, or to Canada. Every time she went, the dangers increased. In 1857 she brought away her old parents, and, as they were too feeble to walk, she was obliged to hire a wagon, which added greatly to the perils of the journey. In 1860 she went for the last time, and among her troop was an infant whom they were obliged to keep stupefied [drugged] with laudanum to prevent its outcries. This was at the period of great excitement, and Moses was not safe even in

New York State; but her anxious friends insisted upon her taking refuge in Canada. So various and interesting are the incidents of the journeys, that we know not how to select from them. She has shown in them all the characteristics of a great leader: courage, foresight, prudence, self-control, ingenuity, subtle perception, command over others' minds. Her nature is at once profoundly practical and highly imaginative. She is economical as Dr. Franklin, and as firm in the conviction of supernatural help as Mahomet. . . . She would never allow more to join her than she could properly care for, though she often gave others directions by which they succeeded in escaping. She always came in the winter when the nights are long and dark, and people who have homes stay in them. She was never seen on the plantation herself; but appointed a rendezvous for her company eight or ten miles distant, so that if they were discovered at the first start she was not compromised. She started on Saturday night; the slaves at that time being allowed to go away from home to visit their friends—so that they would not be missed until Monday morning. Even then they were supposed to have loitered on the way, and it would often be late on Monday afternoon before the flight would be certainly known. If by any further delay the advertisement was not sent out before Tuesday morning, she felt secure of keeping ahead of it; but if it were, it required all her ingenuity to escape. She resorted to various devices, she had confidential friends all along the road. She would hire a man to follow the one who put up the notices, and take them down as soon as his back was turned. She crossed creeks on railroad bridges by night, she hid her company in the woods while she herself not being advertised went into the towns in search of information. If met on the road, her face was always to the south, and she was always a very respectable looking darkey, not at all a poor fugitive. She would get into the cars near her pursuers and manage to hear their plans.

The expedition was governed by the strictest rules. If any man gave out, he must be shot. "Would you really do that?" she was asked. "Yes," she replied, "if he was weak enough to give out, he'd be weak enough to betray us all, and all who had helped us; and do you think I'd let so many die just for one coward man." "Did you ever have to shoot any one?" she was asked. "One time," she said, "a man gave out the second night; his feet were sore and swollen, he couldn't go any further; he'd rather go back and die, if he must." They tried all arguments in vain, bathed his feet, tried to strengthen him, but it was of no use, he would go back. Then she said, "I told the boys to get their guns ready, and shoot him. They'd have done it in a minute; but when he heard that, he jumped right up and went on as well as any body." She can tell the time by the stars, and find her way by natural signs as well as any hunter; and yet she scarcely knows of the existence of England or any other foreign country.

When going on these journeys she often lay alone in the forests all night. Her whole soul was filled with awe of the mysterious Unseen Presence, which thrilled her with such depths of emotion, that all other care and fear vanished. Then she seemed to speak with her Maker "as a man talketh with his friend;" her child-like petitions had direct answers, and beautiful visions lifted her up above all doubt and anxiety into serene trust and faith. No man can be a hero without this faith in some form; the sense that he walks not in his own strength, but leaning on an almighty arm. Call it fate, destiny, what you will, Moses of old, Moses of to-day, believed it to be Almighty God. . . .

. . . she often lay alone in the forests all night.

Her efforts were not confined to the escape of slaves. She conducted them to Canada, watched over their welfare, collected clothing, organized them into societies, and was always occupied with plans for their benefit. She first came to Boston in the spring of 1859, to ask aid of the friends of her race to build a house for her aged father and mother.

She brought recommendations from Gerrit Smith, and at once won many friends who aided her purpose. Her parents are now settled in Auburn, and all that Harriet seems to desire in reward for her labors is the privilege of making their old age comfortable. She has a very affectionate nature, and forms the strongest personal attachments. She has great simplicity of character; she states her wants very freely, and believes you are ready to help her; but if you have nothing to give, or have given to another, she is content. She is not sensitive to indignities to her color in her own person; but knows and claims her rights. She will eat at your table if she sees you really desire it; but she goes as willingly to the kitchen. She is very abstemious [sparing] in her diet, fruit being the only luxury she cares for. Her personal appearance is very peculiar. She is thoroughly negro, and very plain. She has needed disguise so often that she seems to have command over her face, and can banish all expression from her features, and look so stupid that nobody would suspect her of knowing enough to be dangerous; but her eye flashes with intelligence and power when she is roused.

REVIEWING THE READING

1. As a young woman living as a slave in Maryland, what did Tubman pray for? What was her motto in later life?

2. Why did the other slaves call her "Moses"?

3. **Using Your Historical Imagination.** How would you explain Tubman's phenomenal success in returning again and again to the South to bring slaves to the North to freedom?

A Visit to Uncle Tom's Cabin (1851)

70

From *Uncle Tom's Cabin* by Harriet Beecher Stowe.

The 1840s saw a great increase in literature promoting the abolition of slavery. With little doubt the single most important antislavery publication was Harriet Beecher Stowe's Uncle Tom's Cabin: or Life Among the Lowly. *Written by a member of a prominent family of Connecticut and New York, the book sold a remarkable 300,000 copies within a year of its publication in 1851. It was adapted into a play that was performed by scores of professional and amateur troupes in northern cities and small towns. The impact of all this on public opinion was very great. When President Lincoln met Stowe during the Civil War, he said, "So you are the little woman who wrote the book that made this great war." In the following excerpt from Chapter 4, we find Uncle Tom still at home with his original owner. The pleasant circumstances described in the passage are soon to end, because the owner is forced to sell Tom "down the river." As you read the excerpt, consider how the author describes Tom.*

The cabin of Uncle Tom was a small log building close adjoining to "the house," as the negro *par excellence* designates his master's dwelling. In front it had a neat garden-patch, where, every summer, strawberries, raspberries, and a variety of fruits and vegetables flourished under careful tending. The whole front of it was covered by a large scarlet bignonia and a native multiflora rose, which, entwisting and interlacing, left scarce a vestige [bit] of the rough logs to be seen. Here, also, in summer, various brilliant annuals, such as marigolds, petunias, four-

In this illustration from Harriet Beecher Stowe's famous antislavery novel, Uncle Tom leads a prayer meeting in his cabin.

o'clocks, found an indulgent corner in which to unfold their splendors, and were the delight and pride of Aunt Chloe's heart.

Let us enter the dwelling. The evening meal at the house is over, and Aunt Chloe, who presided over its preparation as head cook, has left to inferior officers in the kitchen the business of clearing away and washing dishes, and come out into her own snug territories, to "get her ole man's supper"; therefore, doubt not that it is she you see by the fire, presiding with anxious interest over certain frizzling items in a stewpan, and anon [soon] with grave consideration lifting the cover of a bake-kettle, from whence steam forth indubitable intimations [absolute hints] of "something good." A round, black, shining face is hers, so glossy as to suggest the idea that she might have been washed over with white of eggs, like one of her own tea rusks [hard, baked pieces of bread]. Her whole plump countenance beams with satisfaction and contentment from under her well-starched checked turban [head covering], bearing on it, however, if we must confess it, a little of that tinge of self-consciousness which becomes the first cook of the neighborhood, as Aunt Chloe was universally held and acknowledged to be.

A cook she certainly was, in the very bone and centre of her soul. Not a chicken or turkey or duck in the barnyard but looked grave when they saw her approaching, and seemed evidently to be reflecting on their latter end; and certain it was that she was always meditating on trussing [tieing up], stuffing, and roasting, to a degree that was calculated to inspire terror in any reflecting fowl living. Her corn-cake, in all its varieties of hoe-cake, dodgers, muffins, and other species too numerous to mention, was a sublime mystery to all less practised compounders; and she would shake her fat sides with honest pride and merriment, as she would narrate the fruitless efforts that one and another of her compeers [fellow cooks] had made to attain to her elevation.

The arrival of company at the house, the arranging of dinners and suppers "in style," awoke all the energies of her soul; and no sight was more welcome to her than a pile of travelling trunks launched on the veranda, for then she foresaw fresh efforts and fresh triumphs.

Just at present, however, Aunt Chloe is looking into the bakepan; in which congenial operation [pleasant task] we shall leave her till we finish our picture of the cottage.

In one corner of it stood a bed, covered neatly with a snowy spread; and by the side of it was a piece of carpeting, of some considerable size. On this piece of carpeting Aunt Chloe took her stand, as being decidely in the upper walks of life; and it and the bed by which it lay, and the whole corner, in fact, were treated with distinguished consideration, and made, so far as possible, sacred from the marauding [raiding] inroads and desecrations of little folks. In fact, the corner was the *drawing-room* [room where guests are entertained] of the establishment. In the other corner was a bed of much humbler pretensions, and evidently designed for *use*. The wall over the fireplace was adorned with some very brilliant scriptural prints, and a portrait of general Washington, drawn and colored in a manner which would certainly have astonished that hero, if ever he had happened to meet with its like.

On a rough bench in the corner, a couple of woolly-headed boys, with glistening black eyes and fat shining cheeks, were busy in superintending the first walking operations of the baby, which, as is usually the case, consisted in getting up on its feet, balancing a moment, and then tumbling down,— each successive failure being violently cheered, as something decidedly clever.

A table, somewhat rheumatic in its limbs [with creaky legs], was drawn out in front of the fire, and covered with a cloth, displaying cups and saucers of a decidedly brilliant pattern, with other symptoms of an approaching meal. At this table was seated Uncle Tom, Mr. Shelby's best hand, who, as he is to be the hero of our story, we must daguerreotype [an early kind of photograph] for our readers. He was a large, broad-chested, powerfully made man, of a full glossy black, and a face whose truly African features were characterized by an expression of grave and steady good sense, united with much kindliness and benevolence. There was something about his whole air self-respecting and dignified, yet united with a confiding and humble simplicity.

REVIEWING THE READING

1. How does the author describe her main character, Uncle Tom?

2. What was Aunt Chloe's reputation in the neighborhood?

3. **Using Your Historical Imagination.** What point do you think Stowe was trying to make with this description of Chloe, Tom, and the home in which they live.

Frederick Douglass Describes the Songs of Slavery (1855)

71

From *My Bondage and My Freedom* by Frederick Douglass.

Frederick Douglass, the eloquent writer and lecturer, was himself an escaped slave. In the following excerpts from his autobiography, he explains why slaves sang so frequently. The songs of slaves often had double meanings and contained a kind of "code." On the surface they sounded harmless enough to owners and overseers, but at a deeper level they were about forbidden subjects. This is true of "Go Down, Moses" and "Follow the Drinking Gourd," the two slave songs that follow Douglass' explanation. What do you think may have been the hidden meanings of these two slave songs?

Slaves are generally expected to sing as well as to work. A silent slave is not liked by masters or overseers. *"Make a noise, make a noise,"* and *"bear a hand,"* are the words usually addressed to the slaves when there is silence amongst them. This may account for the almost constant singing heard in the southern states. . . . On allowance day, those who visited the great house farm were peculiarly excited and noisy. While on their way, they would make the dense old woods, for miles around, reverberate with their wild notes. These were not always merry because they were wild. On the contrary, they were mostly of a plaintive [woeful] cast, and told a tale of grief and sorrow. In the most boisterous outbursts of rapturous sentiment, there was ever a tinge of deep melancholy. I have never heard any songs like those anywhere since I left slavery, except when in Ireland. There I heard the same *wailing notes*, and

This illustration was on the cover of the sheet music for a song dedicated to Frederick Douglass.

was much affected by them. It was during the famine of 1845–1846. In all the songs of the slaves, there was ever some expression in praise of the great house farm; something which would flatter the pride of the owner, and, possibly, draw a favorable glance from him. . . .

The hearing of those wild notes always depressed my spirits, and filled my heart with ineffable [unspeakable] sadness. The mere recurrence, even now, affects my spirit, and while I am writing these lines, my tears are falling. To those songs I trace my first glimmering conceptions of the dehumanizing character of slavery. I can never get rid of that conception. Those songs still follow me, to deepen my hatred of slavery, and quicken my sympathies for my brethren in bonds. If any one wishes to be impressed with a sense of the soul-killing power of slavery, let him go to Col. Lloyd's plantation, and, on allowance day, place himself in the deep pine woods, and there let him, in silence, thoughtfully analyze the sounds that shall pass through the chambers of his soul, and if he is not thus impressed, it will only be because "there is no flesh in his obdurate [hard] heart."

Go Down, Moses

Go down, Moses,
Way down in Egypt land
Tell old Pharaoh
To let my people go.

When Israel was in Egypt land
Let my people go
Oppressed so hard they could not stand
Let my people go.

Go down, Moses,
Way down in Egypt land
Tell old Pharaoh
"Let my people go."

"Thus saith the Lord," bold Moses said,
"Let my people go;
If not I'll smite your first-born dead
Let my people go.

Go down, Moses,
Way down in Egypt land,
Tell old Pharaoh,
"Let my people go."

Follow the Drinking Gourd

When the sun comes back and the first quail calls,
    Follow the drinking gourd,
For the old man is a-waiting for to carry you to
        freedom
    If you follow the drinking gourd.

[Refrain] Follow the drinking gourd,
    Follow the drinking gourd,
For the old man is a-waiting for to carry you to
        freedom
    If you follow the drinking gourd.

The river bank will make a very good road,
    The dead trees show you the way,
Left foot, peg foot traveling on
    Follow the drinking gourd. [Refrain]

The river ends between two hills
Follow the drinking gourd.
There's another river on the other side,
Follow the drinking gourd. [Refrain]

Where the little river meets the great big river,
Follow the drinking gourd.
The old man is a-waiting for to carry you to freedom,
If you follow the drinking gourd. [Refrain]

REVIEWING THE READING

1. According to Douglass, why did the slaves sing so much?

2. What is the hidden significance of the "Moses theme" in the first song? Why was Moses such an important Biblical figure to the slaves?

3. **Using Your Historical Imagination.** The "drinking gourd" was the slaves' name for the Big Dipper constellation, the handle of which always points toward the North Star. With that additional information, what do you think is the hidden significance of the second song, "Follow the Drinking Gourd"?

Lucy Stone Calls for Woman's Rights (1855)

72

From *History of Woman Suffrage*, edited by Elizabeth Cady Stanton, Susan B. Anthony, Matilda Joslyn Gage.

Although many people believe that the struggle for women's rights began in the turbulent decade of the 1960s, this struggle actually goes back more than a century. In 1848, for example, more than 300 men and women met at Seneca Falls, New York, to call for the social, political, and economic equality of the sexes. This important meeting encouraged many people to speak out in favor of their beliefs. One tireless worker in the fight for equality was Lucy Stone. The following excerpt is from a speech given by Stone at a national woman's rights convention, held in Cincinnati, Ohio, in 1855. As you read the selection, note what Stone says about women and marriage.

The last speaker alluded [made an indirect reference] to this movement as being that of a few disappointed women. From the first years to which my memory stretches, I have been a disappointed woman. When, with my brothers, I reached forth after the sources of knowledge, I was reproved [scolded] with "It isn't fit for you; it doesn't belong to women." Then there was but one college in the world where women were admitted, and that was in Brazil. I would have found my way there, but by the time I was prepared to go, one was opened in the young state of Ohio—the first in the United States where women and Negroes could enjoy opportunities with white men. I was disappointed when I came to seek a profession worthy an immortal being—every employment was closed to me, except

Woman's rights leader Lucy Stone may have been the first woman to continue to use her maiden name after marriage—a practice that is common today but was not in the 1850s. Other women who followed her example were called "Lucy Stoners."

those of the teacher, the seamstress, and the house-keeper. In education, in marriage, in religion, in everything, disappointment is the lot of woman. It shall be the business of my life to deepen this disappointment in every woman's heart until she bows down to it no longer. I wish that women, instead of being walking show-cases, instead of begging of their fathers and brothers the latest and gayest new bonnet, would ask of them their rights.

The question of Women's Rights is a practical one. The notion has prevailed that it is only an ephemeral [fleeting] idea; that it was but women claiming the right to smoke cigars in the streets, and to frequent bar-rooms. Others have supposed it a question of comparative intellect; others still, of sphere. Too much has already been said and written about women's sphere. Trace all the doctrines to their source and they will be found to have no basis except in the usages and prejudices of the age. This is seen in the fact that what is tolerated in woman in one country is not tolerated in another. In this country women may hold prayer-meetings, etc., but in Mohammedan countries it is written upon their mosques [places of worship], "Women and dogs, and other impure animals, are not permitted to enter." Wendell Phillips says, "The best and greatest thing one is capable of doing, that is his sphere." I have confidence in the Father to believe that when He gives us the capacity to do anything He does not make a blunder. Leave women, then, to find their sphere. And do not tell us before we are born even, that our province is to cook dinners, darn socks, and sew on buttons. We are told woman has all the rights she wants; and even women, I am ashamed to say, tell us so. They mistake the politeness of men for rights—seats while men stand in this hall to-night, and their adulations [flattery]; but these are mere courtesies. We want rights. . . . Women working in tailor-shops are paid one-third as much as men. Some one in Philadelphia has stated that women make fine shirts for twelve and a half cents apiece; that no woman can make more than nine a week, and the sum thus earned, after deducting rent, fuel, etc., leaves her just three and a half cents a day for bread. Is it a wonder that women are driven to prostitution? Female teachers in New York are paid fifty dollars a year, and for every such situation there are five hundred applicants. I know not what you believe of God, but I believe He gave yearnings and longings to be filled, and that He did not mean all our time should be devoted to feeding and clothing the body. The present condition of woman causes a horrible perversion of the marriage relation. It is asked of a lady, "Has she married well?" "Oh, yes, her husband is rich." Women must marry for a home, and you men are the sufferers by this; for a woman who loathes [hates] you may marry you because you have the means to get money which she cannot have. But when woman can enter the lists [fields of competition] with you and make money for herself, she will marry you only for deep and earnest affection.

REVIEWING THE READING

1. How was Stone treated when she sought to be educated like her brothers? What kinds of jobs does she say were open to women?

2. According to Stone, what should be women's proper sphere?

3. **Using Your Historical Imagination.** Why do you think that Stone said the earning of money by women would change the marriage relationship?

73

From *The Irrepressible Conflict: a Speech delivered at Rochester*, October 25, 1858 by William H. Seward.

Senator Seward Foresees an "Irrepressible Conflict" (1858)

Senator William H. Seward of New York predicted the approaching Civil War when he spoke of an "irrepressible conflict." He also told why the conflict was inevitable: "It is an irrepressible conflict between opposing and enduring forces, and it means that the United States must and will sooner or later, become either entirely a slave-holding nation, or entirely a free-labor nation." As you read the following excerpts from Seward's speech on this subject, pay careful attention to what he has to say about the Constitution and the institution of slavery.

O ur country is a theatre, which exhibits, in full operation, two radically different political systems; the one resting on the basis of servile or slave labor, the other on the basis of voluntary labor of freemen. . . .

The two systems are at once perceived to be incongruous [unrelated]. But they are more than incongruous—they are incompatible. They never have permanently existed together in one country, and they never can. It would be easy to demonstrate this impossibility, from the irreconcilable contrast between their great principles and characteristics. But the experience of mankind has conclusively established it. . . .

Hitherto, the two systems have existed in different States, but side by side within the American Union. This has happened because the Union is a confederation of States. But in another aspect the United States constitute only one nation. Increase

Senator William Henry
Seward argued force-
fully against slavery
before the outbreak of the
Civil War and served
as secretary of state for
President Lincoln during
the war years.

of population, which is filling the States out to their
very borders, together with a new and extended
network of railroads and other avenues, and an internal commerce which daily becomes more intimate
[closely related], is rapidly bringing the States into
a higher and more perfect social unity of consolida-
tion. Thus, these antagonistic systems are continually
coming into closer contact, and collision results.

Shall I tell you what this collision means? They
who think that is accidental, unnecessary, the work
of interested and fanatical agitators, and therefore
ephemeral [not likely to last], mistake the case altogether. It is an irrepressible conflict between opposing and enduring forces, and it means that the United
States must and will, sooner or later, become either

entirely a slave-holding nation, or entirely a free-labor nation. Either the cotton and rice fields of South Carolina and the sugar plantations of Louisiana will ultimately be tilled by free labor, and Charleston and New Orleans become marts for legitimate merchandise alone, or else the rye-fields and wheat-fields of Massachusetts and New York must again be surrendered by their farmers to slave culture and to the production of slaves, and Boston and New York become once more markets for trade in the bodies and souls of men. It is the failure to apprehend [understand] this great truth that induces so many unsuccessful attempts at final compromise between the slave and free States, and it is the existence of this great fact that renders all such pretended compromises, when made, vain and ephemeral. . . .

It remains to say on this point only one word, to guard against misapprehension [misunderstanding]. If these States are to again become universally slave-holding, I do not pretend to say with what violations of the Constitution that end shall be accomplished. On the other hand, while I do confidently believe and hope that my country will yet become a land of universal Freedom, I do not expect that it will be made so otherwise than through the action of the several States cooperating with the Federal Government, and all acting in strict conformity with their respective Constitutions.

The strife and contentions concerning Slavery, which gently-disposed persons so habitually deprecate [condemn], are nothing more than the ripening of the conflict which the fathers themselves not only thus regarded with favor, but which they may be said to have instituted.

It is not to be denied, however, that thus far the course of that contest has not been according to their humane anticipations and wishes. . . .

I know, and you know, that a revolution has begun. I know, and all the world knows, that revolutions never go backward. Twenty Senators and a hundred Representatives proclaim boldly in Congress to-day sentiments and opinions and principles of Freedom which hardly so many men, even in this free State, dared to utter in their own homes twenty years ago. While the Government of the United States, under the conduct of the Democratic party, has been all that time surrendering one plain and castle after another to Slavery, the people of the United States have been no less steadily and perseveringly gathering together the forces with which to recover back again all the fields and all the castles which have been lost, and to confound and overthrow, by one decisive blow, the betrayers of the Constitution and Freedom forever.

REVIEWING THE READING

1. What does Seward say is the history of part-slave, part-free societies in other countries?

2. What social and technological changes are making the conflict over slavery even worse?

3. **Using Your Historical Imagination.** Can you see in today's news events irrepressible conflicts? Between whom? What might come of them?

From *Memoirs of Gustave Koerner* II.

74

Gustave Koerner Observes the Lincoln–Douglas Debates (1858)

Although senators were not elected directly by the people in 1858, everyone in Illinois knew that the contest was between Stephen Douglas, a Democrat, and Abraham Lincoln, a Republican. And the issue was slavery—particularly the extension of "the peculiar institution" into the new western territories. Gustave Koerner, the German political leader who wrote this account of the debates, followed the candidates for most of their encounters. Judging from the following excerpts from Koerner's observations, which debater do you think seems more forceful?

On June 15th, the Republican Convention met in Springfield. Twelve hundred delegates attended. Richard Yates was made temporary, and I permanent, chairman. It adopted in the main the Republican State platform of 1856. It disapproved of the Dred Scott decision, maintained the right of Congress to prohibit slavery in the Territories and its duty to exercise it, approved the recent decision of the Supreme Court of Illinois, which declared that property in persons was repugnant [contrary] to the constitution of Illinois, and that slavery was the creature of local and municipal law. A resolution that Abraham Lincoln was the first and only choice of the Republicans of Illinois was adopted with the most deafening applause. James Miller, the old Republican incumbent, was nominated State Treasurer and Newton Bateman for Superintendent of Public Instruction.

The Convention met again in the evening. Mr. Lincoln, having been requested to address the Convention, took his stand on the right hand of the President, and delivered the ever-memorable speech containing the passage: "A house divided against itself cannot stand. I believe this government cannot endure permanently half slave and half free. I do not expect the Union to be dissolved. I do not expect the house to fall, but I do expect it to cease to be divided. It will become all one thing or all the other. Either the opponents of slavery will arrest the further spread of it, and place it where the public mind shall rest in the belief that it is in the course of ultimate extinction,—or its advocates will push it forward until it shall become alike lawful in all the States, old as well as new, North as well as South. Have we no tendency to the latter condition?"

Other speakers followed him and the Convention adjourned amid the wildest enthusiasm. . . .

The first speech Judge Douglas made was at Chicago. His friends had made the most ample preparations for an ovation. Notice had been given for weeks, half-price excursion trains carried large numbers from the country into town. Bands of music and torch-light processions brought large masses to the front of the Tremont House, from the balcony of which he addressed the crowd. Bengal fires illuminated the scene, and when he appeared he was greeted with tumultuous cheers. He was fighting for his political life. His massive form supported his ample head, covered with a thick growth of black hair. His deep-set, dark blue eyes shed their lustre under his heavy brows. The features of his firm, round face were wonderfully expressive of the working of his feelings. Calm in stating facts, passionate when he attacked, disdainful when he was forced to defend, his gestures were sometimes violent, and often exceptionally so. His voice was strong, but not modulated. Bold in his assertions, maledictory [hateful] in his attacks, impressive in language, not caring to persuade, but intent to force the assent of his hearers, he was Danton, not the Mirabeau [both French revolutionists], of oratory. . . .

Lincoln, who happened to be in the city, sat quietly on the same balcony. After Douglas got through, he was loudly called for. He rose, and stated that this ovation was gotten up for his friend Judge Douglas, but that if the good people of Chicago would listen to him, he would speak to them to-morrow evening at the same time and place. Without time for parade or showy demonstration the throng that listened to Lincoln next evening, as might have been expected from the political complexion of the city, was larger and really more enthusiastic than the one of the night before.

No greater contrast could be imagined than the one between Lincoln and Douglas. The latter was really a very little giant physically, measuring five feet and nothing, while Lincoln, when standing erect, towered to six feet three inches. Lincoln, awk-ward in his posture and leaning a little forward, stood calm and collected, addressing his hearers in a somewhat familiar, yet very earnest, way, with a clear, distinct, and far-reaching voice, generally well modulated, but sometimes rather shrill. When un-moved, his features seemed overshadowed by an

In this illustration from 1858, Lincoln and Douglas debate before a crowd in Illinois.

expression of sadness, though at times he could assume a most humorous, and even comical, look; but, when aroused, he appeared like a prophet of old. Neither he nor Douglas indulged in rhetoric; both were mainly argumentative [presented reasonable arguments rather than using exaggeration for effect]. But while Douglas, powerful as was his speech, never showed anything like genius, there came from Lincoln occasionally flashes of genius and burning words, revelations as it were from the unknown, that will live as long as the English language lives. Lincoln was deeply read in the Bible and Shakespeare. He did not quote from them, but his style showed plainly his close intimacy with the Scriptures and the great bard [poet]. Douglas was eminently talented; Lincoln was original. But what made Lincoln vastly more effective in this contest was that even the most obtuse [the dullest] hearer could see at once that Douglas spoke for himself, and Lincoln for his cause.

> . . . there came from Lincoln occasionally flashes of genius and burning words . . .

The day after Lincoln's speech, July 15th, both went down on the train to Springfield,—Lincoln as a quiet passenger, Douglas as a sort of triumphator. He had a special car, had a secretary and a reporter, and a number of devoted friends with him. A band of music accompanied him, and on an attached platform car a gun was planted, which was fired off to announce his arrival at every station. His car was decorated with flags and emblems. Preparations had been made at every station to receive him with music and the booming of cannon. The station platforms were crowded with men, women and children.

At Bloomington, where an appointment had been made for Douglas to speak, processions, salutes of cannon, fireworks, an immense crowd,—everything, in fact,—had been ready to glorify the idol of the Illinois Democracy. Lincoln listened quietly. At Springfield Douglas met with a similar reception, and he spoke in the afternoon at Edwards' Grove for three hours. His friends pronounced it the best speech of his campaign. But now came Lincoln's turn. He spoke in Springfield at night. His speech was not only a masterpiece of argument, but so full of splendid humor that it kept the audience in roars of laughter. . . .

Lincoln now had measured swords, and in spite of his innate [natural] modesty was sagacious [wise] enough to see that he was Douglas's match in every respect. He proposed to canvass the State jointly, dividing the time between them. Douglas alleging that his friends had already made appointments for him, which he could not recall and which occupied nearly all his time, consented, however, to seven joint debates at Ottawa, Freeport, Quincy, Galesburg, Jonesborough, Charleston and Alton. Those joint meetings drew immense crowds. Douglas, impetuous, denunciatory, frequently lost his temper, made unguarded statements of audacity and supreme self-confidence. Lincoln impressed his audiences by his almost too extreme fairness, his always pure and elevated language, and his appeals to their higher nature. Douglas, on the contrary, roused the existing strong prejudices against the negro race to the highest pitch, and not unfrequently resorted to demagogism [rabble-rousing] unworthy of his own great reputation as a statesman.

REVIEWING THE READING

1. Explain Lincoln's phrase, "A house divided against itself cannot stand."

2. Contrast Lincoln and Douglas as debaters, based on Koerner's descriptions.

3. **Using Your Historical Imagination.** Imagine that you have been waiting for the trains carrying the two debaters. Describe in a letter to a friend Douglas' private car and the show he put on, with cannon salutes and fireworks, or Lincoln's simple arrival and his "splendid humor."

John Brown's Last Speech (1859)

75

From *America In Literature*, Volume I, edited by David Levin and Theodore L. Gross.

As you read John Brown's last speech, delivered in court, try to be as impartial as a jury member and consider how you would judge this man. Remember that Brown's accusers have already spoken and he waits only for the verdict. See if you really think he is trying to convince you that he is innocent of the crimes for which he stands accused.

I have, may it please the Court, a few words to say.

In the first place, I deny everything but what I have all along admitted,—the design on my part to free the slaves. I intended certainly to have made a clean thing of that matter, as I did last winter, when I went into Missouri and there took slaves without the snapping of a gun on either side, moved them through the country, and finally left them in Canada. I designed to have done the same thing again, on a larger scale. That was all I intended. I never did intend murder, or treason, or the destruction of property, or to excite or incite slaves to rebellion, or to make insurrection.

I have another objection; and that is, it is unjust that I should suffer such a penalty. Had I interfered in the manner which I admit, and which I admit has been fairly proved (for I admire the truthfulness and candor of the greater portion of the witnesses who have testified in this case),—had I so interfered in behalf of the rich, the powerful, the intelligent, the so-called great, or in behalf of any other of their friends,—either father, mother, brother, sister, wife, or children, or any of that class,—and suffered and sacrificed what I have in this interference, it would have been all right; and every man in this

Abolitionist John Brown was tried for treason after an unsuccessful raid on the arsenal at Harpers Ferry, Virginia. He was hanged on December 2, 1859.

court would have deemed it an act worthy of reward rather than punishment.

This court acknowledges, as I suppose, the validity of the law of God. I see a book kissed here which I suppose to be the Bible, or at least the New Testament. That teaches me that all things whatsoever I would that men should do to me, I should do even so to them. It teaches me, further, to "remember them that are in bonds, as bound with them." I endeavored to act up to that instruction. I say, I am yet too young to understand that God is any respecter of persons. I believe that to have interfered as I have done—as I have always freely admitted I have done—in behalf of His despised poor, was not wrong, but right. Now, if it is deemed necessary that I should forfeit my life for the furtherance of the ends of justice, and mingle my blood further with the blood of my children and with the blood of millions in this slave country whose rights are disregarded by wicked, cruel, and unjust enactments,—I submit; so let it be done!

Let me say one word further.

I feel entirely satisfied with the treatment I have received on my trial. Considering all the circumstances, it has been more generous than I expected. But I felt no consciousness of guilt. I have stated from the first what was my intention, and what was not. I never had any design against the life of any person, nor any disposition to commit treason, or excite slaves to rebel, or make any general insurrection. I never encouraged any man to do so, but always discouraged any idea of that kind.

Let me say, also, a word in regard to the statements made by some of those connected with me. I hear it has been stated by some of them that I have induced them to join me. But the contrary is true. I do not say this to injure them, but as regretting their weakness. There is not one of them but joined me of his own accord, and the greater part of them at their own expense. A number of them I never saw, and never had a word of conversation with, till the day they came to me; and that was for the purpose I have stated.

Now I have done.

REVIEWING THE READING

1. What does John Brown admit that he intended to accomplish at Harpers Ferry?

2. From evidence in his speech, what does he stand accused of?

3. **Using Your Historical Imagination.** Read John Brown's speech again carefully. What do you think Brown was trying to accomplish with this speech, since he apparently believed the verdict would go against him? To whom was he speaking, and why?

76 At a Slave Auction (1859)

From the *New-York Daily Tribune*, March 9, 1859.

Horace Greeley, editor of the New York Tribune, had a great influence on the views held by his readers concerning slavery. The readers were mostly farmers and village people, and the weekly and semi-weekly issues of the Tribune often carried sensational articles about the abuses of slavery that—over time—profoundly affected their opinions. In 1859 a reporter from the Tribune covered a great slave auction in Savannah, Georgia, and published his account in Greeley's newspaper. As you read the following excerpts from the reporter's article, note why the sale attracted so much attention.

The largest sale of human chattels that has been made in Star-Spangled America for several years took place on Wednesday and Thursday of last week, at the Race Course near the City of Savannah, Georgia. The lot consisted of four hundred and thirty-six men, women, children and infants, being that half of the negro stock remaining on the old Major Butler plantations which fell to one of the two heirs to that estate. . . .

The sale had been advertised largely for many weeks, and as the negroes were known to be a choice lot and very desirable property, the attendance of buyers was large. The breaking up of an old family estate is so uncommon an occurrence that the affair was regarded with unusual interest throughout the South. For several days before the sale every hotel in Savannah was crowded with negro speculators from North and South Carolina, Virginia, Georgia, Alabama and Louisiana, who had been attracted hither by the prospects of making good bargains. Nothing was heard for days, in the bar-rooms and

public rooms but talk of the great sale, criticisms
of the business affairs of Mr. Butler, and speculations
as to the probable prices the stock would bring.
The office of Joseph Bryan the negro broker who
had the management of the sale, was thronged every
day by eager inquirers in search of information, and
by some who were anxious to buy, but were uncertain
as to whether their securities would prove acceptable.
Little parties were made up from the various hotels
every day to visit the Race-Course, distant some
three miles from the city, to look over the chattels,
discuss their points, and make memoranda for guid-
ance on the day of sale. The buyers were generally
of a rough breed, slangy, profane and bearish, being
for the most part, from the back river and swamp
plantations, where the elegancies of polite life are
not perhaps developed to their fullest extent. . . .

. . . **The buyers were generally of rough breed, slangy, profane and bearish . . .**

The negroes came from two plantations, the
one a rice plantation near Darien . . . and the other
a cotton plantation. . . .

None of the Butler slaves have ever been sold
before, but have been on these two plantations since
they were born. . . .

It is true they were sold "in families;" but let
us see: a man and his wife were called a "family,"
their parents and kindred were not taken into account. . . . And no account could be taken of loves
that were as yet unconsummated by marriage, and
how many aching hearts have been divorced by
this summary proceeding, no man can ever
know. . . .

The slaves remained at the race-course, some
of them for more than a week and all of them for
four days before the sale. They were brought in
thus early that buyers who desired to inspect them
might enjoy that privilege, although none of them
were sold at private sale. For these preliminary days
their shed was constantly visited by speculators. The
negroes were examined with as little consideration
as if they had been brutes indeed; the buyers pulling
their mouths open to see their teeth, pinching their

limbs to find how muscular they were, walking them up and down to detect any signs of lameness, making them stoop and bend in different ways that they might be certain there was no concealed rupture or wound; and in addition to all this treatment, asking them scores of questions relative to their qualifications and accomplishments. All these humiliations were submitted to without a murmur, and in some instances with good-natured cheerfulness—where the slave liked the appearance of the proposed buyer, and fancied that he might prove a kind "mas'r."

The following curiously sad scene is the type of a score of others that were there enacted:

"Elisha," chattel No. 5 in the catalogue, had taken a fancy to a benevolent looking middle-aged gentleman, who was inspecting stock, and thus used his powers of persuasion to induce the benevolent man to purchase him, with his wife, boy and girl, Molly, Israel and Sevanda, chattels Nos. 6, 7 and 8. The earnestness with which the poor fellow pressed his suit, knowing, as he did, that perhaps the happiness of his whole life depended on his success, was interesting, and the arguments he used were most pathetic. He made no appeal to the feelings of the buyer; he rested no hope on his charity and kindness, but only strove to show how well worth his dollars were the bone and blood he was entreating [begging] him to buy.

"Look at me, mas'r, am prime rice planter; sho' you won't find a better man den me; no better on de whole plantation; not a bit old yet; do mo' work den ever; do carpenter work, too, little; better buy me, Mas'r; I'se be good sarvant, Mas'r. Molly, too, my wife, Sa, fus rate rice hand; mos as good as me. Stan' out yer, Molly, and let the gen'lm'n see."

Molly advances, with her hands crossed on her bosom, and makes a quick short curtsy, and stands mute, looking appealingly in the benevolent man's face. But Elisha talks all the faster.

"Show mas'r yer arm Molly—good arm dat mas'r—she do a heap of work mo' with dat arm

yet. Let good mas'r see yer teeth Molly—see dat mas'r, teeth all reg'lar, all good-she'm young gal yet. Come out yer Israel, walk aroun' an' let the gen'lm'n see how spry you be"—

Then, pointing to the three-year-old girl who stood with her chubby hand to her mouth, holding on to her mother's dress, and uncertain what to make of the strange scene.

"Little Vardy's on'y a chile yet; make prime gal by-and-by. Better buy us mas'r, we'm fus' rate bargain"—and so on. But the benevolent gentlemen found where he could drive a closer bargain, and so bought somebody else. . . .

Mr. Walsh mounted the stand and announced the terms of the sale, "one-third cash, the remainder payable in two equal annual installments, bearing interest from the day of sale, to be secured by ap-

Auctions such as the one depicted in this engraving were what abolitionists found most hateful about slavery.

proved mortgage and personal security, or approved acceptances on Savannah, Ga., or Charleston, S. C. Purchasers to pay for papers." The buyers, who were present to the number of about two hundred, clustered around the platform; while the negroes, who were not likely to be immediately wanted, gathered into sad groups in the background to watch the progress of the selling in which they were so sorrowfully interested. The wind howled outside, and through the open side of the building the driving rain came pouring in; the bar down stairs ceased for a short time its brisk trade; the buyers lit fresh cigars, got ready their catalogues and pencils, and the first lot of human chattels are led upon the stand, not by a white man, but by a sleek mulatto, himself a slave, and who seems to regard the selling of his brethren, in which he so glibly assists, as a capital joke. It had been announced that the negroes would be sold in "families," that is to say, a man would not be parted from his wife, or a mother from a very young child. There is perhaps as much policy as humanity in this arrangement, for thereby many aged and unserviceable people are disposed of, who otherwise would not find a ready sale. . . .

The expression on the faces of all who stepped on the block was always the same, and told of more anguish than it is in the power of words to express. Blighted homes, crushed hopes and broken hearts was the sad story to be read in all the anxious faces. Some of them regarded the sale with perfect indifference, never making a motion save to turn from one side to the other at the word of the dapper Mr. Bryan, that all the crown might have a fair view of their proportions, and then, when the sale was accomplished, stepping down from the block without caring to cast even a look at the buyer, who now held all their happiness in his hands. Others, again, strained their eyes with eager glances from one buyer to another as the bidding went on, trying with earnest attention to follow the rapid voice of the auctioneer.

Sometimes, two persons only would be bidding for the same chattel, all the others having resigned the contest, and then the poor creature on the block, conceiving an instantaneous preference for one of the buyers over the other, would regard the rivalry with the intensest interest, the expression of his face changing with every bid, settling into a half smile of joy if the favorite buyer persevered unto the end and secured the property, and settling down into a look of hopeless despair if the other won the victory. . . .

The auctioneer brought up Joshua's Molly and family. He announced that Molly insisted that she was lame in her left foot, and perversely would walk lame, although, for his part, he did not believe a word of it. He had caused her to be examined by an eminent physician in Savannah, which medical light had declared that Joshua's Molly was not lame, but was only shamming [pretending]. However, the gentlemen must judge for themselves and bid accordingly. So Molly was put through her paces, and compelled to trot up and down along the stage, to go up and down the steps, and to exercise her feet in various ways, but always with the same result, the left foot *would* be lame. She was finally sold for $695.

Whether she really was lame or not, no one knows but herself, but it must be remembered that to a slave a lameness, or anything that decreases his market value, is a thing to be rejoiced over. A man in the prime of life, worth $1,600 or thereabouts, can have little hope of ever being able, by any little savings of his own, to purchase his liberty. But, let him have a rupture, or lose a limb, or sustain any other injury that renders him of much less service to his owner, and reduces his value to $300 or $400, and he may hope to accumulate that sum, and eventually to purchase his liberty. Freedom without health is infinitely sweeter than health without freedom.

And so the Great Sale went on for two long days, during which time there were sold 429 men,

> . . . She was finally sold for $695.

women and children. There were 436 announced to be sold, but a few were detained on the plantations by sickness. . . .

The total amount of the sale foots up [adds up to] $303,850—the proceeds of the first day being $161,480, and of the second day $142,370. . . .

Leaving the Race buildings, where the scenes we have described took place, a crowd of negroes were seen gathered eagerly about a man in their midst. The man was Mr. Pierce M. Butler of the free city of Philadelphia, who was solacing [soothing] the wounded hearts of the people he had sold from their firesides and their homes, by doling out to them small change at the rate of a dollar a head. To every negro he had sold, who presented his claim for the paltry pittance, he gave the munificent stipend [magnificent sum] of one whole dollar, in specie; he being provided with two canvas bags of 25 cent pieces, fresh from the mint, to give an additional glitter to his munificent generosity.

REVIEWING THE READING

1. Why was the slave auction at the Savannah race course regarded with so much interest?

2. Why was the auctioneer playing with the truth when he announced that only "families" would be sold?

3. **Using Your Historical Imagination.** The slaves in the auction were almost powerless to alter what was happening to them, but not quite. What strategies were being used by some of the slaves to better their situations? Can you think of other strategies that the slaves might have used on the plantations to make their lives a little easier?

Mark Twain Describes the Pony Express (1860)

77

From *Roughing It* by Mark Twain.

In Roughing It *Mark Twain vividly describes the transfer of a single mail bag from one pony express rider to another. Eighty pony riders were in the saddle at the same time, 40 west, 40 east, riding 24 hours a day to cover a route of 1,900 miles. Yet history compels us to point out that the fabled pony express went out of business in just 18 months. As you read the following excerpt from Chapter 8 of Twain's book, consider what may have been the reason that the pony express closed down after such a short period of time.*

In a little while all interest was taken up in stretching our necks and watching for the "pony-rider"—the fleet messenger who sped across the continent from St. Joe to Sacramento, carrying letters nineteen hundred miles in eight days! Think of that for perishable horse and human flesh and blood to do! The pony-rider was usually a little bit of a man, brimful of spirit and endurance. No matter what time of the day or night his watch came on, and no matter whether it was winter or summer, raining, snowing, hailing, or sleeting, or whether his "beat" was a level straight road or crazy trail over mountain crags and precipices [steep cliffs], or whether it led through peaceful regions or regions that swarmed with hostile Indians, he must be always ready to leap into the saddle and be off like the wind! There was no idling-time for a pony-rider on duty. He rode fifty miles without stopping, by daylight, moonlight, starlight, or through the blackness of darkness—just as it happened. He rode a splendid horse

For a short period in the 1800s, pony express riders provided a link between the eastern and western United States. But telegraph lines helped make the speeding horsemen unnecessary.

that was born for a racer and fed and lodged like a gentleman; kept him at his utmost speed for ten miles, and then, as he came crashing up to the station where stood two men holding fast a fresh, impatient steed, the transfer of rider and mail-bag was made in the twinkling of an eye, and away flew the eager pair and were out of sight before the spectator could get hardly the ghost of a look. Both rider and horse went "flying light." The rider's dress was thin, and fitted close; he wore a "round-about," [short, close-fitting jacket] and a skull-cap, and tucked his pantaloons into his boot-tops like a race-rider. He carried no arms—he carried nothing that was not absolutely necessary, for even the postage on his literary freight was worth *five dollars a letter*. He got but little frivolous correspondence to carry—his bag had business letters in it, mostly. His horse was stripped of all unnecessary weight, too. He wore a little wafer of a racing-saddle, and no visible blanket. He wore light shoes, or none at all. The little flat mail-pockets strapped under the rider's thighs would each hold about the bulk of a child's primer. They held many and many an important business chapter and newspaper letter, but these were written on paper as airy and thin as gold-leaf, nearly, and thus bulk and weight were economized. The stage-coach traveled about a hundred to a hundred and twenty-five miles a day (twenty-four hours), the pony-rider about two hundred and fifty.

There were about eighty pony-riders in the saddle all the time, night and day, stretching in a long, scattering procession from Missouri to California, forty flying eastward, and forty toward the west, and among them making four hundred gallant horses earn a stirring livelihood and see a great deal of scenery every single day in the year. . . .

Away across the endless dead level of the prairie a black speck appears against the sky, and it is plain that it moves. Well, I should think so! In a second or two it becomes a horse and rider, rising and falling—sweeping toward us nearer and nearer—growing more and more distinct, more and more sharply defined—nearer and still nearer, and the flutter of the hoofs comes faintly to the ear—another instant a whoop and a hurrah from our upper deck, a wave of the rider's hand, but no reply, and man and horse burst past our excited faces, and go winging away like a belated fragment of a storm!

REVIEWING THE READING

1. How many miles was a bag of mail carried each 24-hour period by the pony express? How many miles did each rider ride each day?

2. Describe some of the measures used to keep rider and pony as light as possible.

3. **Using Your Historical Imagination.** You have decided to become a rider in the pony express. How will you convince the agent to hire you?

Plantation Life During the War (1860s)

78

From *White and Black Under the Old Regime* by Victoria V. Clayton.

Victoria Virginia Clayton, like many of the wives of southern plantation owners, managed the plantation while her husband fought at the front. As the war dragged on, Union blockades made even the simplest items impossible to obtain. Yet southerners invented their own brand of Yankee ingenuity when the need arose. In the following selection, excerpted from her published journal, Clayton tells how she improvised to take care of herself, her children, and her plantation during the war. Consider the role played by slaves during this period of hard times and deprivation.

While my husband was at the front doing active service, suffering fatigue, privations, and the many ills attendant on a soldier's life, I was at home struggling to keep the family comfortable.

We were blockaded on every side, could get nothing from without, so had to make everything at home; and having been heretofore only an agricultural people, it became necessary for every home to be supplied with spinning wheels and the old-fashioned loom, in order to manufacture clothing for the members of the family. This was no small undertaking. I knew nothing about spinning and weaving cloth. I had to learn myself, and then to teach the negroes. Fortunately for me, most of the negroes knew how to spin thread, the first step towards cloth-making. Our work was hard and continuous. To this we did not object, but our hearts sorrowed for our loved ones in the field.

Our home was situated a mile from the town of Clayton. On going to town one day I discovered a small bridge over which we had to pass that needed repairing. It was almost impassable. I went home, called some of our men, and gave them instructions to get up the necessary articles and put the bridge in condition to be passed over safely. I was there giving instructions about the work, when an old gentleman, our Probate Judge, came along. He stopped to see what we were doing. When satisfied, he said to me:

"Madam, I think we will never be conquered, possessing such noble women as we do." . . .

There was no white person on the plantation beside myself and children, the oldest of whom was attending school in Eufaula, as our Clayton schools were closed, and my time was so occupied that it was impossible for me to teach my children. Four small children and myself constituted the white family at home.

I entrusted the planting and cultivation of the various crops to old Joe. He had been my husband's nurse in infancy, and we always loved and trusted him. I kept a gentle saddle horse, and occasionally, accompanied by Joe, would ride over the entire plantation on a tour of inspection. Each night, when the day's work was done, Joe came in to make a report of everything that had been done on the plantation that day. When Mr. Clayton was where he could receive my letters, I wrote him a letter every night before retiring, and in this way he, being kept informed about the work at home, could write and make suggestions about various things to help me manage successfully.

We made good crops every year, but after the second year we planted provision crops entirely, except enough cotton for home use.

All the coloring matter for cloth had to be gathered from the forest. We would get roots and herbs and experiment with them until we found the color desired, or a near approach to it. We also found out what would dye cotton and what woolen fabrics. We had about one hundred head of sheep;

This photo from the 1860s shows slaves on a South Carolina plantation planting sweet potatoes.

and the wool yielded by these sheep and the cotton grown in the fields furnished us the material for our looms. After much hard work and experience we learned to make very comfortable clothing, some of our cloth being really pretty.

Our ladies would attend services in the church of God, dressed in their home-spun goods, and felt well pleased with their appearances; indeed, better pleased than if they had been dressed in silk of the finest fabric.

We made good warm flannels and other articles of apparel for our soldiers, and every woman learned to knit socks and stockings for her household, and many of the former were sent to the army.

In these dark days the Southern matron, when she sat down at night feeling that the day's work was over, took her knitting in her hands as a pastime, instead of the fancy work which ladies so frequently indulge in now.

I kept one woman at the loom weaving, and several spinning all the time, but found that I could not get sufficient cloth made at home; consequently I gave employment to many a poor woman whose husband was far away. Many a time have I gone ten miles in the country with my buggy filled with thread, to get one of these ladies to weave a piece of cloth for me, and then in return for her labor sent her syrup, sugar, or any of our home produce she wished.

We always planted and raised large crops of wheat, rice, sugar cane, and potatoes. In fact, we grew almost everything that would make food for man or beast. Our land is particularly blessed in this respect. I venture to say there is no land under the sun that will grow a greater variety of products than the land in these Southern states.

Being blockaded, we were obliged to put our ingenuity to work to meet the demands on us as heads of families. Some things we could not raise; for instance, the accustomed necessary luxury of every home—coffee. So we went to work to hunt up a substitute. Various articles were tried, but the best of all was the sweet potato. The potatoes were peeled, sliced, and cut into pieces as large as a coffee bean, dried, and then roasted just as we prepared coffee. This substitute, mixed with genuine coffee, makes a very palatable drink for breakfast. . . .

Another accustomed luxury of which we were deprived was white sugar. We had, however, a good substitute with which we soon became satisfied; our home-made brown sugar, from the sugar cane. It had the redeeming quality of being pure. . . .

We made many gallons of wine from the scuppernong and other grapes every year. One year I remember particularly. Sheets were spread under the long scuppernong arbors, little negro boys put on top to throw the grapes down, and grown men underneath to gather them in baskets as they fell. When brought to the house they measured thirty-two bushels, and made one hundred and twenty gallons of wine. I did not make so large a quantity from the other varieties of grapes. This wine was kept in the cellar and used for the common benefit. When the negroes would get caught out in the rain, and come to the house wet, they did not hesitate to say, "Mistus, please give me a little wine to keep cold away;" and they always received it. There never was any ill result from the use of domestic wine. We were a temperate family and the use was invariably beneficial.

Closed in as we were on every side, with nearly every white man of proper age and health enlisted in the army, with the country filled with white women, children, and old, infirm men, with thousands of slaves to be controlled, and caused through their systematic labor to feed and clothe the people at home, and to provide for our army, I often wonder, as I contemplate those by-gone days of labor and sorrow, and recall how peacefully we moved on and accomplished what we did.

We were required to give one-tenth of all that was raised, to the government. There being no educated white person on the plantation except myself, it was necessary that I should attend to the gathering and measuring of every crop and the delivery of the tenth to the government authorities. This one-tenth we gave cheerfully and often wished we had more to give.

My duties, as will be seen, were numerous and often laborious; the family on the increase continually, and every one added increased labor and responsibility. And this was the case with the typical Southern woman.

REVIEWING THE READING

1. What crops were raised on the plantation during the war, in comparison to before the war?

2. What substitutes were devised for coffee and white sugar?

3. **Using Your Historical Imagination.** Two severe—ultimately fatal—weaknesses of the Confederacy are mentioned in this reading. What were these weaknesses, and what was the cause of each?

From a Confederate Receipt Book

From *Confederate Receipt Book: A Compilation of Over One Hundred Receipts, Adapted to the Times.*

The recipes on this page are typical of those used by southern women trying to feed their families with limited resources during the Civil War.

Pumpkin Bread.

Boil a good pumpkin in water till it is quite thick, pass it through a sieve, and mix flour so as to make a good dough. This makes an excellent bread.

Indian Bread.

One quart of butter milk, one quart of corn meal, one quart of coarse flour, one cup of molasses, add a little [baking] soda and salt.

Apple Pie Without Apples.

To one small bowl of crackers, that have been soaked until no hard parts remain, add one teaspoonful of tartaric acid, sweeten to your taste, add some butter, and a very little nutmeg.

Artificial Oysters.

Take young green corn, grate it in a dish; to one pint of this add one egg, well beaten, a small teacup of flour, two or three tablespoonfuls of butter, some salt and pepper, mix them all together.

A tablespoonful of the batter will make the size of an oyster. Fry them light brown, and when done butter them. Cream if it can be procured is better.

Indian Sagamite.

Three parts of Indian meal and one of brown sugar, mixed and browned over the fire, will make the food known as "Sagamite." Used in small quantities, it not only appeases hunger but allays thirst, and is therefore useful to soldiers on a scout.

Preserving Meat Without Salt.

We need salt as a relish to our food, but it is not essential in the preservation of our meats. The Indians used little or no salt, yet they preserved meat and even fish in abundance by drying. This can be accomplished by fire, by smoke, or by sunshine, but the most rapid and reliable mode is by all of these agents combined. To do this select a spot having fullest command of sunshine. Erect there a wigwam five or six feet high, with an open top, in size proportioned to the quantity of meat to be cured, and protected from the winds, so that all the smoke must pass through the open top. The meat cut into pieces suitable for drying (the thinner the better) to be suspended on rods in the open comb, and a vigorous smoke made of decayed wood is to be kept up without cessation. Exposed thus to the combined influence of sunshine, heat and smoke, meat cut into slices not over an inch thick can be thoroughly cured in twenty-four hours. For thicker pieces there must be, of course, a longer time, and the curing of oily meat, such as pork, is more difficult than that of beef, venison or mutton.

To cure meat *in the sun* hang it on the South side of your house, as near to the wall as possible without touching.

Substitute for Coffee.

Take sound ripe acorns, wash them while in the shell, dry them, and parch [roast] until they open, take the shell off, roast with a little bacon fat, and you will have a splendid cup of coffee.

79

From *The Red Badge of Courage* by Stephen Crane.

Stephen Crane Describes an Infantry Attack (1860s)

Stephen Crane wrote some of the most brilliant descriptions of battles in the Civil and Spanish-American wars, yet he was an eyewitness to neither. He read widely, looked at the famous battle photographs taken by Matthew Brady, talked to war veterans, and thought deeply about the psychological impact of war on ordinary people.

In Chapter 23 of The Red Badge of Courage *the youthful narrator, Henry Fleming, is plunged into battle in a daring attempt to capture the enemy flag. This action takes place at the bloody battle of Chancellorsville. As you read the following excerpt from Crane's book, consider the psychological factors that motivated Fleming and the others to make this ferocious charge.*

The colonel came running along back of the line. There were other officers following him. "We must charge'm!" they shouted. "We must charge'm!" they cried with resentful voices, as if anticipating a rebellion against this plan by the men.

The youth, upon hearing the shouts, began to study the distance between him and the enemy. He made vague calculations. He saw that to be firm soldiers they must go forward. It would be death to stay in the present place, and with all the circumstances to go backward would exalt too many others. Their hope was to push the galling foes away from the fence.

He expected that his companions, weary and stiffened, would have to be driven to this assault, but as he turned toward them he perceived with a certain surprise that they were giving quick and un-qualified expressions of assent. There was an omi-nous, clanging overture to the charge when the shafts of the bayonets rattled upon the rifle barrels. At the yelled words of command the soldiers sprang forward in eager leaps. There was new and unex-pected force in the movement of the regiment. A knowledge of its faded and jaded condition made the charge appear like a paroxysm, a display of the strength that comes before a final feebleness. The men scampered in insane fever of haste, racing as if to achieve a sudden success before an exhilarating fluid should leave them. It was a blind and despairing rush by the collection of men in dusty and tattered blue, over a green sward [grassy land] and under a sapphire sky, toward a fence, dimly outlined in smoke, from behind which spluttered the fierce rifles of enemies.

It was a blind and despairing rush . . .

The youth kept the bright colors to the front. He was waving his free arm in furious circles, the while shrieking mad calls and appeals, urging on those that did not need to be urged, for it seemed that the mob of blue men hurling themselves on the dangerous group of rifles were again grown sud-denly wild with an enthusiasm of unselfishness. From the many firings starting toward them, it looked as if they would merely succeed in making a great sprinkling of corpses on the grass between their former position and the fence. But they were in a state of frenzy, perhaps because of forgotten vanities, and it made an exhibition of sublime recklessness. There was no obvious questioning, nor figurings, nor diagrams. There was, apparently no considered loopholes. It appeared that the swift wings of their desires would have shattered against the iron gates of the impossible.

He himself felt the daring spirit of a savage religion-mad. He was capable of profound sacrifices, a tremendous death. He had no time for dissections, but he knew that he thought of the bullets only as things that could prevent him from reaching the place of his endeavor. There were subtle flashings of joy within him that thus should be his mind.

He strained all his strength. His eyesight was shaken and dazzled by the tension of thought and muscle. He did not see anything excepting the mist of smoke gashed by the little knives of fire, but he knew that in it lay the aged fence of a vanished farmer protecting the snuggled bodies of the gray men.

As he ran a thought of the shock of contact gleamed in his mind. He expected a great concussion when the two bodies of troops crashed together. This became a part of his wild battle madness. He could feel the onward swing of the regiment about him and he conceived of a thunderous, crushing blow that would prostrate the resistance and spread consternation and amazement for miles. The flying regiment was going to have a catapultian effect. This dream made him run faster among his comrades, who were giving vent to hoarse and frantic cheers.

But presently he could see that many of the men in gray did not intend to abide the blow. The smoke, rolling, disclosed men who ran, their faces still turned. These grew to a crowd, who retired stubbornly. Individuals wheeled frequently to send a bullet at the blue wave.

But at one part of the line there was a grim and obdurate [stubborn] group that made no movement. They were settled firmly down behind posts and rails. A flag, ruffled and fierce, waved over them and their rifles dinned fiercely.

The blue whirl of men got very near, until it seemed that in truth there would be a close and frightful scuffle There was an expressed disdain in the opposition of the little group, that changed the meaning of the cheers of the men in blue. They became yells of wrath, directed, personal. The cries of the two parties were now in sound an interchange of scathing [bitter] insults.

They in blue showed their teeth; their eyes shone all white. They launched themselves as at the throats of those who stood resisting. The space between dwindled to an insignificant distance.

The youth had centered the gaze of his soul upon that other flag. Its possession would be high pride. It would express bloody minglings, near blows. He had a gigantic hatred for those who made great difficulties and complications. They caused it to be as a craved treasure of mythology, hung amid tasks and contrivances of danger.

He plunged like a mad horse at it. He was resolved it should not escape if wild blows and darings of blows could seize it. His own emblem, quivering and aflare, was winging toward the other. It seemed there would shortly be an encounter of strange beaks and claws, as of eagles.

The swirling body of the blue men came to a sudden halt at close and disastrous range and roared a swift volley. The group in gray was split and broken by this fire, but its riddled body still fought. The men in blue yelled again and rushed in upon it.

The youth, in his leapings, saw, as through a mist, a picture of four or five men stretched upon the ground or writhing upon their knees with bowed heads as if they had been stricken by bolts from the sky. Tottering among them was the rival color bearer, whom the youth saw had been bitten vitally by the bullets of the last formidable volley. He perceived this man fighting a last struggle, the struggle of one whose legs are grasped by demons. It was a ghastly battle. Over his face was the bleach of death, but set upon it was the dark and hard lines of desperate purpose. With this terrible grin of resolution he hugged his precious flag to him and was stumbling and staggering in his design to go the way that led to safety for it.

Over his face was the bleach of death . . .

But his wounds always made it seem that his feet were retarded, held, and he fought a grim fight, as with invisible ghouls fastened greedily upon his

This lithograph shows the Fifty-fourth Massachusetts Regiment attacking the Confederate defenders of Fort Wagner, near Charleston, South Carolina. The regiment was made up of free African Americans.

limbs. Those in advance of the scampering blue men, howling cheers, leaped at the fence. The despair of the lost was in his eyes as he glanced back at them.

The youth's friend went over the obstruction in a tumbling heap and sprang at the flag as a panther at prey. He pulled at it and wrenching it free, swung up its red brilliancy with a mad cry of exultation even as the color bearer, gasping, lurched over in a final throe and, stiffening convulsively, turned his dead face to the ground. There was much blood upon the grass blades.

At the place of success there began more wild clamorings of cheers. The men gesticulated [gestured] and bellowed in ecstasy. When they spoke it was as if they considered their listener to be a mile away. What hats and caps were left to them they often slung high in the air.

At one part of the line four men had been swooped upon, and they now sat as prisoners. Some blue men were about them in an eager and curious circle. The soldiers had trapped strange birds, and there was an examination. A flurry of fast questions was in the air.

One of the prisoners was nursing a superficial wound in the foot. He cuddled it, babywise, but he looked up from it often to curse with an astonishing utter abandon straight at the noses of his captors. He consigned them to red regions; he called upon the pestilential wrath of strange gods. And with it all he was singularly free from recognition of the finer points of the conduct of prisoners of war. It was as if a clumsy clod had trod upon his toe and he conceived it to be his privilege, his duty, to use deep, resentful oaths.

Another, who was a boy in years, took his plight with great calmness and apparent good nature. He conversed with the men in blue, studying their faces with his bright and keen eyes. They spoke of battle and conditions. There was an acute interest in all their faces during this exchange of viewpoints. It seemed a great satisfaction to hear voices from where all had been darkness and speculation.

The third captive sat with a morose countenance [gloomy face]. He preserved a stoical and cold attitude. To all advances he made one reply without variation, "Ah, go t'——!"

The last of the four was always silent, and, for the most part, kept his face turned in unmolested directions. From the views of the youth received he seemed to be in a state of absolute dejection. Shame was upon him, and with it profound regret that he was, perhaps, no more to be counted in the ranks of his fellows. The youth could detect no expression that would allow him to believe that the other was giving a thought to his narrowed future, the pictured dungeons, perhaps, and starvations and brutalities, liable to the imagination. All to be seen was shame for captivity and regret for the right to antagonize.

After the men had celebrated sufficiently they settled down behind the old rail fence, on the opposite side to the one from which their foes had been driven. A few shot perfunctorily at distant marks.

There was some long grass. The youth nestled in it and rested, making a convenient rail support the flag. His friend, jubiliant and glorified, holding his treasure with vanity, came to him there. They sat side by side and congratulated each other.

REVIEWING THE READING

1. According to Crane, what factors motivated Fleming and the others to make the successful charge?

2. Why was the enemy battle flag so important to the charging Union troops?

3. **Using Your Historical Imagination.** Reread the section on the treatment of the Confederate prisoners after the charge. Can you imagine this scene taking place after the battle of Okinawa during World War II, or the Tet Offensive in Vietnam? What does this indicate about the special nature of the Civil War?

War Songs of the Blue and Gray

In times of war songs have always inspired people to patriotism, loyalty, and courage. The Civil War was no exception. The first two songs were sung by Union troops; the next two were confederate songs; and the final song was sung by black troops.

Glory! Glory! Hallelujah!

John Brown's Body

Anonymous

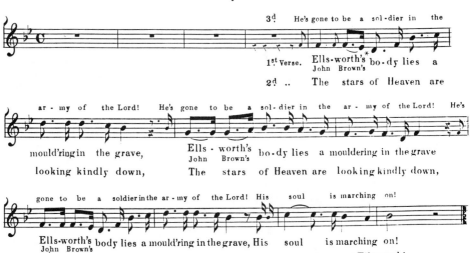

* Elmer Ephraim Ellsworth was an early victim of the war, shot while tearing down a Southern flag.

Glo - ry! Glo-ry Hal - le - lu - -jah! His soul is marching on.

Repeat Chorus.

John Brown's knapsack is strapped upon his back,
His soul is marching on.—*Chorus.*

His pet lambs will meet him on the way,
And they'll go marching on.—*Chorus.*

They'll hang Jeff Davis on a sour apple tree,
As they march along.—*Chorus.*

Let's give three good rousing cheers for the Union,
As we're marching on.—*Chorus.*
Hip, hip, hip, hip, Hurrah!

We Are Coming Father Abra'am

by James Sloan Gibbons; music by L. O. Emerson

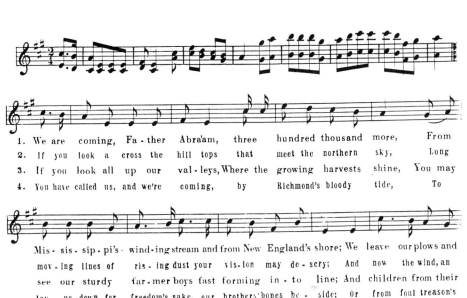

1. We are coming, Fa - ther Abra'am, three hundred thousand more, From
2. If you look a cross the hill tops that meet the northern sky, Long
3. If you look all up our val - leys, Where the growing harvests shine, You may
4. You have called us, and we're coming, by Richmond's bloody tide, To

Mis - sis - sip - pi's wind-ing stream and from New England's shore; We leave our plows and
mov - ing lines of ris - ing dust your vis - ion may de - scry; And now the wind, an
see our sturdy far - mer boys fast forming in - to line; And children from their
lay us down for freedom's sake, our brothers' bones be - side; Or from foul treason's

workshops our wives and children dear, With hearts too full for ut - terance, with
in - stant, tears the cloudy veil a - - side, And floats aloft our spangled flag in
mother's knees are pulling at the weeds, And learning how to reap and sow, a -
savage group, to wrench the murderous blade, And in the face of fo - reign foes its

but a si - lent tear; We dare not look be - hind us, but steadfastly be -
glo - ry and in pride; And bayonets in the sunlight gleam, and bands brave mu - sic
gainst their country's needs; And a farewell group stands weep - ing at every cot - tage
frag - ments to pa - rade; Six hundred thousand loy-al men and true have gone be -

fore _
pour _   We are coming, Father Abra'am _ three hundred thousand more!
door _
fore _

The Bonnie Blue Flag

by Harry Macarthy

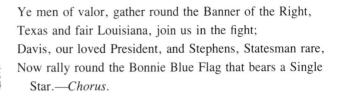

Ye men of valor, gather round the Banner of the Right,
Texas and fair Louisiana, join us in the fight;
Davis, our loved President, and Stephens, Statesman rare,
Now rally round the Bonnie Blue Flag that bears a Single
    Star.—*Chorus.*

And here's to brave Virginia! the Old Dominion State
With the young Confederacy at length has link'd her fate;
Impell'd by her example, now other States prepare
To hoist on high the Bonnie Blue Flag that bears a Single
    star.—*Chorus.*

Then cheer, boys, raise the joyous shout,
    For Arkansas and North Carolina now have both gone
      out;
    And let another rousing cheer for Tennessee be given,
    The Single Star of the Bonnie Blue Flag has grown
      to be eleven!—*Chorus.*

Then here's to our Confederacy, strong we are and brave,
Like patriots of old, we'll fight our heritage to save;
And rather than submit to shame, to die we would prefer,
So cheer for the Bonnie Blue Flag that bears a Single
    Star.— *Chorus.*

From *The Civil War Songbook.*

Dixie
by Albert Pike

From *American History told by Contemporaries,*
Volume IV, edited by Albert Bushnell Hart.

Southrons, hear your Country call you!
Up! lest worse than death befall you!
    To arms! To arms! To arms! in Dixie!
Lo! all the beacon-fires are lighted,
Let all hearts be now united!
    To arms! To arms! To arms! in Dixie!
        Advance the flag of Dixie!
            Hurah! hurrah!

For Dixie's land we take our stand,
    And live or die for Dixie!
        To arms! To arms!
            And conquer peace for Dixie!
        To arms! To arms!
            And conquer peace for Dixie!

Hear the Northern thunders mutter!
Northern flags in South wind flutter!
    [To arms, etc.
Send them back your fierce defiance!
Stamp upon the accursed alliance!]
    To arms, etc.
        Advance the flag of Dixie! etc.
Fear no danger! Shun no labor!
Lift up rifle, pike, and sabre!
    To arms, etc.
Shoulder pressing close to shoulder,
Let the odds make each heart bolder!
    To arms, etc.
        Advance the flag of Dixie! etc.

How the South's great heart rejoices,
At your cannons' ringing voices;
    To arms! etc.
For faith betrayed and pledges broken,

Wrongs inflicted, insults spoken;
    To arms! etc.
        Advance the flag of Dixie! etc.

Strong as lions, swift as eagles,
Back to their kennels hunt these beagles;
    To arms! etc.
Cut the unequal words [bonds?] asunder!
Let them then each other plunder!
    To arms! etc.
        Advance the flag of Dixie! etc.

Swear upon your Country's altar,
Never to submit or falter;
    To arms! etc.
Till the spoilers are defeated,
Till the Lord's work is completed.
    To arms! etc.
        Advance the flag of Dixie! etc.

Halt not, till our Federation
Secures among Earth's Powers its station!
    To arms! etc.
Then at peace, and crowned with glory,
Hear your children tell the story!
    To arms! etc.
        Advance the flag of Dixie! etc.

If the loved ones weep in sadness,
Victory soon shall bring them gladness:
    To arms! etc.
Exultant pride soon banish sorrow;
Smiles chase tears away to-morrow.
    To arms! etc.
        Advance the flag of Dixie! etc.

Many Thousands Gone

From *Folk Songs of North America* by Alan Lomax.

Slow march or freely ♩ = 48   GUITAR / BANJO } *FREE OR RHYTHMIC STRUM*

No more auc - tion block for me, No more, no more,

455

No more auc - tion block for me, Ma - ny thou - sands gone.

1 No more auction block for me,
No more, no more,
No more auction block for me,
Many thousands gone.

2 No more peck o' corn for me, *etc.**

3 No more driver's lash for me, *etc.*

4 No more pint of salt for me, *etc.**

5 No more hundred lash for me, *etc.*

6 No more mistress call for me, *etc.*

* Corn and salt were slave rations.

From *Specimen Days* and *Leaves of Grass* by Walt Whitman, in *Walt Whitman: Complete Poetry and Collected Prose,* edited by Justin Kaplan; and *Selected Poems of Herman Melville,* edited by Robert Penn Warren.

80

The Poets' View of War: Whitman and Melville (1860s)

Here in prose and in verse are the wartime thoughts of Walt Whitman and his contemporary Herman Melville, two of America's greatest writers. We read first an excerpt from a sketchbook Whitman kept, later published as Specimen Days, *and then two of the poems the men wrote about the war. Consider what Whitman meant when he wrote that "the real war will never get in the books."*

And so good-bye to the war. I know not how it may have been, or may be, to others—to me the main interest I found (and still, on recollection, find), in the rank and file of the armies, both sides, and in those specimens amid the hospitals, and even the dead on the field. To me the points illustrating the latent personal character and eligibilities of these States, in the two or three millions of American young and middle-aged, North and South, embodied in those armies—and especially the one-third or one-fourth of their number, stricken by wounds of disease at some time in the course of the contest—were of more significance even than the political interests involved. (As so much of a race depends on how it faces death, and how it stands personal anguish and sickness. As, in the glints of emotions under emergencies, and the indirect traits and asides in Plutarch, we get far profounder clues to the antique world than all its more formal history.)

Future years will never know the seething hell and the black infernal background of countless minor scenes and interiors (not the official surface-courteousness of the Generals, not the few great

A group of Confederate soldiers pose for a photographer in Richmond, Virginia. Photographers traveled with both the Union and Confederate armies, recording events as they took place.

battles) of the Secession war; and it is best they should not—the real war will never get in the books. In the mushy influences of current times, too, the fervid atmosphere and typical events of those years are in danger of being totally forgotten. I have at night watch'd by the side of a sick man in the hospital, one who could not live many hours. I have seen his eyes flash and burn as he raised himself and recurr'd to the cruelties on his surrender'd brother, and mutilations of the corpse afterward. . . .

Such was the war. It was not a quadrille [French dance] in a ball-room. Its interior history will not only never be written—its practicality, minutiae of deeds and passions, will never be suggested. The actual soldier of 1862–'65, North and South, with all his ways, his incredible dauntlessness, habits, practices, tastes, language, his fierce friendship, his appetite, rankness, his superb strength and animality, lawless gait, and a hundred unnamed lights and shades of camp, I say, will never be written—perhaps must not and should not be.

The preceding notes may furnish a few stray glimpses into that life, and into those lurid interiors, never to be fully conveyed to the future. The hospital part of the drama from '61 to '65, deserves indeed to be recorded. Of that many-threaded drama, with its sudden and strange surprises, its confounding of prophecies, its moments of despair, the dread of foreign interference, the interminable [endless] campaigns, the bloody battles, the mighty cumbrous [slow moving] and green armies, the drafts and bounties—the immense money expenditure, like a heavy-pouring constant rain—with, over the whole land, the last three years of the struggle, an unending, universal mourning-wail of women, parents, orphans—the marrow of the tragedy concentrated in those Army Hospitals—(it seem'd sometimes as if the whole interest of the land, North and South, was one vast central hospital, and all the rest of the affair but flanges [attachments])—those forming the untold and unwritten history of the war—infinitely greater (like life's) than the few scraps and distortions that are ever told or written. Think how much, and of importance, will be—how much, civic and military, has already been—buried in the grave, in eternal darkness.

A Sight in Camp in the Daybreak Gray and Dim
by Walt Whitman

A sight in camp in the daybreak gray and dim,
As from my tent I emerge so early sleepless,
As slow I walk in the cool fresh air the path near
  by the hospital tent,

Three forms I see on stretchers lying, brought out
    there untended lying,
Over each the blanket spread, ample brownish
    woolen blanket,
Gray and heavy blanket, folding, covering all.

Curious I halt and silent stand,
Then with light fingers I from the face of the nearest
    the first just lift the blanket;
Who are you elderly man so gaunt and grim, with
    well-gray'd hair, and flesh all sunken about the
    eyes?
Who are you my dear comrade?

Then to the second I step—and who are you my
    child and darling?
Who are you sweet boy with cheeks yet blooming?

Then to the third—a face nor child nor old, very
    calm, as of beautiful yellow-white ivory;
Young man I think I know you—I think this face
    is the face of the Christ himself,
Dead and divine and brother of all, and here again
    he lies.

Shiloh
A Requiem
(April 1862)

by Herman Melville

Skimming lightly, wheeling still,
    The swallows fly low
Over the field in clouded days,
    The forest-field of Shiloh—
Over the field where April rain
Solaced the parched one stretched in pain
Through the pause of night
That followed the Sunday fight
    Around the church of Shiloh—

The church so lone, the log-built one,
That echoed to many a parting groan
   And natural prayer
Of dying foemen mingled there—
Foemen at morn, but friends at eve—
   Fame or country least their care:
(What like a bullet can undeceive!)
   But now they lie low,
While over them the swallows skim,
   And all is hushed at Shiloh.

REVIEWING THE READING

1. What does Whitman mean when he says that the real war will never get in the books?

2. What in Whitman's view was the central characteristic of the American Civil War, particularly in its last years?

3. **Using Your Historical Imagination.** What do the poems of Whitman and Melville have in common? Explain.

An English War Correspondent Observes President Lincoln (1861)

81

From *My Diary North and South* by William Howard Russell.

William Howard Russell seems to have had a keen eye for describing the figures of the Civil War. He was an English lawyer who served as a war correspondent for the London Times. *Both the North and the South read the* Times, *and Russell's criticism of Union military incompetence at the battle of Bull Run drew the wrath of the Lincoln administration. The first paragraph of this report, excerpted from Russell's diary, is classic itself—and not as disrespectful to President Lincoln as one might think on first reading. Look for references by Russell to the greatest problem faced by Lincoln.*

March 27, 1861. Soon afterwards there entered, with a shambling, loose, irregular, almost unsteady gait, a tall, lank, lean man, considerably over six feet in height, with stooping shoulders, long pendulous arms, terminating in hands of extraordinary dimensions, which, however, were far exceeded in proportion by his feet. He was dressed in an ill-fitting, wrinkled suit of black, which put one in mind of an undertaker's uniform at a funeral; round his neck a rope of black silk was knotted in a large bulb, with flying ends projecting beyond the collar of his coat; his turned-down shirt-collar disclosed a sinewy muscular yellow neck, and above that, nestling in a great black mass of hair, bristling and compact like a ruff of mourning pins, rose the strange quaint face and head, covered with its thatch of wild republican hair, of President Lincoln. The im-

. . . the nose itself—a prominent organ—stands out from the face, with an inquiring anxious air . . .

pression produced by the size of his extremities, and by his flapping and wide projecting ears, may be removed by the appearance of kindliness, sagacity [wisdom], and the awkward bonhomie [friendliness] of his face; the mouth is absolutely prodigious; the lips, straggling and extending almost from one line of black beard to the other, are only kept in order by two deep furrows from the nostril to the chin; the nose itself—a prominent organ—stands out from the face, with an inquiring, anxious air, as though it were sniffing for some good thing in the wind; the eyes dark, full, and deeply set, are penetrating, but full of an expression which almost amounts to tenderness; and above them projects the saggy brow, running into the small hard frontal space, the development of which can scarcely be estimated accurately, owing to the irregular flocks of thick hair carelessly brushed across it. One would say that, although the mouth was made to enjoy a joke, it could also utter the severest sentence which the head could dictate, but that Mr. Lincoln would be ever more willing to temper justice with mercy, and to enjoy what he considers the amenities of life, than to take a harsh view of men's nature and of the world, and to estimate things in an ascetic or puritan spirit. A person who met Mr. Lincoln in the street would not take him to be what—according to the usages of European society—is called a "gentleman;" and, indeed since I came to the United States, I have heard more disparaging [rude] allusions made by Americans to him on that account than I could have expected among simple republicans, where all should be equals; but, at the same time, it would not be possible for the most indifferent observer to pass him in the street without notice. . . .

March 28. In the evening I repaired to the White House. . . . Whilst we were waiting, Mr. Seward took me round, and introduced me to the Ministers, and to their wives and daughters, among the latter, Miss Chase, who is very attractive, agreeable, and sprightly. Her father, the Finance Minister, struck me as one of the most intelligent and distinguished persons in the whole assemblage; tall, of a good presence, and with a well-formed head, fine forehead,

Lincoln reads the Emancipation Proclamation to his advisers.

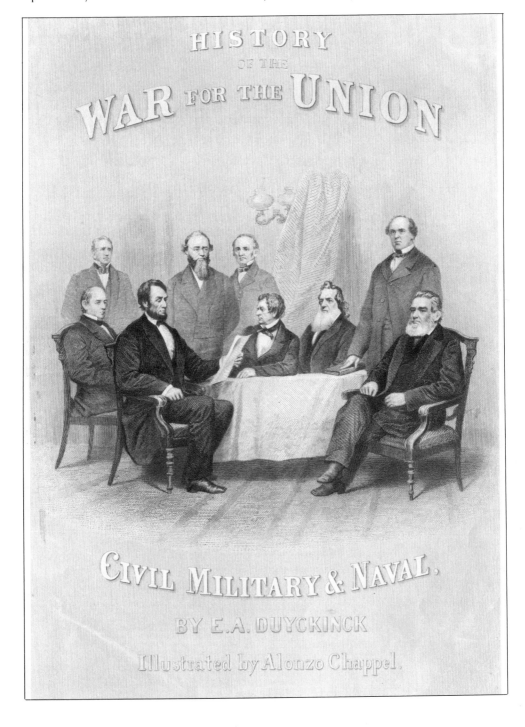

HISTORY OF THE WAR FOR THE UNION

CIVIL MILITARY & NAVAL,

BY E.A. DUYCKINCK

Illustrated by Alonzo Chappel.

and a face indicating energy and power . . . he is
one who would not pass quite unnoticed in a European crowd of the same description. . . .

Mr. Cameron, the Secretary of War, a slight
man, above the middle height, with grey hair, deep-
set keen grey eyes, and a thin mouth, gave me the
idea of a person of ability and adroitness [cleverness].
His colleague, the Secretary of the Navy, a small
man, with a great long beard and spectacles, did
not look like one of much originality or ability;
but people who know Mr. Welles declare that he
is possessed of administrative power, although they
admit that he does not know the stem from the
stern of a ship, and are in doubt whether he ever
saw the sea in his life. Mr. Smith, the Minister of
the Interior, is a bright-eyed, smart (I use the word
in the English sense) gentleman, with the reputation
of being one of the most conservative members of
the cabinet. Mr. Blair, the Postmaster-General, is a
person of much greater influence than his position
would indicate. He has the reputation of being one
of the most determined republicans in the Ministry;
but he held peculiar notions with reference to the
black and white races, which, if carried out, would
not by any means conduce [lead] to the comfort
or happiness of free negroes in the United
States. . . .

In the conversation which occurred before dinner, I was amused to observe the manner in which
Mr. Lincoln used the anecdotes for which he is famous. Where men bred in courts, accustomed to
the world, or versed in diplomacy, would use some
subterfuge, or would make a polite speech, or give
a shrug of the shoulders as the means of getting
out of an embarrassing position, Mr. Lincoln raises
a laugh by some bold west-country anecdote, and
moves off in the cloud of merriment produced by
his joke. . . .

The first "state dinner," as it is called, of the
President was not remarkable for ostentation [showi-
ness]. . . . The conversation was suited to the state

dinner of a cabinet at which women and strangers were present, . . . and except where there was an attentive silence caused by one of the President's stories, there was a Babel of small talk round the table. . . .

October 9. Calling on the General [McClellan] the other night at his usual time of return, I was told by the orderly, who was closing the door, "The General's gone to bed tired, and can see no one. He sent the same message to the President, who came inquiring after him ten minutes ago."

This poor President! He is to be pitied; surrounded by such scenes, and trying with all his might to understand strategy, naval warfare, big guns, the movements of troops, military maps, reconnaissances, occupations, interior and exterior lines, and all the technical details of the art of slaying. He runs from one house to another, armed with plans, papers, reports, recommendations, sometimes good humoured, never angry, occasionally dejected, and always a little fussy. The other night, as I was sitting in the parlour at head-quarters, with an English friend who had come to see his old acquaintance the General, walked in a tall man with a navvy's [laborer's] cap, and an ill-made shooting suit, from the pockets of which protruded paper and bundles. "Well," said he to Brigadier Van Vliet, who rose to receive him, "is George in?"

"Yes, sir. He's come back, but is lying down, very much fatigued. I'll send up, sir, and inform him you wish to see him."

"Oh, no; I can wait. I think I'll take supper with him. Well, and what are you now,—I forget your name—are you a major, or a colonel, or a general?" "Whatever you like to make me, sir."

Seeing that General M'Clellan would be occupied, I walked out with my friend, who asked me when I got into the street why I stood up when that tall fellow came into the room. "Because it was the President." "The President of what?" "Of the

> This poor President! He is to be pitied . . .

United States." "Oh! come, now you're humbugging me. Let me have another look at him." He came back more incredulous than ever, but when I assured him I was quite serious, he exclaimed, "I give up the United States after this."

But for all that, there have been many more courtly presidents who, in a similar crisis, would have displayed less capacity, honesty, and plain dealing than Abraham Lincoln.

REVIEWING THE READING

1. How did Lincoln use wit and humor in his dealings with others?

2. Russell emphasizes (perhaps overemphasizes) President Lincoln's personal awkwardness and the strangeness of his physical appearence. But what seems to have been his true opinion of the American president?

3. **Using Your Historical Imagination.** President Lincoln's great problem in 1861 was how to fight and win a great war. How does Russell depict Lincoln's readiness to play his role as commander-in-chief? Do you think this is a valid description, or not? Justify your answer.

Lincoln Delivers the Gettysburg Address (1863)

82

From *Abraham Lincoln, Complete Works*, edited by John G. Nicolay and John Hay.

The climactic battle of the Civil War was fought at Gettysburg, Pennsylvania, in early July 1863. The battle was a Union victory, and the forces of General Robert E. Lee were turned back, never again to mount an invasion on the North. Nevertheless, the battle was won at terrible cost; the Union lost more than 23,000 men at Gettysburg. In November of 1863 President Lincoln came to Gettysburg to speak during the dedication of a national cemetery at the battlefield. This speech was his famous "Gettysburg address," which is presented in its entirety below. Consider what Lincoln says is the main goal of the North—the reason the soldiers died at Gettysburg.

Fourscore and seven years ago our fathers brought forth on this continent a new nation, conceived in liberty, and dedicated to the proposition that all men are created equal.

Now we are engaged in a great civil war, testing whether that nation, or any nation so conceived and so dedicated, can long endure. We are met [meeting] on a great battle-field of that war. We have come to dedicate a portion of that field as a final resting place for those who here gave their lives that that nation might live. It is altogether [completely] fitting and proper that we should do this.

But, in a larger sense, we cannot dedicate—we cannot consecrate—we cannot hallow—this ground. The brave men, living and dead, who struggle here, have consecrated it far above our poor power to add or detract [lessen]. The world will little note nor for long remember what we say here,

This photo of President Lincoln was taken in 1863, the year he gave his famous Gettysburg Address.

but it can never forget what they did here. It is for us, the living, rather, to be dedicated here to the unfinished work which they who fought here thus far so nobly advanced. It is rather for us to be here dedicated to the great task remaining before us— that from these honored dead we take increased devotion to that cause for which they gave the last full measure of devotion; that we here highly resolve that these dead shall not have died in vain; that this nation, under God, shall have a new birth of freedom; and that government of the people, by the people, for the people, shall not perish from the earth.

REVIEWING THE READING

1. Why does Lincoln say that, in a larger sense, they cannot dedicate the Gettysburg cemetery?

2. What reason does Lincoln offer for the necessity of the sacrifice of Gettysburg?

3. **Using Your Historical Imagination.** Which statement in Lincoln's speech has proven entirely untrue? Why?

Sherman's Army Destroys a Georgia Plantation (1864)

83

From *A Woman's Wartime Journal* by Dolly Sumner Lunt.

On November 15, 1864, General William Tecumseh Sherman sent his armies "marching through Georgia," from Atlanta to the sea. Advancing on a 60-mile (96 kilometer) front, Sherman's troops destroyed much of the civilian property in their path. This was total war, designed to punish the South and help to bring the war to a swift conclusion.

Dolly Sumner Lunt knew nothing of this larger strategy. Born in 1817 in Bowdoinham, Maine, she had come to the south to teach school, married a plantation owner, and in 1864 was running her dead husband's plantation. Unfortunately for the widow, her Burge Plantation, near Covington, Georgia, was directly in the path of Sherman's army. The following excerpts from Lunt's war journal vividly record what happened to one Georgia plantation on the terrible day Sherman passed through. As you read Lunt's account, try to determine the main purpose, or purposes, of Sherman's troops.

November 19, 1864.

Slept in my clothes last night, as I heard that the Yankees went to neighbor Montgomery's on Thursday night at one o'clock, searched his house, drank his wine, and took his money and valuables. As we were not disturbed, I walked after breakfast, with Sadai [her daughter], up to Mr. Joe Perry's, my nearest neighbor, where the Yankees were yesterday. Saw Mrs. Laura [Perry] in the road surrounded by her children, seeming to be looking for some one. She said she was looking for her husband, that old Mrs. Perry had just sent her word that the Yankees went to James Perry's the night before, plundered his house, and drove off all his stock, and that she must drive hers into the old fields. Before we were done talking, up came Joe and Jim Perry from their hiding-place. Jim was very much excited. Happening to turn and look behind, as we stood there, I saw some blue-coats coming down the hill. Jim immediately raised his gun, swearing he would kill them anyhow.

"No, don't!" said I, and ran home as fast as I could, with Sadai.

I could hear them cry, "Halt! Halt!" and their guns went off in quick succession. Oh God, the time of trial has come!

A man passed on his way to Covington. I hallooed to him, asking him if he did not know the Yankees were coming.

"No—are they?"

"Yes," said I; "they are not three hundred yards from here."

"Sure enough," said he. "Well, I'll not go. I don't want them to get my horse." And although within hearing of their guns, he would stop and look for them. Blissful ignorance! Not knowing, not hearing, he has not suffered the suspense, the fear, that I have for the past forty-eight hours. I walked to the gate. There they came filing up.

I hastened [hurried] back to my frightened servants and told them that they had better hide, and then went back to the gate to claim protection and a guard. But like demons they rush in! My yards are full. To my smoke-house, my dairy, pantry, kitchen, and cellar, like famished [starving] wolves they come, breaking locks and whatever is in their way. The thousand pounds of meat in my smoke-house is gone in a twinkling, my flour, my meat, my lard, butter, eggs, pickles of various kinds—both in vinegar and brine—wine, jars, and jugs are all gone. My eighteen fat turkeys, my hens, chickens, and fowls, my young pigs, are shot down in my

yard and hunted as if they were rebels themselves.
Utterly powerless I ran out and appealed to the
guard.

"I cannot help you, Madam; it is orders."

As I stood there, from my lot I saw driven,
first, old Dutch, my dear old buggy horse, who has
carried my beloved husband so many miles, and
who would so quietly wait at the block for him to
mount and dismount, and who at last drew him to
his grave; then came old Mary, my brood mare,
who for years had been too old and stiff for work,
with her three-year-old colt, my two-year-old mule,
and her last little baby colt. There they go! There
go my mules, my sheep, and, worse than all, my
boys [slaves]!

Alas! little did I think while trying to save my
house from plunder and fire that they were forcing
my boys from home at the point of the bayonet.
One, Newton, jumped into bed in his cabin, and
declared himself sick. Another crawled under the
floor,—a lame boy he was,—but they pulled him

*This engraving shows
what it meant for Sher-
man's troops to "live off
the land." The southern
plantation became the
main provider of food
for the Union army.*

In his Memoirs *William Tecumseh Sherman said he hated war. But in 1864 he knew what would end the Civil War quickly. "We must make old and young, rich and poor, feel the hand of war," he wrote Grant.*

out, placed him on a horse, and drove him off. Mid, poor Mid! The last I saw of him, a man had him going around the garden, looking, as I thought, for my sheep, as he was my shepherd. Jack came crying to me, the big tears coursing down his cheeks, saying they were making him go. . . .

My poor boys! My poor boys! What unknown trials are before you! How you have clung to your mistress and assisted her in every way you knew.

Never have I corrected them; a word was sufficient. Never have they known want of any kind. Their parents are with me, and how sadly they lament [mourn] the loss of their boys. Their cabins are rifled of every valuable, the soldiers swearing that their Sunday clothes were the white people's, and that they never had money to get such things as they had. Poor Frank's chest was broken open, his money and tobacco taken. He has always been a money-making and saving boy; not infrequently has his crop brought him five hundred dollars and more. All of his clothes and Rachel's clothes, which dear Lou gave her before her death and which she had packed away, were stolen from her. Ovens, skillets, coffee-mills, of which we had three, coffee-pots— not one have I left. Sifters all gone!

Seeing that the soldiers could not be restrained, the guard ordered me to have their [the slaves] remaining possessions brought into my house, which I did, and they all, poor things, huddled together in my room, fearing every movement that the house would be burned. . . .

Sherman himself and a greater portion of his army passed my house that day. All day, as the sad moments rolled on, were they passing not only in front of my house, but from behind; they tore down my garden palings [fencing], made a road through my back-yard and lot field, driving their stock and riding through, tearing down my fences and desolating [destroying] my home—wantonly doing it when there was no necessity for it.

Such, a day, if I live to the age of Methuselah, may God spare me from ever seeing again!

As night drew its sable curtains around us, the heavens from every point were lit up with flames from burning buildings.

REVIEWING THE READING

1. What did Sherman's troops do to Lunt's plantation?

2. How did the northern troops treat Lunt's slaves?

3. **Using Your Historical Imagination.** Imagine you are General Sherman. What military justifications can you offer for the destruction of civilian property by your soldiers? Can these actions be justified on humanitarian grounds?

84

From *The Andersonville Trial* by Saul Levitt.

The Andersonville Trial (1865)

The Civil War resulted in a vast number of casualties among both the northern and southern forces. Not all of these casualties occurred on the battlefield, however. Many soldiers also lost their lives in military prisons, where unsanitary conditions, poor food, and inadequate medical care were often the order of the day. The worst of these military prisons was Andersonville, operated in Georgia by the Confederacy. Some 13,000 Union men died while being held prisoner there. At a war crimes trial held in August 1865, Captain Henry Wirz, commander of the prison, was court-martialed and convicted for the deaths of these men. Wirz was hanged for his crimes in November of that year.

The following selection is an excerpt from a play written about the Andersonville trial. In this section of Act 1, Scene 1, Lieutenant Colonel Chandler, a Confederate officer, is being questioned by the prosecutor, Lieutenant Colonel Chipman. As you read the selection, note the conditions under which the Union soldiers were forced to live.

CHIPMAN: Before we begin we will state briefly the rule of evidence applying in criminal conspiracy. The evidence of a common design to commit a criminal act is sufficient to convict—and we shall prove that such a common design existed at Andersonville—to which the defendant willingly lent himself.

(GENERAL WALLACE [presiding officer of the court] *indicates that* CHIPMAN *may start interrogation* [questioning]. *We should see* CHANDLER *as a man of breeding and courage, caught through the questioning between loyalty to his defeated cause and his essential humanity*)

Mr. Chandler, please state how you were employed
during the year 1864.

CHANDLER: I served in the Army of the Confederacy,
with the rank of lieutenant colonel.

CHIPMAN: What was your official duty?

CHANDLER: I was assigned by the war office to inspect
and report on the military prisons maintained by
the Confederacy.

CHIPMAN: Did you, in the course of an official assign-
ment, go to the Andersonville military prison situated
in Sumter County, Georgia?

CHANDLER: Yes, sir. There had been civilian complaints forwarded to Richmond.

CHIPMAN: How long did you remain at Andersonville?

CHANDLER: Two weeks.

CHIPMAN: (*Moves to the map* [of the stockade, located
behind the judges' table], *indicating with a pointer*) I
ask you if that is a fair [accurate] map of the Andersonville stockade?

CHANDLER: Yes, it is.

CHIPMAN: Will you state the dimensions of the stockade—its area?

CHANDLER: A thousand feet on the longer side, from
north to south. Eight hundred feet from east to west,
covering about sixteen acres of ground.

CHIPMAN: (*Crosses to the prosecution table*) What was
the nature of the terrain?

CHANDLER: Simply earth—bare ground.

CHIPMAN: Was that the condition of the terrain in
advance of it being selected as a site for the camp?

CHANDLER: No, sir. The tract was originally part of
a section of pine woods.

CHIPMAN: And what can you tell us of the climate
in that part of Georgia? I refer now to extremes of
temperature. Of summer heat and winter cold.

CHANDLER: In July and August it would be quite
high, at times over a hundred degrees. Winters, it
could be near freezing and rainy.

. . . at regular intervals there were sentry boxes.

CHIPMAN: Was that camp laid out with provision for shelter of any kind?

CHANDLER: No, sir.

CHIPMAN: (*Moving to the map again, using the pointer*) This outer stockade wall—describe it, sir.

CHANDLER: A wall some fifteen to twenty feet high, consisting of rough-hewn timbers. A platform ran along the top of the wall and at regular intervals there were sentry boxes.

CHIPMAN: This line inside the wall—

CHANDLER: That was a line of posts running parallel to the outer wall—about twenty-five feet inside it.

CHIPMAN: It had a name, did it not?

CHANDLER: The deadline—so called because a prisoner going beyond it could be shot by the guards.

CHIPMAN: This meandering [winding] line?

CHANDLER: That would be the stream that ran through the camp, entering under the wall on the west . . . and emerging under the east wall of the stockade.

CHIPMAN: Its width and depth?

CHANDLER: No more than a yard wide and perhaps a foot in depth. (*As* CHIPMAN *indicates with the pointer*) The marshy area around the stream.

CHIPMAN: That marshy area could better be called a swamp, could it not?

CHANDLER: Yes, sir; swamp.

CHIPMAN: Of what size?

CHANDLER: Extending about a hundred and fifty feet on either side of the stream.

CHIPMAN: And having a considerable oozy depth, did it not?

CHANDLER: Anyone venturing across it would probably sink to his waist . . . (*Following the pointer*) That would be the cookhouse . . . The burial trenches . . . The dead house . . . The main entrance gate—

CHIPMAN: (*Crosses to his table*) Now, sir, as to the history of the camp. Will you state the circumstances under which it was established?

CHANDLER: By the latter part of '63 our prisoner-of-war camps were overcrowded. The War Office then decided to create a new camp.

CHIPMAN: Who was responsible for the establishment of this camp?

CHANDLER: General John H. Winder.

CHIPMAN: Now deceased?

CHANDLER: Yes.

CHIPMAN: And what was his official function?

CHANDLER: He was in charge of all military prisons for the Confederacy, east of the Mississippi.

CHIPMAN: You have said the tract of land on which the camp was located was originally part of a section of pine woods. The cutting down of every tree that might have provided shade—was Winder responsible for that?

CHANDLER: Yes, sir.

CHIPMAN: And this site—and the arrangements made for the care of the prisoners was known to and approved by the War Office?

CHANDLER: (*Tightly*) I cannot say how much knowledge or approval. The Colonel knows how a line of command operates.

CHIPMAN: (*Moves to witness*) Wasn't it their responsibility—? Withdrawn for the time being. Will you now describe conditions in the prison at Andersonville as you observed them?

CHANDLER: The area was tightly crowded with men when I inspected it.

CHIPMAN: Giving each prisoner—how much room, would you say?

CHANDLER: Thirty-five and a half square feet per prisoner.

CHIPMAN: A space equivalent to a cell only six feet on each side. What else did you find at Andersonville?

CHANDLER: (*Tightly*) There was a general insufficiency—of water, shelter, and food. I think that would cover it.

CHIPMAN: (*Over the witness; his intensity is palpable* [easily seen]) I think not. When you say insufficiency of water you mean that the available water supply for all purposes—for drinking, washing, cooking—all came from that narrow brook, is that correct?

CHANDLER: Yes, sir.

CHIPMAN: And that stream was at the same time the repository [receptacle] for all the waste matter at the camp, was it not?

CHANDLER: Yes, sir.

CHIPMAN: All waste was emptied into that stream; the waste from the cookhouse and the bodily waste of the prisoners?

CHANDLER: Yes, sir.

CHIPMAN: Making that stream into a a foul, sluggish sink, isn't that so?

CHANDLER: Yes—

> And that foul, stinking stream was the water supply for forty thousand men . . .

CHIPMAN: (*Circling*) And that foul, stinking stream a few feet wide was the water supply for forty thousand men, and that is what you meant by an insufficiency of water, isn't it?

CHANDLER: Yes.

CHIPMAN: And as to the insufficiency of shelter, there was in fact *no* shelter and the men lived on bare ground winter and summer or dug themselves into the ground, into burrows—is *that* correct?

CHANDLER: Yes, sir.

CHIPMAN: And as to the sort of clothing they had. You will please be specific, sir.

CHANDLER: (*More and more uneasy*) Some wore shirts and trousers—

CHIPMAN: *Some.* You mean the newly arrived prisoners *still* had their shirts and trousers, don't you?

CHANDLER: Yes.

CHIPMAN: You mean the rest, the vast number of them, were in rags, don't you?

CHANDLER: Yes.

CHIPMAN: You mean those men were simply in a state of nakedness and near nakedness under the terrible weather conditions you described a moment ago—isn't that so?

CHANDLER: Yes.

HARPER'S WEEKLY.

JOURNAL OF CIVILIZATION.

VOL. IX.—No. 455.]   NEW YORK, SATURDAY, SEPTEMBER 16, 1865.   [SINGLE COPIES TEN CENTS.
[$4.00 PER YEAR IN ADVANCE.

Entered according to Act of Congress, in the Year 1865, by Harper & Brothers, in the Clerk's Office of the District Court for the Southern District of New York.

THE MEETING IN RICHMOND.

We publish on page 580 a sketch, by Mr. J. R. HAMILTON, of the mass meeting of the citizens of Richmond, held on August 29, in the beautiful Capitol grounds of that city. The object of the meeting was ostensibly to give a denial to the imputations so frequently made, in the press of the North, that the loyalty of the people of Virginia, in spite of their protestations, is but of a sullen, discontented, and ephemeral nature. Judge WILLIAM H. LYONS presided at the meeting, which adopted a series of resolutions expressive of the people's unfeigned loyalty and devotion to the Union; and speeches were made by Judge LYONS, R. T. DANIEL, late Prosecuting-Attorney for the Commonwealth, W. H. MACFARLAND, President of the late Farmer's Bank, and the Hon. JAMES LYONS, member of the late Confederate Congress.

The meeting, although large (there may have been some 500 or 600 present, a large number of whom were colored), was not by any means either as numerous or enthusiastic as might have been desired, considering that the occasion was one of the most important that ever convened the citizens of Richmond together; and, looking to the objects proposed, it was a circumstance to be regretted. On the platform, however, were many of the most prominent men of the city and State, and nearly all the leading members of the press, under whose auspices the whole movement may be said to have been inaugurated. At the conclusion of the meeting a committee of three—Messrs. W. H. MACFARLAND, ROBERT RIDGWAY, and CHARLES PALMER—were appointed to present the resolutions to President JOHNSON, and to request him to visit the city of Richmond.

The large central building against which the speaker's platform was erected is the celebrated Capitol, containing the Senate Chamber, the House of Representatives, and all the various offices so recently occupied by the Confederate Government.

The view presented being from the beautifully wooded grounds of the Governor's mansion, the latter is, of course, not visible. To the right of the picture is seen CRAWFORD's celebrated bronze statue of WASHINGTON, with its base surrounded by some of Virginia's great men, also in bronze. The church beyond with the tall steeple is St. Paul's, the Episcopal church which JEFFERSON DAVIS usually attended, and where he was seated when he received the telegram from General LEE, announcing that all further resistance was useless. Down in the hollow, to the left of the picture, is seen the upper part of the Custom-house, in which is also at present located the Post-office, the National Bank of Virginia, and the First National Bank of Richmond. Although the Capitol grounds are not spacious, and are not at present in the fine order in which they were formerly kept, few cities in the world possess a spot in their midst more attractive and full of natural beauty.

The meeting at Richmond, while it shows that many prominent citizens of Virginia have sufficient common-sense to see the folly of secession, does not materially alter the situation as presented in the late election. We can not expect that the ideas of Virginians or of the citizens of any other Southern State are to be reversed by their defeat on the battle-field. We have now to oppose in politics the very heresy which we have defeated in a hundred severe battles. We have settled conclusively the question whether the union of States shall be maintained. But there remains much yet to be settled in regard to the prerogatives of the several States as related to the General Government. The English Revolution was not consummated by the victories of Cromwell and the decapitation of Charles the First, but in the peaceful victory of the English people forty years later, when William of Orange succeeded James the Second. Fortunately for us the Slave Power can have no restoration; with the removal of the cause of our troubles our future is ultimately secure.

THE COURT-ROOM IN WHICH CAPTAIN WIRZ, THE ANDERSONVILLE JAILER, IS BEING TRIED AT WASHINGTON.—[SEE PAGE 582.]

CHIPMAN: And the food?

CHANDLER: Mostly corn meal.

CHIPMAN: Ground fine or coarse?

CHANDLER: Unbolted meal.

CHIPMAN: Unbolted meal. Meaning meal ground so coarse it was as good as swallowing a knife for what it did to a man's insides considering the weakened condition those men were in. Isn't that so, Mr. Chandler?

CHANDLER: Yes, sir.

CHIPMAN: Did the men ever get anything to eat outside of this meal?

CHANDLER: A bit of meat now and then.

CHIPMAN: What sort of meat?

CHANDLER: Not very good.

CHIPMAN: (*Moves to* CHANDLER) Not very good. The prisoners had a joke about that meat, didn't they? A grim kind of a soldier joke to describe that meat from sick, dying mules and horses. They told you that the animal that meat came from—it had to be held up on its legs to be slaughtered—didn't they?

CHANDLER: Jokes of that sort—yes.

CHIPMAN: And you saw with your own eyes it was rotten, maggot-ridden meat, and that is what you meant when you said it wasn't very good, didn't you?

CHANDLER: Yes—

CHIPMAN: And the conditions they were living under drove them to extreme measures in the effort to survive, isn't that so?

CHANDLER: Extreme—yes, sir.

CHIPMAN: (*Moving*) To the point where they regarded rats as a delicacy, isn't that so?

CHANDLER: Yes, sir.

CHIPMAN: To the point that when one of them died, the others, in the desperation they had been driven to, stripped his body clean of whatever was on it in five minutes—of boots or trousers if he had any, or bread, or greenbacks to bribe the guards—

anything that might help them stay alive—isn't that correct?

CHANDLER: Yes, sir.

CHIPMAN: Driven in their desperation to the point of cannibalism, isn't that so?

CHANDLER: Yes—

CHIPMAN: You were able to establish that in your mind for a fact?

CHANDLER: Yes.

CHIPMAN: (*Close to the witness*) How? (*As* CHANDLER *hesitates*) As delicately as you wish, Mr. Chandler.

CHANDLER: (*After a moment, with difficulty*) Well—by the condition of some bodies—very rough surgery had been performed.

CHIPMAN: And so, in that place, men had been driven to the disposition of beasts—

CHANDLER: Yes.

CHIPMAN: (*Crosses to the map, his voice flaring*) And if I were now to sum up Andersonville as a pit—an animal pit in which men wallowed—the sick, the dying, the insane wallowing among the dead—would I exaggerate the picture of that place?

CHANDLER: No.

CHIPMAN: Concerning what you saw there . . . you submitted a report with recommendations to General Winder and your War Office, did you not?

CHANDLER: I did.

CHIPMAN: (*Handing over a document to* CHANDLER) This is a copy of that report?

CHANDLER: (*Glancing at it and handing it back*) That is the report.

CHIPMAN: Offered in evidence. (*He hands the report to* WALLACE *who scans it and returns it to* CHIPMAN) You say in this report that Andersonville is a blot on the Confederacy. You recommend that all prisoners be transferred to other prisons without delay and that Andersonville be immediately closed down.

CHANDLER: I did; yes.

(CHIPMAN *hands the report to the* CLERK)

CLERK: Exhibit one, for the government.

CHIPMAN: And that report was ignored, was it not? Ignored, disregarded, the condition allowed to continue—?

CHANDLER: Colonel, I am not here to indict the leaders of the cause for which I fought, as plotting the murder of defenseless men.

CHIPMAN: (*Boring in*) The report revealing how Winder and Wirz were operating that camp was ignored—

CHANDLER: I have told you I could not endure Andersonville. You people act as though you were better human beings than we were!

CHIPMAN: No, but our cause was. Your report was ignored?

CHANDLER: Due to the crisis—the bitterness—the disorder—with General Sherman marching through Georgia burning his way—

CHIPMAN: It was ignored—?

CHANDLER: As your officers would have ignored it, sir, if it had been General Lee marching through Pennsylvania into New York!

CHIPMAN: Mr. Chandler—

CHANDLER: This situation is difficult for me.

CHIPMAN: (*Stern, but not hard; he respects* CHANDLER) Nevertheless, you must answer the question. The Judge Advocate will repeat the question and you *will* answer it.

CHIPMAN: Your report on Andersonville was ignored, was it not?

CHANDLER: Yes, sir.

CHIPMAN: Did General Winder ever express to you his disposition [attitude] toward those prisoners?

CHANDLER: When I spoke to General Winder he had hard and bitter feelings toward them.

CHIPMAN: And how did he express those feelings?

CHANDLER: He finally said that if half of the prisoners died, there would then be twice as much room for the rest—

CHIPMAN: And the half slated for the grave were well on their way at Andersonville, weren't they?

. . . **General Winder . . . had hard and bitter feelings toward them.**

Mr. Wirz set up certain rules for that camp, rules relative to punishing prisoners attempting to escape—?

CHANDLER: Yes, sir.

CHIPMAN: His command of that camp conforming to Winder's inhuman disposition toward those men?

BAKER [the defense attorney]: I must ask the Judge Advocate what he means by that suggestive, ambiguous phrase, *conforming to*.

CHIPMAN: Withdrawn. Those rules Mr. Wirz set up at Andersonville—were they rules violating the customs of war?

CHANDLER: Well—yes.

CHIPMAN: Were they, in addition, cruel and inhuman rules?

CHANDLER: Yes.

CHIPMAN: Was Wirz the personal choice of Winder for superintendent of that camp?

CHANDLER: Yes.

CHIPMAN: That will be all. (*He crosses to his table*)

BAKER: Colonel Chandler, you made a second report on Andersonville to the Confederate war office, did you not?

CHANDLER: I did, yes, sir.

BAKER: This is a copy of that report? (*He hands the report to* SCHADE, *who shows it to* CHANDLER)

CHANDLER: (*Scrutinizing it briefly and handing it back to* SCHADE) It is.

(SCHADE *hands it to* WALLACE, *who examines it quickly and indicates that it is acceptable*)

SCHADE: Submitted for the Defense—(*Handing the report to the* CLERK) Entered in evidence.

CLERK: Exhibit one for the defense.

BAKER: In this report—to which the Judge Advocate has failed to call attention—you recommend the dismissal of General Winder.

CHANDLER: Yes.

BAKER: But *not* of Captain Wirz.

CHANDLER: No.

BAKER: Why not?

CHANDLER: At the time I inspected Andersonville, I saw nothing in Captain Wirz's conduct of a malignant disposition toward those men, that would have justified asking for his dismissal.

BAKER: I note in the same report that you took various prisoners aside, urging them to speak freely as to any instance of ill treatment by Captain Wirz—and they had no complaints on that score?

CHANDLER: No, sir.

BAKER: In other words, neither you nor the prisoners, who were presumably being subjected to Captain Wirz's cruel and inhuman treatment, blamed him for it, did you?

CHANDLER: No, sir.

BAKER: No more questions. Thank you, sir.

CHIPMAN: Mr. Chandler, very often, as you know, commanders are forwarned of inspection and dress up their commands in advance. Couldn't that have occurred in your case?

CHANDLER: Possibly.

CHIPMAN: And isn't it possible that they would fear the consequences of complaints against Wirz? Those men did not know you, and Wirz would still be in command after you were gone. And under those circumstances, isn't it very possible that they would not answer you truthfully?

CHANDLER: Perhaps. I did the best I could with that Andersonville situation—

CHIPMAN: (*Inwardly raging; silent for a moment*) Did Wirz do the best he could? (*Rises and crosses to witness*) In spite of Winder's orders, couldn't he have chosen to . . . (*Frustrated*) . . . there are ways!

BAKER: Ways of doing what? Evading the orders of a superior? What is the Judge Advocate suggesting?

CHIPMAN: (*Crosses to his table, sits*) Withdrawn. That will be all, thank you, Mr. Chandler.

WALLACE: If there are no other questions the witness may step down. The Court thanks the witness.

REVIEWING THE READING

1. What was Colonel Chandler's official job for the Army of the Confederacy?

2. According to Chandler, why was there insufficient water in the camp? Why was unbolted meal dangerous for the prisoners to eat?

3. **Using Your Historical Imagination.** In your opinion, should Wirz have been held responsible for the deaths at the prison, considering the fact that he was only following the orders given him by General Winder? Give reasons for your response.

85

From the *Proceeding of the Convention of the Colored People of Virginia.*

Proceedings of the Convention of the Colored People of Virginia (1865)

Although the Civil War brought slavery to an end, many African Americans realized that the Emancipation Proclamation would not guarantee their political equality. After the war they organized to protect their newly won freedom. As you read the following excerpt from the statement issued by the convention held in Virginia in 1865, notice the measures the members of the convention call for in order to safeguard the economic and political freedom of all African Americans.

We, the undersigned members of a convention of colored citizens of the state of Virginia, would respectfully represent that, although we have been held as slaves and denied all recognition as a constituent of your nationality for almost the entire period of the duration of your government, and that . . . we have been . . . deprived of the dearest rights of human nature; yet when you and our immediate oppressors met in deadly conflict, ... *we*, with scarce an exception, in our inmost souls espoused your cause. . . .

When the contest waxed long and the result hung doubtfully, you appealed to us for help, and how well we answered is written in the rosters of the 200,000 colored troops now enrolled in your service; and as to our undying devotion to your cause, let the uniform acclamation of escaped prisoners, "whenever we saw a black face we felt sure of a friend," answer.

Well, the war is over, the rebellion is "put down," and we are *declared* free! Four-fifths of our enemies are paroled or amnestied, and the other fifth are being pardoned, and the President has, in his efforts at the reconstruction of the civil government of the states late in rebellion, left us entirely at the mercy of these subjugated but unconverted Rebels, in *everything* save the privilege of bringing us, our wives, and little ones to the auction block. . . . We *know* these men—know them *well*—and we assure you that, with the majority of them, loyalty is only "lip deep," and that their professions of loyalty are used as a cover to the cherished design of getting restored to their former relations with the Federal government, and then, by all sorts of "unfriendly legislation," to render the freedom you have given us more intolerable than the slavery they intended for us.

We warn you in time that our only safety is in keeping them under [military] governors . . . until you have so amended the Federal Constitution that it will prohibit the states from making any distinction between citizens on account of race or color. In one word, the only salvation for us besides the power of the government is in the *possession of the ballot.* Give us this, and we will protect ourselves. . . . But, 'tis said we are ignorant. Admit it. Yet who denies we know a traitor from a loyal man, a gentleman from a rowdy, a friend from an enemy? The 12,000 colored votes of the state of New York sent Governor Seymour home and Reuben E. Fenton to Albany. Did not they know who to vote for? . . . All we ask is an *equal chance* with the white traitors varnished and japanned [given a hard brilliant finish] with the oath of amnesty. Can you deny us this and still keep faith with us? . . .

. . . All we ask is an equal chance . . .

Do not then, we beseech you, give to one of these "wayward sisters" the rights they abandoned and forfeited when they rebelled until you have secured *our* rights by the aforementioned amendment to the Constitution. . . .

Trusting that you will not be deaf to the appeal herein made, . . . and that you will rise to the height of being just for the sake of justice, we remain yours for our flag, our country, and humanity.

REVIEWING THE READING

1. Why did the members of the convention believe that they should have the right to vote?

2. With the war over, what did the members of the convention fear would happen to African Americans?

3. **Using Your Historical Imagination.** Do you think that most African Americans in the North would have supported the Convention's statement? Explain your answer.

Photo Acknowledgments

Cover: HRW Photo

Table of Contents: Page iii(t), Werner Wolff/Black Star; iii(b), iv(t), iv(b), v, vi, vii(t), vii(b), Culver Pictures; viii(t), The Bettmann Archive; viii(b), ix(t), Culver Pictures; ix(b), The Bettmann Archive; x, Library of Congress.

Page 5: The Granger Collection; 9, Historical Pictures Service; 12, The Granger Collection; 17, The Bettmann Archive; 20, 28, 31, 37, The Granger Collection; 42, Scala/Art Resource; 47, Virginia State Library; 51, 57, Historical Pictures Service; 63, 68, The Granger Collection; 74, Historical Pictures Service; 79, Taylor/Art Resource; 88, Culver Pictures; 93, Historical Pictures Service; 98, Library of Congress; 101, 105, Culver Pictures; 109, The Bettmann Archive; 114, Culver Pictures; 120, The Granger Collection; 124, Historical Pictures Service; 128, The Bettmann Archive; 132, The Granger Collection; 139, The Franklin Institute; 142, Free Library of Philadelphia; 145, The Bettmann Archive; 150, The Granger Collection; 155, Library of Congress; 160, Metropolitan Museum of Art, Bequest of Charles Allen Munn, 1924 (24:109.82); 163, Culver Pictures; 168, The Bettmann Archive; 174, 178, Library of Congress; 181, The Granger Collection; 185, New York Historical Society; 189, 193, Culver Pictures; 196, 197: 1, Franklin Institute, Science Museum; 2, 3, Lee Boltin; 4, New York Public Library; 5, American Antiquarian Society; 6, 7, 8, Lee Boltin; 199, Denver Public Library, Western Collection; 204, New York Public Library, Parsons Collection; 210, 211, Culver Pictures; 216, Library of Congress; 223, American Historical Prints; 228, 233, Culver Pictures; 238, 245, Historical Pictures Service; 251, Nawrocki Stock Photo; 259, 266, Culver Pictures; 273, 277, Historical Pictures Service; 282, Valentine Museum, Cook Collection; 287, The Bettmann Archive; 292, 297, Historical Pictures Service; 302, 303, 308, 314, Culver Pictures; 318, 324, Historical Pictures Service; 328, The Bettmann Archive; 333, Culver Pictures; 338, Library of Congress; 343, Culver Pictures; 348, Historical Pictures Service; 352, Library of Congress; 356, The Bettmann Archive; 359, Culver Pictures; 364, Nawrocki Stock Photos; 368, Library of the Boston Atheneum; 373, Historical Pictures Service; 378, Library of Congress; 382, New York Historical Society; 390, Chicago Historical Society; 394, Library of Congress; 397, Virginia State Library; 399, Howard University Library; 401, Nawrocki Stock Photo; 407, Culver Pictures; 412, Library of Congress; 415, Historical Pictures Service; 416, The Bettmann Archive; 423, Nawrocki Stock Photo.